Mystic Musings in Religions

Mystic Musings in Religions

Selected Papers
from the International Conference
'Mysticism without Bounds'

Editor
Dr. Kurian Kachappilly, CMI

Christian World Imprints™

First Published in 2013 by

Christian World Imprints™
Christian Publishing & Books from India
H-12 Bali Nagar, **New Delhi-110015**
info@christianworldimprints.com
www.ChristianWorldImprints.com
More at: www.kkagencies.co.in/sitemap
Phone: +91 11 25465925 Fax: +91 11 25173055

(Interfaith Treasures Uncovered - 2)

ISBN-13: 978-81-925121-8-1 ISBN-10: 81-925121-8-5

Cataloging in Publication Data--DK
Courtesy: D.K. Agencies (P) Ltd. <docinfo@dkagencies.com>

International Conference: 'Mysticism without Bounds' (2011 : Bangalore, India)
Mystic musings in religions : selected papers from the International Conference 'Mysticism without Bounds' / editor, Kurian Kachappilly.
p. cm. -- (Interfaith treasures uncovered ; 2)
Includes bibliographical references.
ISBN 9788192512181
ISBN 8192512185

1. Mysticism--Comparative studies--Congresses. 2. Spiritual life--Congresses. I. Kachappilly, Kurian. II. Title. III. Series: Interfaith treasures uncovered ; 2.

DDC 204.22 23

Printed at Chawla Offset Printers

Dedication

To

Mrs. Annam Joseph Kachappilly

- my beloved mother -

who instilled in me

a quest for the glimpse of the ‘Beyond’

revealed in the religions of the world.

The Book

'Mysticism' is "the pursuit of communion with, identity with, or conscious awareness of an ultimate reality, divinity, spiritual truth, or God, through direct experience, intuition or insight." The International Conference "Mysticism without Bounds" makes an attempt to explore the "mystical consciousness" from different disciplines, like religions (Hinduism, Judaism, Christianity, Islam, Buddhism, Sufism, Taoism, etc), sciences (biology, new physics, neuroscience, and logic), humanities (philosophy, theology, spirituality, psychology, etc.), and art forms (poetry, music, dance, visual arts and rituals).

Researches reveal that certain common grounds do exist among the various forms of consciousness, scattered among the world's religions, theologies, sciences, philosophies and art forms. The discovery of such points of convergence holds out the possibility of creating a 'new worldview', and this new world view can create an awareness of the essential 'unity' of humanity. Let these scholarly and challenging papers from different religious experiences create an awareness among the inquisitive readers of the need of overcoming the 'bounds' of individuation and discovering the 'unity' of self.

The Editor

Dr. Kurian Kachappilly is the Professor of Philosophy and Religion at the DVK, Bangalore, India; and Associate Director, Research Centre, Christ University, Bangalore, India. He holds Master's Degrees in English Literature and Psychology, and a Licentiate and Doctorate in Philosophy from the Katholieke Universiteit Leuven, Belgium. He is a Visiting Fellow at the Bangalore University, Bangalore; Katholieke Universiteit Leuven (KUL), Belgium; Fakultät für Informatik & Wirtschaftsinformatik, Würzburg, Germany; the University of Santo Tomas, Manila, the Philippines; and other institutions.

He is the Executive Editor of *Tattva*, Journal of Philosophy, Christ University, Bangalore; a Member of the International Advisory Board, *Process Studies*, Claremont, USA; a Member of the Pontifical Organization, Militia Christi, and a Member of the Governing Board, International Process Network (IPN). Dr. Kachappilly is a prolific writer with several books and many scientific articles to his credit. Some of the books include *God of Love Revisited* (1998), *Between Partners* (1999), *Word of God Retold* (2001), *God of Love: A Neoclassical Inquiry* (2002), *God-Talk Reconstructed: An Introduction to Philosophy of God* (2006), *Process: Implications and Applications* (2006), *Mystic Musings in Art and Poetry: Thematic Essays from the International Conference 'Mysticism without Bounds'* (2013), etc. His major areas of research are 'Indian Roots of Process Philosophy', 'Whitehead and Philosophical Doctrines of Buddhism', 'Innovative Experiments in Pedagogy', 'Religion vis a vis Society', 'Inquiry into Religious Experience' and 'Corporate Social Responsibility'.

Contents

1. A Note from the Editor 1
   Dr. Kurian Kachappilly, CMI

2. Mystics are Beyond Religions. 9
   His Holiness Swami Paramananda

3. *Dukkha* – Passio: Buddhist and Christian Meanings of Suffering in the Context of Mystical Experience 21
   Dr. Jakub Urbaniak

4. The Abiding Density of Light: Light and Sound Carved and Chiseled Across the Luminous Black Light of the Islamic and Sufi Void. 53
   Dr. Barbara A. Amodio

5. Sufi Inspired Devotional Islam in Egypt. 69
   Dr. Emilio Giuseppe Platti

6. The Place of the Word of God in Mystical Experience. 83
   Dr. Luke Emehiele Ijezie

7. Buddhist Epistemology of *Vipassana* and its Meaning. 101
   Dr. Hoang Thi Tho

8. Mysticism without Bounds: Islamic Perspective 117
   Dr. Gnanapragasam Lazar, SVD

9. Mysticism and Sociability in Daoism from a Christian Point of View 141
   Dr. Romualdas Dulskis

10. In Quest for the Unbound: Sufi Ritual as Sacred and Secular 153
Dr. Kashshaf Ghani

11. Significance of "You Have No Part with Me" in John 13:8: A Potential Mystical Interpretation 171
Sr. Bincy Mathew

12. Dialogue along Mystics' Spirituality: Models of Effective Interreligious Dialogue in Religious Pluralistic Societies. 197
Dr. Marinus C. Iwuchukwu

Contributors 217

Index of Subjects. 221

Index of Authors 231

1

A Note from the Editor

Dr. Kurian Kachappilly, CMI
Christ University, Bengaluru, India

'Mysticism' (from the Greek *mystikos*) is "the pursuit of communion with, identity with, or conscious awareness of an ultimate reality, divinity, spiritual truth, or God, through direct experience, intuition or insight."[1] In fact, there is no one single definition or common description of mysticism, for mysticism is a trans-cultural phenomenon, found in all different religions. Strictly speaking, mysticism is not to be connected with religions per se, for its scope is very wide, embracing all realms of human thought. Hence in "Mysticism without Bounds" (MwB2011) an attempt is made to explore the "mystical consciousness" from different disciplines, like religions (Hinduism, Judaism, Christianity, Islam, Buddhism, Taoism, etc), sciences (biology, new physics, neuroscience, and logic), humanities (philosophy, theology, spirituality, psychology, etc.), and art forms (poetry, music, dance, visual arts and rituals).

The MwB2011 was jointly organized by Christ University and the DVK, under the aegis of Dharmaram College, which was attended by over 320 delegates from thirty countries, like Australia, Belgium, Canada, China, Congo, Germany, Korea, Japan, Nigeria, Philippines, South Africa, Sweden, Thailand, UK and USA. There were about 200 Indian delegates from different universities, faculties, institutes and centres across the Indian Subcontinent. There were also representatives from

[1] http://en.wikipedia.org/wiki/Mysticism

various Indian Associations, like Association of Christian Philosophers of India (ACPI), Bangalore Academy of Philosophers (BAP), Kerala Philosophical Congress (KPC), and Indian Leuven Alumni Association Meeting (ILAAM). About 150 scholarly papers were presented in five parallel sessions, chaired by delegates, participants and invited guests, in addition to the key-note papers. Some of the highlights of the MwB2011 include (i) Inauguration by Rev. Jose Panthaplamthottiyil, (ii) Presidential Address by Swami Veda Bharati, (iii) Key-note papers by Dr. Bernard McGinn (USA), Dr. Paul Moyaert (Belgium), Dr. Peter Tyler (UK), Dr. Reimund Bieringer (Belgium), Dr. Una Agnew (Ireland) and Dr. Francis Vineeth (India).

May I place on record my heartfelt thanks and appreciation to all the delegates, presenters, participants, event partners, who have extended their wholehearted support toward the successful organization of the MwB2011, especially to all the heads of the institutions: Dr. Augustine Thottakara (Rector, Dharmaram College), Dr. Thomas C. Mathew (Vice Chancellor, Christ University) and Dr. Francis Thonippara (President, DVK); Dr. Lieven Boeve (Dean, Faculty of Theology, KUL, Belgium); Dr. Antoon Vandevelde (Dean, Institute of Philosophy, KUL, Belgium); Dr. Annette Meuthrath (Asia Desk, Institute of Missiology Missio, Aachen, Germany), and Fr. Geo Edakalathur (Webmaster). In a special way, I do acknowledge with thanks my great indebtedness to the administration and office-bearers of the **Institute of Missiology Missio**, Aachen, Germany, for their generous contribution and support toward the organization of the International Conference, 'Mysticism without Bounds' (MwB2011), from January 05 – 08, 2011.

'Religion', derived from the Latin *religare* (which means 'to bind fast'), refers to an 'institution with recognized body of communicants who gather together for worship and accept a set of doctrines, offering some means of relating the individual to what is taken to be the ultimate reality' (W.L. Reese, 488). Any attempt to define religion throws light on some important aspect of religion, but fails to do complete justice to it. This difficulty is felt because there are various kinds of religions, involving different kinds of behaviours, cognitions and emotions; and it is not possible to comprehend in one definition all possible aspects of a particular discipline.

There are so many religious institutions and religious codes serving good or bad, right or wrong, beneficial or harmful ends. But the fact that they are called "religious" necessitates a definition of religion that comprehends them all. The difficulty is not merely of diversity or variety, but a more fundamental one. An analysis of religious life reveals that there is a 'first-order' religious consciousness over and above the 'second-order' religious life. Within most of the world religions there are polarities of 'exoteric' (second-order) and 'esoteric' (first order), along with shades of gray between these two aspects of religions. In general, exoteric religion is the external form of religious practice, and is what most of us are accustomed to seeing in majority of the religious institutions and organizations. Esoteric religion, on the other hand, has more to do with the inner experience, and the pursuits of direct experience of the spiritual principles. Mystics, with the risk of simplification, are those who have *moved from mere belief systems or from belonging to particular systems to actual inner experience.*

All religious and spiritual traditions agree that such a movement is possible, desirable, and available to everyone. But if this is to be possible, as Richard Rohr explains citing the medieval Christian Philosopher, Richard of St. Victor, there is an urgent need for "contemplative seeing" *or "the third-eye seeing," which is the way the mystics see (The Naked Now*, 2009, III). According to Richard of St. Victor humanity is endowed with three different sets of eyes, each building on the previous one. The first eye is the eye of the flesh, namely *thought* or *sight*; the second is the eye of reason, that is *meditation* or *reflection;* and the third eye is the eye of true understanding, i.e., *contemplation* (Cf. *Classics of Western Spirituality: The Mystical Ark*, III-IV).

At the core of all the major religions, there exists a current of mystical consciousness, which, when compared to one another, exhibit a startling degree of cross-cultural agreement. Pluralists often refer to the fact that, just as there are many paths up Mt. Fuji, so there are many paths to God" (Rick Rood). Rig Veda states that, "The real is one; [but] the wise declare it as many: *Ekam sad vipra bahudha vadanti* (I.164.46). All religions, it is thus argued, have one common ideal; worship of the Lord; and all of them proclaim that there is but one God. This 'unitive awareness of the Beyond, or God' has been examined, down through the history of mysticism, from different points of view, 'as a type of experience, as a way of knowledge, and as a state of consciousness' (Happold, *Mysticism*, 1970, 39).

"*Mystics are beyond Religions*" by His Holiness Swami Paramananda is an attempt to capture the very essence of 'mysticism'. Mysticism, for Swamiji, is the experience of the mystic, and a mystic is an individual whose being has merged into the truth that he calls 'Mystery'. Enlightenment or consciousness of the 'Mystery' is attained by using certain means, which later evolved into religions. All the methods, parables, stories and koans, used by enlightened people, are only means to help the seeker. In fact different masters used different devices according to the evolution of the people, time, circumstances and environment where they incarnated. The paths may be different but the destination, argues, Swamiji, is one – merging with the Whole.

In "*Dukkha - Passio: Buddhist and Christian Meanings of Suffering*," Dr. Jakub Urbaniak explores various meanings ascribed to suffering by the mystical traditions of Buddhism and Christianity. On the one hand, looking at the writings of great figures of Christian mysticism, the author concludes that an intense experience of suffering is a *conditio sine qua non* of being a Christian mystic. On the other hand, a Buddhist sage seeks liberation from suffering; and even when afflicted with bodily pain, he endures such a feeling patiently, since for him suffering remains an external object of contemplation. Critically analyzing these two contrasting images of mystical experience with regard to suffering, Dr. Urbaniak tries to understand how suffering is integrated in these two mystical traditions.

Dr. Barbara Amodio, in her paper "*The Abiding Density of Light*," explores a wide spectrum of Islamic and Sufi sacred arts spread across the world '*ummah* with an eye toward extracting a unified aesthetics grounded in the requirements of the mystical Void, a primordial aniconic Silence from which emanate all Light and Sound. The Sufi mystical paradox (*shat'ih*) of Black Luminous Light is complemented by the *Anahatta* (Unstruck) analysis of Sound in the Indian tradition. She also analyses the philosophical distinctions between sacred and secular arts and aesthetics to the point of recovering authentic and ancient meanings of aesthetics; and the neglected differences between secular idols and sacred icons that have been a particular source of conflict in Islam's intercultural spread.

In "*Sufi inspired devotional Islam in Egypt*," Dr. Emilio Giuseppe Platti argues that the popular devotional Islam in Egypt is linked to the tombs of the saints who are spread in the Northern Delta, what is called "the Sa'îd", the land South of Cairo. According to Platti there are several 'types' of saints in Egypt; and in particular the famous medieval Muslim scholars, such as al-Imâm al-Shâfi'î, or al-Imâm Layth. However, more important, he observes, are the so-called "*Ahl al-Bayt*", or "*Âl-al-Bayt*", members of the family of the Prophet, Muhammad, whose devotion was established in Egypt by the Fatimids, a Shi'î dynasty, connected with the Ismâ'îlîs.

Dr. Luke Emehiele Ijezie, in "*The Place of the Word of God in Mystical Experience*" argues that the word, both in its spoken form and in its incarnate form, can be regarded as the unique basis of mystical union. This argument is developed on four levels by examining (i) the Christian understanding of mystical experience in general, (ii) the significance of the word of God in the Old Testament as the basis for union between God and humanity, (iii) the mystical dimensions of the word in the New Testament, and (iv) the implications of the biblical portrait of the word in the contemporary world and society.

According to Dr. Hoang Thi Tho "*Buddhist Epistemology of Vipassana*" was a particular produce of ancient Indian thinking, and Buddhism inherited this method from Brahman tradition and through Yoga-sutras. However, it was further developed by different Buddhist Mahayana philosophers to be a method of introspection or inward-looking in India. Later when Buddhism was introduced into China this method was integrated with Taoist method of forget-oneself-sitting and Zen method of direct enlightenment. Buddhist epistemology of Vipassana, he concludes, should be considered as one of the remarkable features of Asian thinking and it can be a candidate to solve some problems of personality in modern society.

Dr. Gnanapragasam Lazar in "*Mysticism without Bounds: An Islamic Perspective*" dwells on the mystical movement within Islam, Sufism, which arose as an organized movement after the death of Muhammad, among different groups who found orthodox Islam to be spiritually stifling. Sufism, which is the inner, mystical dimension of Islam, is 'a science whose objective is reparation of the heart and turning it away from all else but God;' "a science through which one can know how to travel into the presence of the Divine, purify one's inner self from filth, and beautify it with a variety of praise worthy traits". Although the mystic is right to emphasize his closeness to God, the author contends, the contrast between the transcendence and immanence of God is a familiar problem in many religions, but particularly so in Islam, with its explicit stand against idolatry.

Although Daoism is generally considered as a doctrine concentrated on mystical experience alone and utterly disinterested in the problems of politics and community life, Dr. Romualdas Dulskis in "*Mysticism and Socializing in Daoism*" contends that recent investigations provide an entirely different picture of Daoism. An intensive internal life is meant to assist the harmonizing, not only with an individual's internal being, but also with his/her relationships with other people as well. Daoism thus clearly speaks about the relation between a person's mystical experience and social activity. A Daoist, for example, does not only seek to live in wisdom but also to make an impact on the world. His/her purpose is to assimilate Dao and then to participate in the lives of people with this new quality in his/her heart.

In "*Quest for the Unbound: Sufi Ritual as Sacred and Secular*," Mr. Kashshaf Ghani attempts to deal with the spiritual exercise of audition (*sama*) as the integrating *symbol* of Sufi orders in south Asia, where Islamic mysticism has left a rich tradition of practice and preaching. The paper also aims at situating this ritual within the broader cultural canvas of the subcontinent, arguing that, although Islamic mystical practices retained its profound individuality, it, at the same time, could not free itself completely from the influences of the resident cultures/religions. Mr. Ghani seems to suggest that it is through these interstices of cross-cultural interactions that Islamic mysticism expands its boundaries of thought and practice, in their quest for the unbound.

In the paper "*Significance of 'You have no part with me' in John 13:8*," Sr. Bincy Mathew brings out the underpinnings of mystical elements in the Fourth Gospel, by making a re-reading of the 'Foot Washing' pericope, paying soecial attention to the word "meros" found in John 13:8. In order to make the arguments convincing, the author discusses the possible mystical background of the Fouth Gospel, and the way it is reflected in it. The main contention of Sr. Bincy Mathew is that an in-depth study of the literary-exegetical reading of "meros" with its parallel texts confirms the relevance of the mystical explanation for the Fouth Gospel.

Dr. Marinus Iwuchukwu in "*Dialogue along Mystics' Spirituality: Models of Effective Interreligious Dialogue in Religious Pluralistic Societies*" critically evaluates the relationship of some Christian, Hindu, Muslim, and Jewish mystics to peoples of other faith traditions with whom they interacted. He tries to highlight the dialogic values decipherable from mystics like Francis of Assisi, Rabia al-Adawiyya, Sri Ram Thakur, and Azriel ben Menahem that will benefit people living in religious pluralists' societies. According to Dr. Iwuchukwu the exemplary qualities and dialogic values these mystics radiate stem from their life activities in relation to people of other faith traditions, their philosophy of life, and their theological assumptions, and two of the common threads that run through the ministries of these mystics are compassion and love.

Let these scholarly and challenging papers from different religious experiences create an awareness among the inquisitive readers of the need of overcoming the 'bounds' of individuation and discovering the 'unity' of self, which the international conference 'Mysticism without Bounds' (MwB2011) aims at: "One who knows only the differentiated experience [...] comes to know an undifferentiated experience," the experience of "the primal self, *das Urselbst*" (Martin Buber, 1909). The unity of self is often conceived and interpreted in terms of 'God-experience' with its basis within non-phenomenal self, and a unity that promises the unity of all experiences within the phenomenal world.

2

Mystics are Beyond Religions

His Holiness Swami Paramananda
Satyam Gyanam Anandam Society, Vacoas, Mauritius

Mysticism is an experience and without experience, religion, spirituality and even mysticism itself become mere philosophy; and philosophy is a mental affair. All bounds, discussions and discrimination are created by the mind. Mysticism beyond bounds means to go beyond the mind. That is linked to the science of spirituality or the science of meditation; therefore the whole question is about practice, not talk or debate. We have to ask ourselves the following question: Are we practising something that will break the barrier created by the mind, or are we trying to involve the mind, which is itself the barrier?

Mysticism alone is without bounds. Mysticism is the experience of the mystic and a mystic is an individual whose being has flourished and merged into the truth that I call 'The Mystery'. God or Truth remains a mystery even after the great experience of enlightenment, Buddhahood or Nirvana. "The most beautiful thing that one can experience is the mysterious. It is the source of all true art and science," said Albert Einstein. But I say it is the source of this wonderful universe and countless other universes! That which is beyond human mind is indeed mysterious and if God is not mysterious, then what is it? Those who have known will definitely say that It is mysterious or a mystery.

God has always been and will always remain a mystery because even after the ultimate experience, It is not fully known and cannot be expressed in words. It is beyond the mind that one experiences oneness and unity and from that spring love and all the known virtues which flow spontaneously. The mystic is one who has merged into and become one with that mystery. He has transcended or gone beyond the mind after years of intense meditation, which is the art and science that leads to a profound understanding of the nature of the mind. Mystics are not necessarily knowledgeable people. Jesus, Kabir, Ramakrishna and many others were illiterate and did not even know the scriptures. Experiencing God does not imply knowing everything. On the contrary, it implies losing all knowledge and what remains is self-knowledge. One sees nothing but oneself and even that remains a mystery by its very nature.

When I say God is a mystery, it does not imply that God cannot be known at all. I simply mean that though it can be known, felt and tasted, yet it remains a mystery. This may seem contradictory, but that is the nature of truth. The art and science that can make such a union possible is called mysticism, pure religion or spirituality. To realise God, our human nature has to die through the practice of meditation. That is what Jesus meant, when he said that man should be born again in order to have eternal life. The Hindus call it to become a *dwij*, a twice-born.

Enlightenment or cosmic consciousness is attained by using certain means, which after an advanced stage are of no use. These means later evolve into religions. The paths may be different but the destination is one – merging with the Whole. Some rare mystics are at ease with a multitude of paths and methods and can guide seekers on specific paths according to each one's temperament and inclination. All the methods, words, parables, stories, *koans* and scriptures used by prophets, and enlightened beings are only means to help the seeker to attain a no-mind state or to develop an interest towards that state. The words are not the truth but simply pointing fingers. Alas! In their ignorance, people have caught the finger, moulded it in their own way and according to their own likeness and have given it the name of religion or God. Different masters use different devices according to the evolution of the people, time, circumstances and environment where they incarnate.

Pure religion or spirituality cannot be taught by lay people or even highly intellectual ones. It brings messages from beyond the mind, senses and body, beyond matter and beyond perceptive reality. Expert guidance is needed. It is like the study of highly advanced physics and mathematics, which requires guidance of accomplished physicists and mathematicians. Many people have done and are still doing much harm by explaining religions though they have no spiritual experience. They lead people, exploit them and are themselves misguided by their ego. Such people even have degrees in religious scriptures: MA's, PhD's and what not! They are, however, like the person who knows the abc of making sugar, but has never seen or tasted it. Kabir, a famous Indian mystic, Sai Baba of Shirdi, Ramakrishna, Jesus and Mohammed were all academically illiterate, yet that did not prevent them from being the stars of the earth.

1. The Mystery

The Bible says that no man has ever seen the face of God. Then why so much talk of that Which has never been seen? Scriptures cannot be taken literally; we should know how to read in between the lines. The truth is that to know or to experience It, the mind must dissolve and When this happens, Who will know, Who will describe, Who will be the witness? Fortunately, many who have merged with the Infinite have retained, by the will of that mystery, a little humanness and it is that which helps to give a faint idea of the unknown to others. They are the mystics.

The mysterious is such because even after experiencing It, one feels that one does not really know It and one becomes aware of one's 'nothingness'. Thus Socrates said, "The only thing I know is that I know nothing." Indeed, in front of that mystery, one realises how much one is nothing, ignorant and tiny. The mind thinks it knows a lot. But when it dissolves in That, all its knowledge vanishes like a dewdrop in the morning sun. That is what I call *Vedanta* - the end of knowledge.

God has infinite faces. The Upanishads talk about *Sat-Cit-Ananda* and *Atma*. *Sat* means existence, *Cit* is consciousness and *Ananda* is bliss. The Upanishads and the Vedas lay emphasis on the absolute nature of God. It is formless, eternal, infinite and untouched by the whole existence of names and forms. The universe is like a mirage, a dream in His mind. Ancient Indian mystics or *rishis* refer to God as Atma or the Self as He is uncreated, eternal and wisdom infinite. They do not see creation as being separate from God; for them creation is nothing but God, just like waves are a modification of the ocean.

Creation, Preservation and Dissolution are characteristics of 'Brahm' or the Supreme Mind, who is a witness to the universal drama. Creation is not an act of desire, but a spontaneous overflow of ideas. And since God is perfect, whatever comes out of Him is perfect. However, the idea of being perfect as understood in the Christian religion and in the mind of people is different from what it is in reality. For instance, a layperson will say, "If God is perfect, then Why is there so much imperfection in His creation?" From his point of view, the question seems logical, but How does God see things? And How can you give the right answer when your perception is fragmented and blurred? This is why enlightened beings will say that God is a mystery and they say so not because they do not know or are evading the question. The truth is that until and unless your mind is not completely freed from impressions, you cannot have direct perception.

2. The Ultimate Stuff of the Universe as Experienced by Mystics

For the mystic, the world is nothing but the waves, ripples and bubbles of an infinite ocean of energy. Existence is energy and energy is conscious and boundless. Matter is, in the words of Professor David Bohm, but a drop in an infinite ocean of energy. The mere presence of that conscious force brings about the birth of the universe. This implies that God does not create but simply witnesses the birth, evolution and dissolution of the universe. From this angle, it does not interfere with the good march of the cosmos.

That which appears to be void or filled with air for the layman is, in fact, filled with an extremely subtle stuff which is the real space. It is known that space contains atoms, molecules, particles, waves and finally light, which is the subtlest. The latest discovery is that even space and creation are only an aspect of an infinite ocean of energy. With the penetrating eyes of meditation, the mystic goes to that ultimate stuff and beholds it as a blue 'substance' which is beyond light as is known by science. The blue substance beheld by the mystic is an infinite ocean of power. My guru, Swami Veervasantha says that this is the subtle Blue Matter or Space Blue and the purest form of energy. When Professor

David Bohm said that matter is only a drop from an infinite ocean of energy, he was unknowingly referring to that pure homogeneous substance, which is the ultimate building block of the universe.

Professor Bohm has also spoken about the implicate order and explicate order. The implicate order has infinite depth. He has proposed that in its inward recesses, both matter and consciousness have their source and get unified. The subtle Blue Matter or Space Blue to which Swami Veervasantha referred is mind, and mind is both matter and consciousness. It is both energy and the void; it is Satti-Shiva, Prakriti-Purusha. Therefore, the infinite Space Blue or the Mind of God can be compared to the implicate order of Professor Bohm. At times, some scientists have glimpses of the Beyond, but given that they depend solely on logic, mathematics and theory and do not practise meditation, they evade the glimpses and thus the very truth is missed.

Mystics go further than science to say that the essence of the universe is not only energy of infinite density and vibration but the highest truth is that it is also pure consciousness, as if a living void completely free of all motion, wave, form and colour. Buddha named the same thing Nirvana, but since he did not explain it in scientific terms, he was taxed with being an atheist. How do we know that the universe is pure consciousness, sheer bliss and ineffable peace? This is indeed a very challenging question! The answer is the mind, which is also energy congealed. And since the mind does not die but simply undergoes transformation, the mind can be transformed to merge with the essence of the universe to experience the above-mentioned qualities. William Blake, the famous mystic-poet, has made a very beautiful statement: “Energy is delight.” I am sure he must have tasted the truth of his declaration at least to a little extent. Yes, indeed! The more we are filled with energy, the more delightful we feel. Therefore if we can make our mind merge with the essence of the universe, then we will no doubt experience delight, peace, consciousness and from these, many other virtues will spring.

3. The Freedom of Enlightenment

Only a mystic or an enlightened person is free and here I am referring to mental freedom, which is the real and ultimate freedom. It is freedom from unconsciousness, from the notion of 'I am separate from the Whole', from ceaseless thinking, greed, lust, hatred, from the duality of evil-good, morality-immorality. It is freedom from the weight of body consciousness and bookish knowledge, from the notion of 'I-you, mine-thine', from action and inaction, from humility and arrogance, from belief and disbelief and other dualities. Such a state, however, is inconceivable to a lay mind. This is why when an enlightened being behaves at times like an ordinary mortal, lay people think, "But he is like us!" People usually think an enlightened being should behave in a particular manner, be strictly vegetarian, be a celibate and abstain from any form of enjoyment. This is totally absurd.

Enlightenment is a state of being, a state of absolute freedom. The person is not; instead it is the fire of pure consciousness which is constantly manifesting. For such a soul to stay in his body, he has to retain some human features which are like the ash of a burnt wick. For him, the world is nothing but the waves, ripples and bubbles of an infinite ocean of energy.

It is strange that many people of meagre intelligence believe that such great souls should be disciplined, follow norms and live according to a certain pattern while they themselves do not do these things. God knows from where people get such stupid ideas! Who is freer to enjoy, the student or the teacher? The teacher is free as he has no exam behind the door. He can therefore enjoy, but the student still has to work hard and make sacrifices. An enlightened being is free; he now lives as part and parcel of the whole, not as a separate unit. His every move is that of the whole. The state of enlightenment is transcendental.

Any person who attains enlightenment is identified to that state, some fully, others not so fully. The reason that some are not totally identified is that they have to come down to a lower level of consciousness to help others. However, their state of consciousness is nevertheless very high in comparison to aspirants and meditators. Also, they identify themselves with a state of being, not with the ego or the body. Such beings always live in the '*Aham Brahmasmi*' state, meaning 'I am Brahman – the Absolute.' It is impossible for non-meditators to comprehend that. This is why enlightened beings have few disciples when they are alive, but many followers after their demise. Every individual is essentially as free as space and even more, we are all *chit* or space consciousness, free, pure and unblemished. Enlightened beings are not 'good' in the sense worldly people understand it, nor are they moralistic. They are virtuous but their virtuosity is a natural spontaneous overflow of their being. Dharma or righteous living is not a straight line that should be followed. Many a time, it is based on circumstances and is therefore fluid. So are the enlightened ones, thus they can easily adapt to circumstances. For example, they can be meat-eaters; Moses, Jesus and Mohammed are but a few examples. Krishna, Rama, Mohammed had to take up arms, but that did not make them violent people.

It may be very difficult to understand that they were the most non-violent people who ever lived. Their non-violence was a state of their being; it was not mechanical, moralistic or based on any bookish principle. They were simply practical individuals. Having waged a war, they do not feel guilty or regret because they know that it is the body that dies, not the soul. Besides, a person may have a human body but a devilish mind and such individuals who are threats to human society should be eliminated. In fact, enlightened beings such as Krishna, Rama and Mohammed act only in self-defence.

Rama killed Bali from behind when the latter was engaged in a dual with his brother Sugriv. Mohammed had taken the sword, which is a sign of violence, blood and killing in the mind of people. Krishna and the Pandavas, who were the very symbol of dharma, had won the war by breaking many rules. Most of those who criticise or do not understand such behaviours of the great ones are themselves not spiritual and non-virtuous, but rather moralistic and mechanically virtuous.

Laypeople are caught in the duality of good and evil without being practical, thus they suffer when they are faced with certain circumstances. 'Good' and 'Bad' reflect the materialistic and dual attitude of the mind while enlightenment or God-realisation is holistic, non-dual and transcendental. Only people who have transcended duality can be really practical in situations that seem most conflicting and confused. They can play with the laws. The cosmos is a play and the liberated ones know this.

For them, commandments, religions and the whole world are mere illusions; there are no do's and don'ts. They have no aim as they have reached home. However, society or the mob cannot understand that. This is why they have always condemned them. When Jesus healed during the Sabbath, he was said to have broken the laws and he was criticised for that. When Krishna stole the clothes of young damsels who were bathing in the river and asked them to come out, he seemed to be immoral in the eyes of some people. But Krishna is free from morality and immorality because he is free from lust.

When do we need norms, laws, and rules? We need all sorts of regulations, when people are unintelligent, unpractical, dishonest, complexed and selfish. What's the use of the laws if one is free from them? Being alone and free from the laws of matter, morality and immorality, good and evil and all other dualities, they do not make wrong use of their freedom, they only use it to help other individuals. Krishna, for example, did not make the Pandavas break the rules of the war for his own sake, but rather for the welfare of society. Jesus did not heal during the Sabbath for vested interests; he was motivated by mere compassion.

A mystic understands that not everyone is enlightened; therefore at times he will have to behave like an ordinary person in order to fit in society. Otherwise, he will not be able to help others. But that is not always possible. Few people will understand the esoteric dimension behind certain instances such as when Jesus cursed a fig tree. The mystic usually becomes a misfit in society. Most people are unconscious or with very little consciousness. When Jesus proclaimed himself as the Son of God, his people said, "Is this not the son of Joseph and Mary? Is he not the one who was helping his father in his workshop? How come that now he is proclaiming himself as the Son of God?" Similarly, when Al-Hillaj Mansoor uttered, "*Anal-haq*," he was chopped to pieces.

Many mystics have run into trouble because they could not conceal their realisation. It is indeed very difficult to conceal such a vast and blissful happening. The behaviour of different mystics varies. Songs, dance, poems and strange statements about love, God and so on emanate from those who express through the heart, whereas those who express through the head will write, talk and make unusual statements. Those who are enlightened are no more. They have to be understood: it is the divine energy manifesting through them with a very little human consciousness. But how can those who are nearly asleep and a prey to greed, anger, lust, and hatred, understand those who live in the realm of light and consciousness?

God enjoys the world through the mystics. That is why they say, "Not I, my Lord, but thou." Krishna said, "I am the Supreme Enjoyer." What a wonderful truth! Yes, if there is only One, how can there be many doers? The greatest illusion of the mind is that it thinks of itself as a body, hence the doer. The mystic or the devotee will say, "God is doing actions through me." The joy of such a realisation is inexpressible.

4. The Transformation and Silencing of the Mind

Man, as he is now, is only a potential. It is only when he has realised and lived fully his oneness with the Absolute that he is fulfilled. Why should anyone seek to live in oneness with existence or God? That seems to be very far-fetched to most people, even for the so-called religious people. The question is not of goal or aim, philosophy or morality, but that of perception. It is like a man who is blind and believes that there is darkness everywhere, which he finds very natural. He even believes that everyone is like him. Similarly, existence is one, homogenous and boundless, but man's perception is limited to his body and mind.

Though the ultimate possibility of human life is to realise his oneness with God, there are many relative possibilities or opportunities in life. Human life was not meant only to attain union with the Absolute. If such were the case, then life would have been completely different. That vast illusion came into being to be enjoyed both materially and spiritually. Materially, it can be enjoyed through the senses when one is still in duality and ignorance. However, such enjoyment has its own risk. The other way of enjoying the world is spiritually and this means that now I am aware, I see the world as a play, a dream or an illusion. Before enlightenment, I used to do everything like a sleepwalker, now I do the same fully conscious.

The process of transforming the mind that can lead to the ultimate realisation is what I call spirituality. In this process we need no Bible, Gita, Quran or other scriptures. Who can deny that our body is a replica of the universe in miniature? If our body can dissolve into it, then why not the mind? This simple understanding and logic can make us deeply religious. If our body is a tiny universe, then its essence is the essence of the universe. Then what does one have to do apart from simply relaxing and merging one's mind into the universal mind?

When the body dies, the mind does not die because it is too subtle. Its death can come only through certain methods. In fact, its death brings a new regeneration, a new life, an oceanic feeling or oneness with the whole existence. What I find more wonderful is that this experience is the right of one and all in this very body. Once this experience is acquired, the whole of humanity can become paradise-like. Ancient mystics knew this, but they had no scientific explanation. When Jesus talked of 'one earth, one humanity', he was not dreaming. I have myself gone through the experience. In fact, anyone else can go through it, provided that one is willing to learn and ready to undergo the great transformation.

Silence of the mind is the key. That is why, in the Bible, God says, "Be still and know that I am." Normally, the mind is constantly active with thoughts, ideas, dreams, desires, ambitions, negative and positive moods and above all an incredibly thick layer of unconsciousness. Silence is the complete cessation of all mental activities leading to the total dissipation of the unconscious layers. Consequently, there is a state of pure consciousness, a peace that is boundless, ineffable, transcendental and bubbling with infinite potentialities.

The state of pure consciousness is everything. It is the energy that becomes the whole existence. We function by its virtue. When Jesus said, "You have eyes but you do not see; you have ears but you do not hear," he was referring to the blockage of the subtle senses of hearing and seeing. In other words, our perception is greatly reduced due to our blurred mind. This means that we listen, see and perform every activity with the mind; the body and the senses are only the medium. Therefore, if the mind is loaded with thoughts, impressions, emotions, concepts and ideas, How can it see, listen, think, reason and hear correctly?

The whole of the mystical or spiritual science is based on silencing the mind. It means bringing the mind to its original state of Pure Consciousness. I would say that silence is the dawn of intelligence. Krishnamurti exhorts people to be attentive and calm; these are aspects of the state of a pure mind. Attentiveness is of paramount importance if we wish to learn. The silence of the mind is like the sharp penetrating rays of the most sophisticated apparatus by which scientists probe the womb of matter and the world of sub-atomic particles. From silence is born the whole existence. In silence it exists and to silence it will go back. Deep within matter is silence. The harmony of existence is due to an ineffable silence.

5. Mysticism is Beyond Knowledge

Mysticism can be compared to the particle-wave duality. The particle is relative reality while the wave is the ultimate reality. Similarly, the individuality of an unenlightened person is a relative reality, while the mystic's experience of being pure consciousness is the ultimate reality. The perception of life through the relative reality of individuality is an illusion as the person is covered with a thick layer of unconsciousness, which itself is formed by an amalgamation of habits, beliefs, impression and many other conditionings. Therefore, first the individual has to be liberated from them, then he can flower and merge into the Mystery. The process and the experience are what I call mysticism. It has nothing to do with any belief or religion.

The scholar or the pundit has much knowledge, while the mystic knows but his self. So far as knowledge is concerned, one will always have to learn if one so wishes, but that concerns the person who has not reached his destination. The fact is that the enlightened one has reached his destination. If he decides to stay in the world, it is for the purpose of guiding others to grow spiritually. If you can conceive and think about something, then it is no longer boundless; it is limited. So-called religious people think that God can be known as it has been revealed and defined in the scriptures – this implies that He is within bounds. For those 'people of the book', everything is contained in the scriptures. This form of limitation is called *maya* – the great illusion. There are also people who use the pretext of being always a seeker or a learner just to avoid facing themselves or a spiritual guide, who is an ego-cracker. They think they are humble when in reality it is the ego clad in humility.

The mystic has stopped learning because he has reached the ultimate goal. Learning involves action and effort, while enlightenment is rest, silence, awareness, pure knowing, bliss, love and freedom. Life is like a university; the yogi has learnt his lessons and thus is free. There is nothing else left to be learnt for one who has known his self. What would one who has merged with that, from which all material as well as spiritual knowledge flows, learn from the scriptures or any person?

This is what the Upanishads imply when they say, "Know that by knowing which all else gets known." What could that be if not the self? The Upanishads form part of the last part of the Vedas and are thus referred to as Vedanta. However, there is a secret behind it and Who else apart from an enlightened being can speak out the truth that the word Vedanta conceals? My realisation is that the word Vedanta means 'the end of all knowledge' or 'beyond knowledge', from the root words *vid* meaning knowledge and *anta* meaning end.

Knowledge is only a ladder with the help of which one may ascend to the realm of the Absolute. Once the Absolute is attained, then all knowledge becomes useless, at least for the enlightened one. The world is full of knowledgeable people, but very poor in experienced people so far as spirituality is concerned. What avails a man if he has abundant knowledge yet is self-ignorant! If the world is extremely sick today, it is just because people have drifted from self-knowledge to secular knowledge. We have even reduced self-knowledge to bookish knowledge – such is the cunningness of the mind.

When all knowledge ends, when the mind is completely silent but fully awake, then experience dawns. This is self-realisation. Only the realisation of knowledge can bestow on you the highest good – all else is secondary. And only the guidance of a mystic can lead to self-realisation or enlightenment. He alone can reveal the esoteric truth behind scriptures and then share the effulgence of the Beyond with humankind.

3

Dukkha – Passio

Buddhist and Christian Meanings of Suffering in the Context of Mystical Experience

Dr. Jakub Urbaniak
Department of Church History
University of Pretoria, Pretoria, South Africa

"Man is ready and willing to shoulder any suffering, as soon and as long as he can see a meaning in it."[1]

"It would be a grave error to suppose that Buddhism and Christianity merely offer various explanations of suffering, or worse, justifications and mystifications built on this ineluctable fact. [...] Suffering, as both Buddhism and Christianity see, each in its own way, is part of our very ego-identity and empirical existence, and the only thing to do about it is to plunge right into the middle of contradiction and confusion in order to be transformed by what Zen calls the 'Great Death' and Christianity calls 'dying and rising with Christ'."[2]

---

[1] As quoted in Dalai Lama & Howard C. Cutler, *The Art of Happiness: A Handbook for Living*, London: Hodder & Stoughton, 1998, 167. Victor Frankl was a Jewish psychiatrist imprisoned by the Nazis in World War II.

[2] Thomas Merton, *Thoughts on the East*, New York: New Directions Bibelot, 1995, 41.

In my paper, I attempt to show how the mystical approaches to suffering characteristic of Buddhism differ from those which can be found in Christianity and in what sense the meanings these two traditions ascribe to suffering in general and to the suffering as a "component" of the mystical experience in particular may challenge and stimulate both Buddhists and Christians.

1. Suffering: A Problem or a Mystery?

Before I will focus on the proper, mystical, context of my analysis, I find it necessary to summarise the doctrinal understanding of suffering in Buddhism and Christianity.

What associated the mendicant monks assembled around Gautama Buddha, and became thereby the main distinguishing feature of their earnest spiritual world, is the overwhelming and clear consciousness that every earthly being is full of suffering, and thus human being can liberate himself or herself from pain only through resignation and eternal peace. Regarding the Buddha's teaching, it is much more evident than in the case of all revealed religions that his doctrine appears as a response to the tensions at the heart of the human condition.

In Buddhism, suffering constitutes an original fact. How ought we to understand this statement? Firstly, in an empirical sense: the experience of *dukkha*, being absolutely universal and inevitable, is shared by every living creature. Secondly, as concerning the inner logics of the Dharma; the truth about common painfulness is not only the starting point of the Buddha's teaching, but it plays indeed the role of a necessary assumption without which the entire Buddhist doctrinal system lacks the reason for existence. However, this statement should not be understood in a metaphysical sense; suffering is neither the result of some cosmic disaster (a sort of stigma), nor the consequence of some particular historical event. To find its sources one has to examine one's "actual" – mental and ethical – attitude whose effects, according to Buddhists, spread over numerous, karmically conditioned existences.

Even though the inconvenience of being appears in Buddhism as an original fact, it should by no means be considered an "insurmountable" aspect of the human condition. What makes people suffer, by setting and keeping the wheel of *samsara* in motion, is ultimately ignorance which generates the will to live and all sorts of unwholesome states of mind. Anyone who uproots ignorance liberates himself from suffering, *eo ipso* existence. Thus *dukkha* is nothing more than an obstacle that has to be overcome, a problem to be solved.

From the perspective of the Judeo-Christian tradition, temporality can be compared to a prenatal period; being on earth, the human person ripens like a "fruit of life"; She learns what is good, develops her personality, and somehow exceeds herself. Among many components of this process, the experience of suffering occupies a crucial position as the instrument of justice and pedagogy, as a cure, and so forth.

Even though relatively early (namely in later texts of the Old Testament), the conception of suffering as a direct punishment for sins (committed by man himself or by his ancestors) was overcome and replaced by the understanding of suffering as a mystery which largely evades any schematic explanations and calculations, the relation between the truth about sin and the truth about suffering remains the hallmark of the Christian faith. Sin appears thus as an existential "situation," a common "fact" which concerns each and every one, as a trans-historical reality penetrating the whole history, from its beginning to its end. Ranging from the Pauline theology, through the Fathers' (particularly Augustine's) teaching, to modern times, what plays a central part in the reflection on suffering is Adam's sin conceived as a prototype, the "matrix" of any human sin. It is the symbolic presentation of the original event and at the same time the figure of human tragedy in general. However, the fundamental message of Christianity is that in Jesus Christ humanity is saved, i.e., liberated from any evil which touches its present life. In this very context, Adam's fall, as well as every human sin, turns out to be secondary in comparison with God's grace that comes from the cross, and therefore – as far as it is admitted and remorsefully confessed – can be called a *felix culpa*, a "blessed fault," that is something necessary for recognising the depth of the *even more abundant* grace of God's mercy.

Christian theology discerns – more or less distinctly – also those aspects and dimensions of suffering which are not the result of original sin. Since everything has been created in Christ, and it is in him that the whole of history is recapitulated, suffering must have been from the very beginning, some meaning for the life plan of every single person and for humanity as such. Jesus from the Old Testament, the son of Sirach, repeats, “A man cannot say, ‘This is worse than that’, for in time [*kairos*] they shall all be well approved” (Sir 39:21.34). Believing that evil is unable to overstep the order established by God, to become absolutely independent of good, Christian theology opens onto a more profound interpretation of all the painful aspects of man’s experience (as well as of the entire natural order) which are difficult to reconcile with the “revealed goodness” of creation. Implying a trust in God’s plan Judeo-Christian faith allows believers to tolerate various forms of suffering more easily, since they *trust* that every misery they experience will be outweighed by the ultimate good it produces. As the Talmud puts it, “Everything God does, he does for the best.”[3]

The deepest, salvific sense of suffering becomes visible only in the light of the Passover of Jesus. For the baptised who together with Christ are buried into death in order to rise with him from the dead by the glory of the Father and walk in the newness of life,[4] suffering is not a radical evil, but rather a *difficult good*. That is why, as modern Christian teaching underscores, the truth about suffering cannot be examined in isolation from its natural theological environment, nor apart from its personalistic background. The salvific sense of the mystery of suffering appears only at the intersection of these coordinates.

Throughout the ages, religions, and philosophical systems have formulated many different explanations of the state of the human condition, thus also of suffering as its constitutive component. As far as Buddhism looks at our existential situation mainly through the prism of a concrete experience, marked by a common painfulness – a burden from which a human being should simply liberate itself, the Christian faith interprets it in reference to God’s plan regarding humanity: the plan spoiled (and being spoiled on and on) by human sin, but ultimately accomplished by Jesus-the-Son. Even though these two traditions start from different points (the first one from a certain empirical statement, and the second one from the truth of the Revelation), they meet each other at least in two important aspects, namely the conviction that suffering is

---

[3] Cf. Dalai Lama, *The Art of Happiness*, 168.

[4] Cf. Rom 6:4.

"part of our very ego-identity and empirical existence"[5] and a readiness and wish to "carry" human being through the abyss of suffering to the other shore (of nirvana / of eternal life), i.e., an explicitly soteriological character.

For Buddhism *dukkha* is simply a "state" of all living beings; suffering – in all its aspects – is identified with existence. Therefore, the only *positive* meaning of *dukkha,* a Buddhist can be interested in is its didactic meaning (i.e., the experience of suffering as a motivation to follow the Dharma). As for the Christian *passio*, one has to distinguish between What is in a certain sense inscribed into God's vision of the creation? and What – being the result of sin – is actually a curse that humanity has brought (and is still bringing) on itself by misusing its freedom? In view of the mentioned distinction, eliminating or overcoming every form of pain certainly cannot be considered the superior aim of a religious practice. A Christian ought rather to accept the mysterious character of suffering and be able to assume an adequate attitude depending on circumstances; the particular manifestations of suffering should be surrounded by compassion and possibly soothed, while trying to regard those which evade one's forces as "good in time," and to bear them in unity with Christ dead and risen.

Referring to Gabriel Marcel's distinction between problem and mystery, it can be therefore assumed that for Buddhism suffering (*dukkha*) constitutes an original fact which, being the universal *problem* of the whole mankind, needs to be understood and then practically solved; whereas for Christianity suffering is most of all a *mystery*, at least to some extent rooted in *mysterium iniquitatis* – a mystery whose salvific sense is to be found by a personal participation in *passio Christi.*

To complete the picture emerging from the doctrinal understandings of suffering, it must be added that in both Buddhism and Christianity a number of rather surprising approaches may be found, which – although seemingly exceptional – brings an essential novelty to the panorama of religious meanings ascribed to suffering. My thesis is that these subtleties become more visible and graspable in the field of mystical experience in the respective religions. Let us therefore explore now

[5] Thomas Merton, *Thoughts*, 41.

various meanings ascribed to suffering by the mystical traditions of Buddhism and Christianity.

2. Saint or Sage? Two Models of Mysticism

Spelled out briefly, within the general category of religion, "Buddhism and Christianity appear to occupy opposite poles; over against a religion of enlightenment, a religion of faith. On the one hand a religion of experience, on the other a religion of dogma; a religion of wisdom facing a religion of love; a religion centered on the human self over against a religion centered on God; on the one hand, a religion of introversion and equanimity and on the other, a religion of extraversion and desire."[6] It is then understandable that while the Buddhist-Christian dialogue on the level of doctrine or theology is fraught with formidable difficulties, at the same time, it turns out to be very fruitful on the mystical level. Indeed, it can be said that the central role in this dialogue is played by mysticism.[7] As Thomas Merton pointed out, "While on the level of philosophical and doctrinal formulations there may be tremendous obstacles to meet, it is often possible to come to a very frank, simple, and totally satisfying understanding in comparing notes on the contemplative life, its disciplines, its vagaries and its rewards."[8] In a nutshell, it seems that what rationality cannot grasp can be touched by concrete mystical experience.[9]

However, Buddhism and Christianity are not "mystical" in the same sense and to the same degree. The characteristic Buddhist approach

---

[6] Paul Mommaers & Jan Van Bragt, *Mysticism Buddhist and Christian. Encounters with Jan van Ruusbroec*, Crossroad: New York, 1995, 28.

[7] Buddhists engaged in the dialogue with Christianity spontaneously focus on Christian mysticism. They willingly refer to St. Francis of Assisi and to the Spanish mystics, St. Teresa of Avila and St. John of the Cross, but "the lion's share of their attention clearly goes to the 'metaphysical mysticism' of Meister Eckhart." Paul Mommaers, *Mysticism*, 30.

[8] Thomas Merton, *Mystics and Zen Masters*, New York: Dell Publishing Co., 1980, 209. The author of this assertion, Thomas Merton, found himself in extraordinary harmony with many representatives of Eastern spiritual traditions, for instance with D. T. Suzuki. Cf. Paul Mommaers, *Mysticism*, 28-29.

[9] Cf. Edward Stevens, *An Introduction*, 97.

to reality is through the "silent non-rational path of mysticism."[10] In other words, mysticism is congenial to the Buddhist way of thinking and practical for the Buddhist way of living.[11] Christianity, instead, as a prophetic religion, has never made mysticism central and essential to salvation, although it developed its own rich mystical tradition (to mention only such outstanding personages as Meister Eckhart, Teresa of Avila, or John of the Cross).[12]

At first glance, the experience of suffering plays totally different roles within each of these two mystical traditions. On the one hand, a Buddhist sage, not attached to favourable conditions and not repelled by unfavourable ones, seeks first and foremost liberation from suffering. Even when afflicted with bodily pain, he endures such a feeling patiently, with equanimity, since for him *dukkha* is nothing but an external object of contemplation.[13] As D. T. Suzuki accurately puts it, in Buddhism "there is no ego to be crucified."[14] On the other hand, looking at the writings of great Christian saints one may reach a conclusion that an intense experience of suffering is a *sine qua non* condition of being a Christian mystic.[15] The Cross seems to be the only way of uniting with

---

[10] Edward Stevens, *An Introduction*, 97-98. Buddhist pragmatism expresses itself in the fact that it is short on speculation, and long on practice. The house is on fire, *dukkha* is omnipresent, and therefore the need for liberation is urgent. Metaphysical questions, generally speaking, are unanswerable and, what is more, they have no bearing on man's practical life *here and now*. Reality remains mysterious and the proper response to mystery is not discourse, but silence. In this sense, "Buddhism is a mystical religion with mysticism's mistrust of words." Edward Stevens, *An Introduction*, 105.

[11] Cf. Edward Stevens, *An Introduction*, 161. Cf. also Paul Mommaers, *Mysticism*, 31-32. The author reflects on the question, *Does it make sense to speak of "Buddhist mysticism?"*.

[12] Cf. Edward Stevens, *An Introduction*, 161. "Christianity, indeed, contains mysticism, but cannot be called a mystical religion in the same strong sense of the word, because salvation in Christianity is not as intimately linked [as in Buddhism] with the mystical path." Paul Mommaers, *Mysticism*, 39.

[13] Cf. Bhikkhu Bodhi, *In the Buddha's Words*, 21.

[14] D. T. Suzuki, *Mysticism: Christian and Buddhist*, London & New York: Routledge Classics, 2002, 113.

[15] For instance, St. Ignatius of Loyola is praised in his Litany for being "constant in the practice of corporal penance"; St. Thérèse of the Child Jesus, according to her biographer, "took the discipline three times a week, scourging herself with all the strength and speed of which she was capable, smiling at the crucifix through the tears which bedewed her

Christ, which is so impressively reflected in the cry usually inscribed as a motto upon images of St. Teresa of Avila, "Lord, either let me suffer or let me die!"

This gives us two contrasting images of mystical experience with regard to suffering. Emile Cioran, a twentieth-century Romanian existentialist who spent most of his adult life in Paris writing rather pessimistic and yet surprisingly stimulating aphoristic texts, achieved a real mastery in stressing the above mentioned contrast. "After twenty centuries" – Cioran writes in one of his books – "in which *convulsion* was regarded as a sign of spiritual advancement [...] accustomed to a racked, ruined, grimacing Saviour, we are unsuited to enjoy [...] the inexhaustible smile of a Buddha plunged into a vegetable beatitude."[16] Such a caricature and hyperbole of Western (Christian) and Eastern (Buddhist) attitudes to suffering may of course be reproached for being too simplistic. Nonetheless, it rightly indicates the two opposed tendencies represented by the passionate saint eagerly plunging into suffering and the indifferent monk detached from all earthly miseries.

However, stopping at this stage, i.e., confronting "sage-the-robot" with "saint-the-sufferer," would be a serious mistake. This scheme can be challenged by numerous testimonies of mystics, both Buddhist and Christian. Taking this diversity into account is critical for understanding how suffering is integrated in the two mystical traditions under discussion.

3. 'No Ego to be Crucified': Mysticism as Uprooting Suffering

In Theravāda, with its ideal of the *arhat*, no positive meanings are attributed to suffering except for its didactic function. In consequence, from the point of view of the original Buddhism, a monk voluntarily plunging into suffering or ascribing some positive senses to it would have to be seen as a "mystical failure." At the same time, in Buddhism as such, and particularly in the oldest forms of Buddhism, the suffering and transiency of the world constitute the object of contemplation *par*

eyelashes" (Cf. Henry Petitot, *Saint Teresa of Lisieux*, Burns Oates and Washbourne LTD., London, 1927, 37).

[16] Emile Cioran, *The Fall into Time*, trans. R. Howard, Chicago: Quadrangle Books, 970,139.

excellence.[17] In this sense, being the result of our own negative past actions, *dukkha* is also seen as an effective "catalyst for seeking spiritual liberation."[18] Meditation on suffering is a fundamental way of uprooting it. Indeed, enlightenment itself is a fruit of *prajñā*, clear insight into the Four Noble Truths about the "inconvenience of being."

The first three Noble Truths give the disease, the cause, and the cure, whereas the fourth one is to be considered the doctor's prescription. And it is at this point that the Buddhist mystical practice has its essential role to play. The Eightfold Noble Path to Enlightenment constitutes a "manual for the practice of the Middle Way."[19] The first two steps call for commitment: (1) Right Understanding, (2) Right Attitude of Mind; the following three – (3) Right Speech, (4) Right Action, and (5) Right Livelihood – indicate that understanding and consequent commitment must translate into action, that is, find their expression in a moral attitude. Finally, the last three – (6) Right Effort, (7) Right Awareness, and (8) Right Concentration – cover the mystical dimensions of the Dharma. In fact, both commitment and moral action prepare man for meditation which is, without doubt, the highest form of the Buddhist practice.[20]

A double movement is to be found within Buddhist mystical practice. On the one hand, there is the doctrine of *anatta* (No-Self), on the other, the discovery of one's Buddha-nature.[21] They can be seen as the two sides of the same experience in which the monk-mystic overcomes *dukkha* by meditating on it and ultimately by realising that there is no personal subject such as "I," or "you," thereby *suffering lacks in sufferer*. One ought to remember that in Buddhism meditation does not mean rational analysis. For the mystic, existential problems such as death, suffering, failure, or frustration are not to be rationally solved, but rather "transrationally *dis*-solved."[22] It is underscored especially

[17] Cf. Paul Mommaers, *Mysticism*, 37. As Heinrich Dumoulin points out, "The peculiar mixture of rationality and mysticism might be the most surprising characteristic and astonishing paradox of Theravāda Buddhism." Heinrich Dumoulin, *Östliche Meditation und Christliche Mystik,* Freiburg: Karl Alber, 1966, 200.

[18] Dalai Lama, *The Art of Happiness*, 168.

[19] Edward Stevens, *An Introduction*, 106.

[20] Cf. Edward Stevens, *An Introduction*, 106-107.

[21] Cf. Edward Stevens, *An Introduction*, 163.

[22] Edward Stevens, *An Introduction*, 170.

in Zen Buddhism that *bodhi*, awakening, is not to be attained by any particular effort. The monk must only *allow* the "flame of existence" to be extinguished. As one of Zen koans says, "Sitting quietly, doing nothing, Spring comes, and the grass grows by itself."[23]

One might ask, does individual human death and suffering, experiences belonging to the realm of *samsara* and *maya* (illusion) matter, If man is already liberated? As for the suffering, it does not affect an enlightened one in the same manner as it does average people. The worldling reacts to all objective aspects of suffering, and therefore, on top of painful bodily feelings, he or she experiences also painful mental feelings (sorrow, resentment, distress, and so forth).[24] In contrast to that, anyone who has discovered the emptiness (the lack of self) of all things, is thus able to reduce the suffering resulting from pain to its elementary, strictly bodily aspect. Also death loses its common meaning. Even though the liberated one is subject to physical death, as the Buddha himself was, he is no longer in its power, for in his case death leads not to rebirth in a next existence, but directly to Nirvana: *The Buddha did not die! The Arhats [...] do not die! They don't die as people and animals do. [...] Earth, water, fire, air, the four elements, simply split up; there is no person in these things. [...] Dirt, they call it. A pile of dirt! By seeing that there are only earth, water, fire, and air, they conquer death.*[25]

In his famous book *Mysticism: Christian and Buddhist*, Suzuki discusses the Buddhist "spirituality of suffering" as contrasted with the Christian one. "Christian symbolism" – he begins – "has much to do with the suffering of man. The crucifixion is the climax of all suffering. Buddhists also speak much about suffering and its climax is the Buddha serenely sitting under the Bodhi tree [...]. Christ carries his suffering to

---

[23] Edward Stevens, *An Introduction*, 45.

[24] "How you perceive life as a whole" – the Dalai Lama says – "plays a role in your attitude about suffering. For instance, if your basic outlook is that suffering is negative and must be avoided at all costs [...], this will add a distinct psychological component of anxiety and intolerance when you encounter difficult circumstances [...]. On the other hand, if your basic outlook accepts that suffering is a natural part of your existence, this will undoubtedly make you more tolerant towards the adversities of life." Dalai Lama, *The Art of Happiness*, 116.

[25] Pabongka Rinpoche, *Liberation in our hands. Part two: The Fundamentals*, trans. Trijang Rinpoche with Sermey Khensuar Lobsang Tharchin and Artemus B. Engle, New Jersey: Mahayana Sutra and Tantra Press, Howell, 1994, 74-75.

the end of his earthly life, whereas Buddha puts an end to it while living and afterwards goes on preaching the Gospel of enlightenment until he quietly passes away under the twin Sala trees. [...]" What a contrast? – Suzuki concludes – "between the crucifixion-image of Christ and the picture of Buddha lying on a bed surrounded by his disciples and other beings non-human as well as human!"[26]

As a Japanese author explains, the sight of Christ hanging helpless, full of sadness on the vertically erected cross is almost unbearable to the Oriental mind.[27] Why? Because by elevating the Cross to the level of God's central Revelation, Christianity makes Man combative; it encourages him to crucify 'the self' because it is considered to be the threatening enemy. "Christians would say that crucifixion means crucifying the self or the flesh, since without subduing the self we cannot attain moral perfection. This is where Buddhism differs from Christianity. Buddhism declares that there is from the very beginning no self to crucify. [...] As there is no self, no crucifixion is needed, no sadism is to be practiced, no shocking sight is to be displayed by the road-side."[28]

4. 'To Suffer or to Die': Mystical Elevation of Suffering

It has to be stressed that the very concept of suffering as a component of the mystical path differs significantly according to particular currents of mysticism. For instance, Meister Eckhart's[29] focus is on the state of detachment understood as complete self-abandonment, and thus his

[26] D. T. Suzuki, *Mysticism*, 117, 120.

[27] Cf. D. T. Suzuki, *Mysticism*, 117. "The crucified Christ is a terrible sight and I cannot help associating it with the sadistic impulse of a physically affected brain. [...] Christianity tends to emphasize the corporeality of our existence. Hence its crucifixion, and hence also the symbolism of eating the flesh and drinking the blood. To non-Christians, the very thought of drinking the blood is distasteful." D. T. Suzuki, *Mysticism*, 120.

[28] D. T. Suzuki, *Mysticism*, 119-120. "[...] when you clearly perceive that this deadly enemy who keeps you on the alert is non-existent, when you understand that it is no more than a nightmare, a mere delusion to posit a self as something trying to overpower you, you then will be for the first time at peace with yourself and also with the world at large" (D. T. Suzuki, *Mysticism*, 121).

[29] Cf. William Harmless, *Mystics*, Oxford: University Press, 2008, 107-134.

approach is almost purely intellectual and metaphysical.[30] Julian of Norwich, on the other hand, describes her relation with Jesus in a very imaginative and affective way emphasising the Lord's Humanity and the bodily aspect of his and her own sufferings; the vividness of her visions is most impressive.[31] Teresa of Avilla, in turn, tends to meditate on Jesus' passion, so to say, looking down on it "from the blissful height of 'perfect contemplation',"[32] as though all images and intermediaries, the Christ's Humanity included, had been a kind of necessary evil, but also a necessary condition of *unio mystica*.[33]

Suffering is first of all present in the experience of Christian mystics as a topic of visions and apparitions as well as a theme or image stimulating and nourishing their contemplation: in this case, it is about the suffering of Christ and, sometimes, the fellow-suffering of Mary. There is probably no religious event more likely to fill and fix a mystic's imagination and affection than what happened on the Via Dolorosa and on the hill of Calvary.[34] This Christocentrism is to be considered the central characteristics of Christian mystical experience.

For instance, Julian of Norwich (1342 – c. 1416) prayed for the grace of the painful bodily presence of Jesus; "I longed to be shown him in the flesh so that I might have more knowledge of our Saviour's bodily suffering."[35] And indeed in her "showings," Julian very often saw Jesus' passion. In LT chapter 16, his body hanging on the cross is shown as slowly drying out; in her first *Revelation*, in turn, she describes "the red blood trickling down from under the crown of thorns, hot and fresh and very plentiful"[36]; elsewhere, we read about hot blood running out so abundantly that no skin or wound could be seen, and so forth.

---

[30] Cf. Olivier Davies, *Meister Eckhart: Mystical Theologian*, London: SPCK, 1991, 170.

[31] Cf. Paul Mommaers, *The Riddle of Christian Mystical Experience: the Role of the Humanity of Jesus*, Louvain: Peeters Press, 2003, 50.

[32] Cf. Paul Mommaers, *The Riddle of Christian Mystical Experience,* 72.

[33] Cf. Paul Mommaers, *The Riddle of Christian Mystical Experience*, 72-73.

[34] Cf. Paul Mommaers, *The Riddle of Christian Mystical Experience*, 105.

[35] LT Ch. 2, 43. Cf. Edmund Colledge & James Walsh, eds., *A Book of Showings to the Anchoress Julian of Norwich,* Toronto: Pontifical Institute of Mediaeval Studies, 1978, 286: 12-17.

[36] LT ch. 4, p. 45. Cf. Edmund Colledge, *A Book of Showings*, 294: 3-6.

The Passion of Christ does not, however, capture the mystic's attention to keep it on itself; the ultimate aim of the contemplation on Jesus' one-time suffering in Jerusalem is to realise his actual suffering in the mystic himself or herself, here and now. In other words, the mystics are not satisfied with the mere visions of a suffering Christ, their appetites are bigger: they long for the active participation in his salvific Passion. Let us look again at Julian's wishes: "That my whole body," the Norwegian saint confesses, "should be filled with remembrance and feeling of his blessed Passion; for I wanted his pains to be my pains, with compassion, and then longing for God [...]. I wanted to suffer with him."[37]

As for Bernard of Clairvaux (1090-1153),[38] although he makes heartfelt love of and for Christ the hub of his spirituality, suffering still plays an essential role in his mystical experience. It is so because the main reason for loving the Godman is, for him, "the price for our redemption."[39] What moves, arouses, and enflames the French saint, making him love Jesus more than all the rest, is precisely the chalice that the Saviour drank for our salvation.[40]

Also Francis of Assisi (1182-1226)[41] experienced suffering as a meaningful reality, integral for his mystical path. Francis, for whom the *conformitas Christi* indicated the lifetime spiritual programme, experiences Christ's crucifixion in his very own body (stigmata) and soul, so as to be "totally transformed into the likeness of Christ crucified,"[42] so as to bear with him "the image of the Crucified (...) engraved in the members of his body."[43] Jacopone da Todi (1230-1306), a Franciscan friar from Umbria, summarises his mystical experience as follows: "Therefore I suffer to see Your wounded heart./ Why did You endure the pain?/ So that I might be healed."[44]

---

[37] LT ch. 2, p. 43 and ch. 3, 45. Cf. Edmund Colledge, *A Book of Showings*, 292: 51.

[38] Cf. William Harmless, *Mystics,* 41-58; Paul Mommaers, *The Riddle*, 117-129.

[39] Bernard of Clairvaux, *On the Song of Songs I*, 148; §2.

[40] Bernard of Clairvaux, *On the Song of Songs I*, 148; §2.

[41] Cf. Bernard McGinn, ed., *The Essential Writings of Christian Mysticism*, New York: The Modern Library, 2006, pp. 225-230; Paul Mommaers, *The Riddle*, 142-157.

[42] Bonaventure, *The Life of St. Francis*, 306; Ch. 13, §3.

[43] Bonaventure, *The Life of St. Francis* 307; ch. 13, §5.

[44] Jacopone da Todi, *How the Soul Through the Senses Finds God in All Creatures*, as quoted in Andrew Harvey, *The Essential Mystics*, 195.

Teresa of Avila (1515-1582),[45] one of the most striking personalities in the history of Christian spirituality, was not only graced with an "overwhelming and multi-faceted mystical experience,"[46] but also had great talent for expression. In one of her spiritual texts, Teresa describes Cherubim who thrusts a long spear of gold into her heart and leaves her all on fire with a great love of God. "The pain was so great" – the Spanish saint says – "that it made me moan; and yet so surpassing was the sweetness of this excessive pain that I could not wish to be rid of it."[47]

In his journal, Father Seraphim Rose (1934-1982), an American hieromonk of the Russian Orthodox Church outside Russia, wrote: "Let us not, who would be Christians, expect anything else from it than to be crucified. For, to be a Christian is to be crucified. [...] We must be crucified personally, mystically; for through crucifixion is the only path to resurrection."[48]

Last but not least, according to Thomas Merton (1915-1968),[49] the entire sense of Christian asceticism is summed up in Mark 8:34, when Jesus said, "If any man would come after me, let him deny himself and take up his cross and follow me."[50]

The common denominator is to be found, again, in a radical Christocentrism of mystical experience in the shape given to it by Christian saints.[51] Christ's suffering within the mystic's personal experience appears as tantamount to the mystic's own suffering as a voluntary participation in the death and resurrection of the Saviour.[52] As Maria Petyt (1623-1677), the rather unknown Flemish mystic, puts it, "the soul does not perceive or feel her abandonment and pains as being in her, but she regards, loves, and embraces them as the pains of

---

[45] Cf. Paul Mommaers, *The Riddle,* 59-94.

[46] Paul Mommaers, *The Riddle* 59.

[47] Teresa of Avila, as quoted in Andrew Harvey, *The Essential Mystics*, 195.

[48] Seraphim Rose, as quoted in "Christianity and Suffering," http://josephpatterson.wordpress.com/2007/05/10/christianity-and-suffering/, accessed on 20.12.2010.

[49] Cf. William Harmless, *Mystics*, Oxford: University Press, 2008, 19-40.

[50] Cf. Raymond Bailey, *Thomas Merton*, 79.

[51] There are only few exceptions in this regard, e.g., Meister Eckhart with his mystical focus on God and the Godhead.

[52] Cf. Paul Mommaers, *The Riddle*, 105.

Christ with whom she is united, and at that moment she is also forgetting herself."[53]

These few examples illustrate the elevation of suffering in the Christian mystical tradition. Of course, we already feel that it is not about the physical pain in and for itself. Indeed, much more is at stake which is why we are going to reinterpret and, so to speak, complete the above examples in due course.

5. Transforming *dukkha*?

Unlike Theravāda, Mahāyāna Buddhism developed a more subtle attitude toward suffering, integrating it, to a higher extent, in its mystical experience. First of all, as the Dalai Lama argues, from the pragmatic point of view, "intentional contemplation of the suffering nature ahead of time – in the sense of developing greater acceptance of suffering as a natural part of existence – can be helpful in preventing one from becoming overwhelmed when difficult situations arise."[54] But meditation on *dukkha* performs also other, much more essential functions. Within the framework of Mahāyāna Buddhism, mysticism is seen chiefly as the path to getting fully in tune with reality by removing from one's consciousness, all the filters. And awareness of suffering is to be conceived as an essential means for such a *purgation of consciousness*, which of course has its practical consequences. From the existential and ethical point of view, reflecting on suffering has tremendous importance because by realising its nature, one can develop "greater resolve to put an end to the causes of suffering and the unwholesome deeds which lead to suffering."[55] The mystic has to be aware of *dukkha*, and even plunge into suffering in order to feel it deeply, since it is commonly known

---

[53] Albert Deblaere, *De mystieke schrijfster Maria Petyt*, 43, as quoted in Paul Mommaers, *The Riddle*, 105.

[54] Dalai Lama, *The Art of Happiness*, 172. "If we can transform our attitude towards suffering," the Dalai Lama continues, "adopt an attitude that allows us greater tolerance of it, then this can do much to help counteract feelings of mental unhappiness, dissatisfaction, and discontent. [...] the strongest and most effective practice to help tolerate suffering is to see and understand that suffering is the underlying nature of Samsara, unenlightened existence" (Dalai Lama, *The Art of Happiness*, 115).

[55] Dalai Lama, *The Art of Happiness*, 172.

that "happy people don't develop wisdom. They are asleep."[56] If human being does not analyse the fact of suffering, she will never understand it, no matter how many births she goes through. While facing pain, she has a chance to enter the mystical path on which she may discover a way out of suffering. The pervasive unsatisfactoriness of existence – *dukkha* itself – can be therefore seen as a "noble truth", and consequently, meditating on it constitutes the starting point of the Buddhist mystical practice.

In a broad sense, three types of meditation can be distinguished: concentration, surrender, and self-emptying. The first type is the outer directed formal "technique"; the second type is the inner directed spontaneous "experience"; and the third type constitutes the "negative path" of detachment.[57] Let us examine at closer range the last approach. The negative way of meditation works to "eliminate 'rational consciousness' so that supra-rational might emerge";[58] its quest is the one for self transcendence.[59] In fact, what underlies Buddhism from the very beginning (though it blossoms most fully in its Tantric version) is the intuition of the transformation of negative psychoenergies into positive ones, understood as the essence of liberating the mind form karmic contamination. It can be reflected on in correlation with what the Western tradition calls the "path of the night" and which involves, so to say, *treatment by means of poison.*

The first of the three examples of the experience of suffering being integrated in the mystical path I would like to mention, namely the practice of *Asubhabhāvanā*, is based on this very principle. It can be summarised as a reflection on death – and even more; its "anticipation," i.e., some kind of *living death* during one's own life-time. The ascetic practices in

---

[56] Ajahn Chah, *Everything arises, everything falls away. Teachings on impermanence and the end of suffering*, trans. P. Breiter, Boston: Shambhala Publications, 2005, 58.
[57] Cf. Edward Stevens, *An Introduction*, 16. For Christian understanding of the mystical "theology of darkness," cf. Raymond Bailey, *Thomas Merton on Mysticism*, New York: Image Books, 1975, 102-106. For comparison of Christian and Buddhist forms and meanings of *via negativa*, cf. James L. Fredericks, *Faith Among Faiths: Christian Theology and the Non-Christian Religions*, Mahwah, New Jersey: Paulist Press, 1999, 83-84.
[58] Edward Stevens, *An Introduction*, 34.
[59] Cf. Edward Stevens, *An Introduction*, 36.

which monks are required to arouse in themselves an aversion towards the body in a state of decay are known in many Oriental traditions, including the oldest forms of Buddhism. What does the practice itself look like? *Asubhabhāvanā* is a form of Yoga contemplation, consisting in meditating on the disgust evoked by a human corpse.[60] To come to realise the hideous and impermanent character of all corporal being, a monk – often sitting in the middle of a crematory ground – is imagining dead bodies at different stages of decay and repeats, "Truly, my body is of the same nature and it will end in the same way."

The task of the "meditation on the impurity of the body" is to recognise visually one of the three main characteristics of any being, namely its impermanence or destructibility (*anicca*), and to develop in oneself a constant, unchangeable spiritual disposition to see the real nature of the world, namely *dukkha*. Thanks to such a change of perspective the monk is better prepared to become independent of various external circumstances and to concentrate his mind on an arduous spiritual practice. In this way, the follower of the negative path of meditation learns to say "no" to enslaving thoughts and desires, so that he or she may say "yes" to higher consciousness, to responsibility for his or her own life, and to acceptance of his or her imminent death.[61] Therefore, the ultimate aim of *Asubhabhāvanā* is not to arouse disgust for life, but to remove attachment, the will to live, and thus to gain serenity, peace, and bliss.

As some claim, a "deep realisation of the interconnectedness of everyone and everything"[62] constitutes a basic aspect of mysticism as such. Some schools of Mahāyāna Buddhism made the ethical consequences of this ontological fact the actual fundament of their mystical approach.[63] According to the Tibetan Buddhism, being aware

---

[60] Cf. Dīghanikāya III, 223.

[61] Cf. Edward Stevens, *An Introduction*, 48.

[62] Wayne Teasdale, *The Mystic Heart: Discovering a Universal Spirituality in the World's Religions*, Novato, CA: New World Library, 1999, 114.

[63] The Buddhists establish their entire religious *praxis* on the metaphysical perception of interconnectedness, which they call *pratiya-samutpada* (dependent origination). The parallel intuition on the Christian side underlies the concept of the Mystical Body of Christ, a community of being rooted in and centred on Christ as the "Head," the essence of the universal Church. Cf. Wayne Teasdale, *The Mystic Heart*, 114.

of suffering helps one to develop the capacity for empathy, to relate to other people's misery, and thus enhances one's capacity for compassion towards fellow beings.[64] Therefore, a *bodhisattva* resolves: "I take upon myself the burden of all suffering [...] the burdens of all beings. [...] The whole world of living beings I must rescue, from the terrors of birth, of old age, of sickness, of death, and rebirth [...]. I myself must grapple with the whole mass of suffering of all beings."[65] This is the idea that underlies the practice of *Tong-len*, the second example I want to briefly discuss referring to the Dalai Lama's teaching.

Tong-len ("giving and receiving") is a Mahāyāna visualisation practice in which one mentally visualises taking on another's pain and suffering, and in turn giving them all of one's own resources, good health, fortune, and so on;[66] it is a kind of "suffering by proxy."[67] "May my suffering be a substitute for the suffering of all other sentient beings. By experiencing this, may I be able to save all other sentient beings who may have to undergo similar suffering"[68] – that is the intention the monk is supposed to arouse in his mind.[69] Practices such as *Tong-len* are based on the conviction that "it is our suffering that is the most basic element that we share with others, the factor that unifies us with all living creatures."[70] *Tong-len* meditation may have a very beneficial influence on one's spiritual practice. First of all, it helps counteract one's selfishness. Besides, it can make a significant difference in how a suffering person responds to the situation of, let's say, illness in terms of his or her mental attitude: instead of being overwhelmed by anxiety and worry, one may save oneself from additional mental (psychological)

---

[64] Cf. Dalai Lama, *The Art of Happiness*, 173.

[65] *The Bodhisattva's Infinite Compassion*, Vajradhvaha Sutra, as quoted in Andrew Harvey, *The Essential Mystics*, 76.

[66] Cf. Dalai Lama, *The Art of Happiness*, 171.

[67] Dalai Lama, *The Art of Happiness*, 178.

[68] Dalai Lama, *The Art of Happiness,* 171.

[69] "[...] it is recommended that doing the visualisation of taking upon oneself the sufferings of other beings one should visualise these sufferings in the form of poisonous substances, dangerous weapons, or terrifying animals, and then absorb them directly into one's heart. Done effectively, such a visualisation makes one feel discomfort and thus is hitting its target: the self-centered, egocentric attitude." Dalai Lama, *The Art of Happiness*, 180.

[70] Dalai Lama, *The Art of Happiness*, 177.

pain and anguish by adopting the right attitude, and in fact, even see one's miserable state as a kind of opportunity and privilege.[71] In such a way, one's suffering "takes on new meaning as it is used as the basis for a religious or spiritual practice."[72]

It is particularly stressed in Zen that most human beings are asleep, deeply immersed in illusion, and that to attain enlightenment is, *de facto*, equivalent to being awaken and starting to live. "We all think we are living" -- D. T. Suzuki states – "we really eat, sleep, walk, talk. But are we really? If we were, we would never be talking about 'dread,' 'insecurity,' 'fear,' 'frustration,' 'courage to be,' 'looking into the vacant,' 'facing death.'"[73] Zen basically speaks of two decisive moments that mark the spiritual practice leading to self-liberation, i.e., entering the path and the moment of enlightenment itself. Of course, there is a place for training which, in a sense, prepares one to enlightenment, yet in no way can such a training be considered a *cause* of enlightenment. Zen practice is therefore presented, especially in the *Lin-chi* or *Rinzai* tradition, in a totally negative way; "All it does is lead the trainee to a dead end of all his faculties, a thorough impotence or despair," which is called "The Great Doubt" or "The Great Death."[74] This is the third and final illustration of suffering's *positive* meaning within the Buddhist mystical tradition. Enlightenment, seen as a "Great Light," a "Great Life," or "Resurrection," cannot break through but from this very point. Zen texts often describe the dialectic of The Great Death and The Great Life. It comes to full force in the words of the Zen master Yüan-wu (1063-1135) who is talking about "coming across a light in thick darkness" or "receiving treasure in poverty."[75] The meaning of The Great Death can also be grasped with the help of the following Zen story; "A disciple came to his master and asked, 'It is terribly hot, and how shall we escape the heat?' And at once the answer came, 'Let us go down to the bottom of the furnace.' So the perplexed disciple asked again, 'But in the furnace how shall we escape the scorching fire?' To

[71] Cf. Dalai Lama, *The Art of Happiness*, 171-178.
[72] Dalai Lama, *The Art of Happiness*, 172.
[73] D. T. Suzuki, *Mysticism*, 30.
[74] Paul Mommaers, *Mysticism*, 184-185.
[75] Yüan-wu, as quoted in Thomas Merton, *Mystics and Zen Masters*, New York: Dell Publishing Co., 1980, 233.

which he received the surprising reply, 'There, no further pains will harass you'."[76]

6. Passio Overcome by Visio

It is time to pose the question whether Christian mysticism is tantamount to masochism or not. Many thinkers, particularly in the West, see the practice of mysticism in general and Christian mysticism in particular as basically masochistic.[77] They consider the self-denial, the withdrawal, and the disappearance of the individual to be anti-human. Thus, they question the role of mysticism as a means of self-realisation, reproaching it for being instead, a way of self-destruction; a pathology which refuses to affirm and develop the self and a symptom of social alienation. In such a context, the mystic appears as a potential rebel, masochist, and a social outcast.[78] But may the self-emptying, purifying process of mysticism, the negative way, be really conceived as a type of physical and psychological suicide?[79]

Apart from obvious perversions of physical discipline sometimes turned into pure masochism, the Christian ideal of ascetic life has often been misunderstood and misrepresented, especially with regard to the meaning and intention lying behind such practices. They are not intended as punishment or rejection of the natural order, but rather as a means for the "subduing of the passions and the control of the senses" which serves, in turn, the purpose of "clearing away the barriers to the

---

[76] "The Furnace of Reality," as quoted in Andrew Harvey, *The Essential Mystics*, 84. For the sake of precision, it has to be clarified that The Great Death is not tantamount to the experience of suffering per se. As another Zen master, Hakuin, explains, when a trainee faces The Great Doubt, "before him there is in all directions only a vast and empty land without birth and without death, like a large plain of ice extending ten thousand miles. As though seated within a vase of lapis lazuli surrounded by absolute purity. [...] Within his heart there is not the slightest thought or emotion." Paul Mommaers & Jan Van Bragt, Mysticism Buddhist and Christian, 186. So the experience under discussion is to be conceived rather in terms of emptiness and purity than actual pain.

[77] Cf. Peter Berger, *The Precarious Vision: A Sociologist Looks at Social Fictions and Christian Faith*, New York: Doubleday and Company, Inc., 1961; Mary Douglas, *Natural Symbols: Explorations in Cosmology*, London: The Cressett Press, 1970.

[78] Cf. Edward Stevens, *An Introduction*, 161-163.

[79] Cf. Edward Stevens, *An Introduction*, 168.

experience of the goodness of creation," of continuing the "work of re-creation begun in, by and through Christ," and finally of "the death of the old for the sake of giving birth to the new."[80] In short, voluntary suffering is for Christian mystics a means of *catharsis*. In this sense, St. Teresa of Avila exhorted her spiritual charges to "spin a cocoon of death for the silkworm that the new creature of beauty might emerge."[81] Let us now retrace at least some of the mystical testimonies signalled earlier.

St. Julian of Norwich, whose "showings" have been briefly discussed above, does not desire bodily pain for itself. Far from that, she has a full appreciation of the suffering body as the seat of real love:[82] a love that "unites with the human person [of Jesus] and at once leads to the divine."[83] In the ninth *Revelation*, we see the divine emerge from the most miserable human and joy emerge from the suffering. Thus, the seeing of the visionary goes along with the mystic's own transformation:[84] "the changing of his blessed expression changed mine," Julian admits, "[...] our Lord made me think happily, 'Where is there now one jot of your pain or your sorrow?'."[85]

In the same spirit, Meister Eckhart claims, "If you suffer for God's sake and for God alone, that suffering does not hurt and is not hard to bear, for God takes the burden of it. [...] What one suffers through God and for God alone is made sweet and easy."[86] In another place, the Dominican mystic underscores the role that the spiritual "desert" plays in achieving *unio mystica*, "The spirit seeks to be broken through by God. God leads this spirit into a desert, into the wilderness and solitude

---

[80] Raymond Bailey, *Thomas Merton*, 78.

[81] Also Meister Eckhart stressed the importance of the "annihilation" of self: "I say that if the soul is to know God, it must forget itself [...] for as long as it is self-aware and self-conscious, it will not see or be conscious of God." Raymond B. Blakney, *Meister Eckhart: A Modern Translation*, New York: Harper & Brothers, 1957, 131.

[82] "I wanted his pains to be my pains, *with compassion, and then longing for God*." LT ch. 2, 43 and ch. 3, p. 45. Cf. Edmund Colledge, *A Book of Showings*, 292: 51 [my emphasis].

[83] Paul Mommaers, *The Riddle*, 48.

[84] Cf. Paul Mommaers, *The Riddle*, 54-55.

[85] LT Ch. 21, 71. Cf. Edmund Colledge, *A Book of Showings*, 379: 3-10.

[86] Meister Eckhart, as quoted in D. T. Suzuki, *Mysticism*, 136.

of the divinity where God is pure unity and where God gushes up within himself."[87]

Bernard of Clairvaux bases his description of contemplation on two pivotal terms: "death" and "rest"; while the former refers to the liberation from the restlessness that holds those still alive, the latter, synonymous with 'sleep,' points to the state of the contemplative who, like the bride, "sweetly sleeps within the arms of her bridegroom, in ecstasy of spirit."[88]

In the case of St. Francis, the means and the ultimate aim of the transformation through suffering is, again love, "the fire of ecstatic love," as St. Bonaventure, the biographer of *Povorello*, puts it.[89] And, like in the case of Bernard, the final word belongs not to bodily pain, but to saving grace, since, according to Bonaventure, in the last analysis, Francis was transformed "not by the martyrdom of his flesh, but by the fire of his love consuming his soul."[90] The revelation of paradise made by Christ to the good thief has also been made to St. Francis, and in a broader sense, to many other mystics. In their case, however, "paradise" has been realised already in this life by way of Christ-centered ecstasy.[91] This mystical experience allowed St. Francis to admit that "it is in dying to self that we are born to eternal life."[92] Only someone gifted with unusual internal freedom could address God with the following words of praise:

> Glory to You, my Lord,
> For those who forgive for love of You
> And bear sicknesses and ordeals. [...]
> Glory be to You, my Lord,

---

[87] Meister Eckhart, *Led to the Desert*, as quoted in Andrew Harvey, *The Essential Mystics*, 191.

[88] Bernard of Clairvaux, *Sermons on the Song of Songs*, 51-52; §7-8.

[89] The climax of this experience is to be found in Francis' "ecstatic contemplation" on Mount Alverna.

[90] Bonaventure, *The Life of St. Francis*, 306; ch. 13, §3. According to the different translation, "[...] through complete conflagration of mind." Cf. Bernard McGinn, *The Essential Writings*, 229.

[91] Cf. Paul Mommaers, *The Riddle*, 156.

[92] Andrew Harvey, *The Essential Mystics*, 193.

For our sister bodily death
From whom no living man can escape.[93]

Reading the works of St. Teresa of Avila, one may conclude that she was almost obsessed from the desire to suffer together with Jesus. But again, her willingness to participate in the Saviour's passion is to be seen as a means for union with God. For instance, the imaginative visions of suffering Christ the bridegroom and spiritual marriage, conceived as taking part in his death and resurrection, led Teresa to the more intellectual vision of the Trinity that brought her into the seventh Mansion.[94] But also the other way round, Teresa admits that "the *divine impression* is such that it causes its *human expression*," that is to say, the deeply spiritual impulse initiates an "interior movement that proceeds from the centre of the soul and awakens the faculties." And what the human powers are so strongly urged to do is precisely to serve and to suffer in the way that Jesus himself did.[95] As Teresa writes, "...these favours [perfect contemplation] are given us to strengthen our weakness [...] so that we may be able to imitate Him [Jesus] in his great sufferings."[96] For the Saint of Avila, the mystical experience of fellow-passion with Jesus is also a call to service, "Do you know when people really become spiritual?" – she asks in her *El Castillo Interior*. "It is when they become the slaves of God and are branded with his sign, which is the sign of the Cross [...]. Then He can sell them as slaves to the whole world, as He Himself was sold [...]."[97]

The two nights referred to by John of the Cross (1542-1591)[98] also imply the idea of *catharsis*.

Upon a dark night,
With anxious love inflamed,

---

[93] St. Francis, *The Song of the Sun*, as quoted in Andrew Harvey, *The Essential Mystics*, 193-194.

[94] Cf. E. Allison Peers, *Complete Works St. Teresa of Avila* [*Interior Castle*], London: Sheed and Ward, 1946, 334; 331-332.

[95] Cf. Paul Mommaers, *The Riddle*, 94.

[96] E. Allison Peers, *Complete Works*, 345.

[97] E. Allison Peers, *Complete Works*, 346. Cf. Paul Mommaers, *The Riddle*, 94.

[98] Cf. Bernard McGinn, *The Essential Writings*, 72-77.

O happy lot!
Forth unobserved I went,
My house being now at rest.[99]

The first night means the purgation of the sensual part of the soul, i.e., the privation of all sensual desires for the outward things of this world, the pleasures of the flesh, and the satisfactions of the will, whereas the second night is about the purification of the spiritual part of the soul led by God into a state of union with him. Therefore, in John's understanding, the traditional concept of asceticism is to be replaced by the mortifications of the desires which is "night to the soul" consisting not merely in bodily discipline, but being a free gift of God's grace.[100] As John puts it, "the privation was done in it [the soul] by God, a condition that is night to the soul."[101]

O night, my guide!
O night more friendly than the dawn!
O tender night that tied
Lover and the loved one,
Loved one in the lover fused as one![102]

In the context of John's reflections, it becomes clear that suffering, in its broad sense, appears in the Christian mystical tradition not only as a component of the *via purgativa*. It can be also seen as a "special gift" from God allowing the mystic to unite even closer with suffering Christ, as a fruit of an intimate love between creature and Creator. This "paradox of the *darkness born of light* is one of the religious experiences attested to by almost all of those who have earned a place of honour in the mystical tradition."[103]

---

[99] John of the Cross, *Dark Night*, as quoted in Bernard McGinn, *The Essential Writings*, 73.
[100] Cf. Bernard McGinn, *The Essential Writings*, 73-76.
[101] Bernard McGinn, *The Essential Writings*, 74.
[102] John of the Cross, *Dark Night*, as quoted in Andrew Harvey, *The Essential Mystics*, 202-203.
[103] Raymond Bailey, *Thomas Merton*, 104.

Also Thomas Merton was aware that in daring to embrace our own demons, we may discover our own truth and divinity.[104] Thus, in *New Seeds of Contemplation*, he states that "prayer and love are really learned in the hour when prayer becomes impossible, and the heart turns to stone."[105] That is also the hour that presents a real challenge to the negative path of detachment, dis-identification, and the entry into darkness.[106] Merton reminds us that a genuine contemplation is "at the same time the source and result of crisis."[107] And yet one also has to remember that monastic discipline, including all sorts of mortification, has only one purpose, namely to emancipate the monk.[108] It is "utterly useless," Merton points out, "if it turns us into freaks."[109] Therefore, on the one hand, misery as such, destitution as such, cannot be treated as the way to contemplative union.[110] On the other hand, to deny oneself and taking up one's cross to follow Christ (cf. Mark 8:34) is a necessary condition of mystical union with God. *Visio beatifica* appears, then not as a compensate, but as a *result* of suffering, yet – it has to be added – of suffering experienced in unity with Christ.[111]

To sum up, what has been said so far, a very crucial observation is to be made: in the experience of Christian mystics, suffering – both with regard to Jesus and to mystics themselves – always appears as an intermediary stage, as an expression of unconditional love, as a step on the way leading to transformation, but the step that cannot be easily dismissed, since the Cross constitutes a *sine qua non* condition of salvation.[112] As Paul Mommaers says, the "imaginative and affective concentration of the senses upon a senselessly suffering and destroyed human figure [of Jesus]," to the point of participating in his suffering,

---

[104] Cf. Edward Stevens, *An Introduction*, 53.

[105] Thomas Merton, *New Seeds of Contemplation*, New York: New Directions Publishing, 2007, 221.

[106] Cf. Edward Stevens, *An Introduction*, 37.

[107] Raymond Bailey, *Thomas Merton*, 104, 125.

[108] Cf. Raymond Bailey, *Thomas Merton*, 104, 125

[109] Thomas Merton, *No Man Is an Island*, Garden City, New York: Image Books, 1967, 94.

[110] Cf. Anne Bancroft, *Twentieth-Century Mystics and Sages*, New York: Arkana, 1989, 37.

[111] Cf. Raymond Bailey, *Thomas Merton*, 176.

[112] Cf. Paul Mommaers, *The Riddle*, 55.

is for the majority of mystics "the only possible way to be personally touched in the spirit [...] by indestructible joy, life, love, and the imageless reality."[113]

7. Buddhist and Christian Mystical Traditions Challenging Each Other

After examining diverse meanings of suffering, we should now ask in what sense mystical traditions of Buddhism and Christianity can challenge and enrich each other. In a broad sense, the fruitfulness of Buddhist-Christian dialogue results chiefly from the distance which divides (in every sense) Banaras from Jerusalem. Even a superficial knowledge of both traditions allows one to presume that in an all-encompassing range of possible answers to the question of suffering (as well as to many other questions) Buddhism and Christianity indicate two opposite poles.[114] It is so because these traditions grow out of basically different pre-philosophical intuitions. In effect, both their spiritualities and their mystical approaches are – at least at first glance – so different that one can hardly speak of "mysticism without bounds."[115]

So it is in relation to suffering as a "component" in the mystical path.[116] As I tended to show in the first part of my paper, "the very starting point of Buddhism, historically and conceptually, is the undesirability of suffering."[117] Christianity, instead, seems to question this presupposition.[118] However, the above analysis of suffering and the roles it plays in the mystical practices of Buddhism and Christianity shows that the picture is not black and white. The mystical experience in its specifically Buddhist form actually opens itself to the various dimensions

[113] Paul Mommaers, *The Riddle*, 57.

[114] This internal discrepancy between the two traditions may be considered as one of the factors of an unusual growth of the Buddhist-Christian dialogue which is practised on many levels (from broadly understood culture to sophisticated theological analyses) since the end of 19th century.

[115] It is clear from the Buddhist point of view, more than from the Christian one, that "what makes the mystic a mystic is simply a particular kind of awareness [...]. In other words, mysticism is primarily a matter of consciousness." Cf. Paul Mommaers, *Mysticism,* 112.

[116] Cf. "Crucifixion and Enlightenment" in D. T. Suzuki, *Mysticism*, 113-122.

[117] Paul Williams, *The Unexpected Way: On Converting from Buddhism to Catholicism*, Edinburgh & New York: T&T Clark, 2002, 60.

[118] Cf. Paul Williams, *The Unexpected Way*, 60-61.

of *dukkha*; whereas Christian mysticism leads to overcoming *passio* for the sake of *unio*. One might even describe the process through which the Buddhist mystic is going in terms of "masochism" and psychological "self-annihilation." For his aim is to destroy his unique individual human reality by disciplining his senses, i.e., by withdrawing them from their natural objects, by stilling his fantasies and feelings, in consequence of which his mind becomes empty, and ultimately, he loses even the sense of his own ego.[119] At this stage, however, *dukkha* consequently loses its *raison d'être*, as one realises that there is no subject to experience it anymore. On the other hand, the Christian mystic, instead of being seen as the "saint-sufferer," may appear as a beneficiary of the blissful union with God. Although, as it was demonstrated above, such a union can only be "built" on the transforming fellow-suffering with Christ the Redeemer.

The element common to Buddhist and Christian contemplatives is the consciousness of "an upheaval, a breakthrough, whereby something in the subject has to 'give,' to break, or to be annihilated."[120] Interestingly enough, this annihilation – painful as it may be at the moment – from the perspective of mystics themselves is not experienced as a loss or sacrifice but on the contrary, as an immeasurable gain, since what is actually broken or annihilated in this process is a negative element, an obstacle or a "cage."[121] In fact, the mystical purgation, *catharsis*, can be described in very similar terms in both Buddhism and Christianity, namely as the giving up of self's selfhood, the process in which "the self begins to realise its own powerlessness and limitations and begins

[119] Cf. Edward Stevens, *An Introduction*, 170. This ideal of mystical "masochism" is epitomised, inter alia, both in the Judeo-Christian canonisation of the suffering Job submitting to complete destruction by the Biblical God and in the *Ch'an* Buddhist story of Bodhidarma who sat for nine years facing a wall until his legs withered away.

[120] Paul Mommaers, *Mysticism*, 95. However, when it comes to speculative interpretation of what exactly the object of this annihilation is, the ways of Buddhism and Christianity part again. While the answer of the former is simple and straightforward, namely: what is annihilated is the "I," the individuality, or the "person" (as far as it is understood as a synonym for the individual), the latter, as it values the person, is obliged to formulate a more subtle distinction: what is annihilated is not the person as such, with its unique capacity of self-presence, but the distorted preoccupation with oneself.

[121] Cf. Paul Mommaers, *Mysticism*, 95.

to find a new happiness in the surrender of its entity."[122] Insofar as it is intimately linked with the apophatic tradition of negative theology, Christian mysticism has therefore much in common with the "tenacious process of negation" that pervades the whole of Buddhism, and particularly Mahāyāna Buddhism.[123]

As Thomas Merton suggests, maybe the most striking dissimilarity between Christian and Buddhist mysticism consists in the fact that, although both "set out in search of the true self," the Buddhist mystic goes no farther than the inner self, whereas the Christian one "presses on through his personal centre to God."[124] Christian mysticism of unity or union (*unio mystica*) is basically the mysticism of love.[125] It is this personal and relational context, the context of the intimate and often passionate love, a kind of "spiritual eros,"[126] in which Christian mystics experience and "equip with meaning" their suffering.[127] On the other hand, Buddhism, as a religion of Wisdom, never came to assign a congruent place to love on the mystical path, even at the time when mercy had come to be considered, in the practice, as the "final outcome of the Buddhist path."[128] It is so because the final state to be achieved by the Buddhist disciple, *upekkha* ("indifference" or, better, "equanimity"), means to get rid of both love and hatred, "to be interested neither in happiness nor in suffering, neither in pleasure nor in sorrow."[129] Thus, Merton concludes,

---

[122] Anne Bancroft, *Twentieth-Century Mystics*, 40.

[123] Cf. Anne Bancroft, *Twentieth-Century Mystics*, 33.

[124] Raymond Bailey, *Thomas Merton*, 203.

[125] Cf. Paul Mommaers, *Mysticism*, 197. It is worth mentioning that around the 12th century this ancient form of mysticism (going back at least to Origen) underwent a basic change: its approach became more human and affective. In short, love now became "the whole thing." Bernard of Clairvaux is one of the most striking examples of this new tendency.

[126] Cf. Louis Dupré, "Mysticism," in M. Eliade, ed., *The Encyclopedia of Religion*, New York: Macmillan, 1987, 10:254.

[127] Cf. Paul Mommaers, *Mysticism*, 196-197.

[128] Cf. Louis Dupré, "Mysticism," 132, 182-183, 191-192.

[129] Gadjin M. Nagao, «Tranquil Flow of Mind: An Interpretation of *Upekṣā*,» *Indianisme et Bouddhisme: Mélanges offerts à Mgr. Etienne Lamotte,* Louvain-la-Neuve: Institut Orientaliste, 1980, 245. And yet in Buddhist practice, especially in Mahāyāna Buddhism with its bodhisattva path, mercy clearly rose to the rank of primary virtue, becoming *de facto* the basic dynamic element of the Buddhist path. Cf. Paul Mommaers, *Mysticism*, 197-199. The mostly routinely repeated "solution" to this paradox is a reduction of

while "in Christianity the confrontation [with Absolute Being, Absolute Love, Absolute Mercy, or Absolute Void] is *theological* and *affective*, through *word* and *love*, in Zen [and generally in Buddhism] it is *metaphysical* and *intellectual*, through *insight* and *emptiness*."[130] One could add to that the very personal and often "passionate" character of mystical experience in Christianity as contrasted to the totally "cool" and purely cognitive character of Buddhist mysticism.[131]

In this context, engaging into dialogue with the Christian mysticism of love, marked with affection and "high temperature," can protect Buddhism from dehumanisation. On the other hand, Buddhist mystics have much to say about the "technical" and intellectual side of meditation which tends to be compromised by their Christian fellow-contemplatives. With regard to suffering, due to its doctrinal focus on the undesirability of *dukkha*, Buddhism may remind Christianity that what lies in the very heart of each genuine mysticism is the transformation of one's mind and heart, which logically excludes the mystic's personal suffering from being a goal in itself. Christianity, in turn, shall continuously emphasise the positive role of the experience of suffering which – seen in a wider context, as part of a greater spiritual path, as a component in the process of purifying the mind – ultimately allows one to achieve a state in which there is no more suffering.[132]

Finally, important contribution Buddhist and Christian mystics can make to the humanity today consists simply in honest and straightforward talk about suffering. The contemporary world, the Western world in particular, seems to be more and more paralysed by the most common facts of human existence such as disease, old age, and death. In this regard, the Dalai Lama rightly points out that "as long as we view suffering as an unnatural state, an abnormal condition that we fear, avoid, and reject, we will never uproot the causes of suffering and begin

mercy to wisdom by a definition of mercy as "the insight into the non-duality of self and other." Paul Mommaers, *Mysticism*, 200.

[130] Thomas Merton, *Zen and the Birds of Appetite*, New York: New Directions Publishing Corporation, 1968, 62.

[131] Cf. Paul Mommaers, *Mysticism*, 39.

[132] Cf. Dalai Lama, *The Art of Happiness*, 118.

to live a happier life."[133] From the Christian point of view, it would be more accurate to say that without fully accepting the human condition, together with suffering and death which constitute its essential aspects, people are not able to truly acknowledge the goodness of creation and engage themselves in the mission of re-creation to which they have been called.

References

01. Bailey, Raymond, *Thomas Merton on Mysticism*, New York: Image Books, 1975.
02. Bancroft, Anne, *Twentieth-Century Mystics and Sages*, New York: Arkana, 1989.
03. Berger, Peter, *The Precarious Vision: A Sociologist Looks at Social Fictions and Christian Faith*, New York: Doubleday and Company, Inc., 1961.
04. Blakney, Raymond B., *Meister Eckhart: A Modern Translation*, New York: Harper & Brothers, 1957.
05. Bodhi, Bhikkhu, *In the Buddha's Words: An Anthology of Discourses from the Pali Canon*, Boston: Wisdom Publications, 2005.
06. Chah, Ajahn, *Everything arises, everything falls away. Teachings on impermanence and the end of suffering*, trans. P. Breiter, Boston: Shambhala Publications, 2005.
07. Cioran, Emile, *The Fall into Time*, trans. R. Howard, Quadrangle Books, Chicago 1970.
08. Colledge, Edmund & Walsh, James, eds., *A Book of Showings to the Anchoress Julian of Norwich*, Toronto: Pontifical Institute of Mediaeval Studies, 1978.
09. Dalai Lama & Cutler, Howard C., *The Art of Happiness. A Handbook for Living*, London: Hodder & Stoughton, 1998.
10. Douglas, Mary, *Natural Symbols: Explorations in Cosmology*, London: The Cressett Press, 1970.
11. Dumoulin, Heinrich, *Östliche Meditation und Christliche Mystik,* Freiburg: Karl Alber, 1966.
12. Eliade, Mircea, ed., *The Encyclopedia of Religion*, New York: Macmillan, 1987.
13. Fredericks, James L., *Faith Among Faiths: Christian Theology and the Non-Christian Religions*, Mahwah, New Jersey: Paulist Press, 1999.

---

[133] Dalai Lama, *The Art of Happiness*, 122.

14. Hanh, Thich Nhat, *Living Buddha, Living Christ*, New York: Riverhead Books, 1995.
15. Hanh, Thich Nhat, *The Blooming of a Lotus: Guided Meditation Exercises for Healing and Transformation*, Boston: Beacon Press, 1999.
16. Harmless, William, *Mystics*, Oxford: University Press, 2008.
17. Harvey, Andrew, ed., *The Essential Mystics: Selections from the World's Great Wisdom Traditions*, New York: Harper San Francisco, 1996.
18. McGinn, Bernard, ed., *The Essential Writings of Christian Mysticism*, New York: The Modern Library, 2006.
19. McGinn, Bernard, *The Mystical Thought of Meister Eckhart: The Man From Whom God Hid Nothing*, New York: The Crossroad Publishing Company, 2001.
20. Merton, Thomas, *Mystics and Zen Masters*, New York: Dell Publishing Co., 1980.
21. Merton, Thomas, *New Seeds of Contemplation*, New York: New Directions Publishing, 2007.
22. Merton, Thomas, *No Man Is an Island*, Garden City, New York: Image Books, 1967.
23 Merton, Thomas, *Thoughts on the East*, New York: New Directions Bibelot, 1995.
24. Merton, Thomas, *Zen and the Birds of Appetite*, New York: New Directions Publishing Corporation, 1968.
25. Mommaers, Paul & Bragt, Jan Van, *Mysticism Buddhist and Christian. Encounters with Jan van Ruusbroec*, Crossroad: New York, 1995.
26. Mommaers, Paul, *The Riddle of Christian Mystical Experience: the Role of the Humanity of Jesus*, Louvain: Peeters Press, 2003.
27. Nagao, Gadjin M., "Tranquil Flow of Mind: An Interpretation of Upekṣā," *Indianisme et Bouddhisme: Mélanges offerts à Mgr. Etienne Lamotte*, Louvain-la-Neuve: Institut Orientaliste, 1980.
28. Pabongka, Rinpoche, *Liberation in our hands. Part two: The Fundamentals*, trans. Trijang Rinpoche with Sermey Khensuar Lobsang Tharchin and Artemus B. Engle, Howell, New Jersey: Mahayana Sutra and Tantra Press, 1994.
29. Peers, Edgar Allison, *Complete Works St. Teresa of Avila*, London: Sheed and Ward, 1946.
30. Petitot, Henry, *Saint Teresa of Lisieux*, Burns Oates and Washbourne LTD., London, 1927.
31. Suzuki, Daisetsu Teitaro, *Mysticism: Christian and Buddhist*, London & New York: Routledge Classics, 2002.
32. Teasdale, Wayne, *The Mystic Heart: Discovering a Universal Spirituality in the World's Religions*, Novato, CA: New World Library, 1999.

33. Thera, Nyanaponika, *The Roots of Good and Evil*, Kandy: Buddhist Publication Society, 1977.
34. Whitson, Robley Edward, *Mysticism and Ecumenism*, New York: Sheed and Ward, 1966.
35. Williams, Paul, *The Unexpected Way: On Converting from Buddhism to Catholicism*, Edinburgh & New York: T&T Clark, 2002.

4

The Abiding Density of Light

Light and Sound Carved and Chiseled Across the Luminous Black Light of the Islamic and Sufi Void

Dr. Barbara A. Amodio
Fairfield University, Norwalk, USA

The abiding image of Islamic and Sufi sacred aesthetics and cosmology is Light. This Light plays over, across and through a Void which is at once an Infinity and a Zero of cosmic, grounding Formlessness, an aniconic mystic Void beyond all name and image.[1] It is the zone of the 100th Name of Allah which, unlike the other more recognizable 99 Names, can neither be pronounced, imagined nor comprehended by the minds of creatures to whom it remains intellectually awesome and overwhelming while yet emanating a core value of constant, unconditional, uninterrupted absolute Love exceeding all limitations of human comprehension. The chattering *nafs* (mind) must be stilled to truly enter and penetrate the realm of Light and Void to *taste* it spiritually by entering the realm of *Ruh* (Soul), and more deeply, entering the jewel of the heart and the

[1] The Islamic Void is here easily recognized in its functionally equivalent perspective of that which is *beyond Nama-Rupa* (Name and Form) in Indian traditions. Each offers a diverse, complementary perspective on cosmic Formlessness that transcends and grounds the more common western (and nonwestern) concept of a Personal (or Creator) God. The aniconic emphasis is tied in Islam to strict proscriptions against idol worship, and idols as fake images of the One and Formless Godhead. No clarification is made between an idol and an icon (sacred symbolic image.) This philosophical issue has lead to intercultural clashes.

heart secret (*Sirr*) abiding in the cosmos and reflecting into the *Ruh* of all persons.[2]

The Void presents the mystical paradox (*shat'h*) of an inner darkness that is yet luminous beyond all ordinary light, denoting the very essence of light before it is manifest to the senses. In the Islamo-Sufi context this connotes the mystical paradox of an Unmanifest Luminous Black Light[3] within a cosmic cave at the heart of the cosmos from which all creation springs.[4] The appearing world (*alam al-mulkh*) of this planet somewhere in the swirling Andromeda Pinwheel of the Milky Way and Northern Lights is in its Qura'nic perspective part of the lowest of seven Spheres

[2] Sufi spiritual states (*ahwal*) by whatever system of naming correspond to the states of any Master, and again, to those delineated authoritatively by Patanjali in the Yoga Sutras (Aphorisms). Cultural inflections, sacred symbols and metaphors vary, while the Yoga of consciousness among authentic Masters of all traditions remains constant. The *silsilah* (initiatic chain) observed is also discerned in Indian and Taoist transmissions from Master or Guru to inner circle disciples (*sishyas*). Initiation frequently may occur by a spiritualizing glance or other transmission of the *barakah* only accomplished by authentic Masters, many of quite ordinary appearance in the world. Patanjali's systematic elaboration of the stages for dissolving the mindstuff is meticulous and standard. The expressions used by Sufi saints and Masters converge on the same meanings with slight nuances applied by different authoritative Masters. In general, the Sufi terminology simplifies and uses didactic models of contraction and expansion, crossing valleys, and climbing the cosmic mountain to its peak, represented by the mystically derived Arabic letter *Qaf* persued in light and sound. Sufi contraction is the experience of dissolving negative mind in stepped stages, then halting at stations while becoming established in higher states (standings) along the way. In a traditionally unifying Qur'anic metaphor, the tip of the cosmic mountain (*Qaf*) touches the footstool leading to the Throne ('arsh) which is the Void.

[3] The luminous black light of the Void is the *sawad a-zam* of Classical Arabic and the *nur-i siyah* of Persian. It is mentioned in the Qur'an. The Void functions much as the Formlessness of Brahman in the Indian tradition, both being completely *arupa* (formless.) The Indian descriptor, beyond *Nama-Rupa (Name and Form)*, implies the Supreme (Para) state of the Ground of the cosmos, namely, Brahman, and carries the same cosmological and metaphysical distinctions and functions as the 100th Name of Allah. Both traditions emphasize that what is in the macrocosm is also all-pervading throughout the cosmos and into the microcosm. The emphases each cosmology gives to Sound and Light are non-contradictory and complementary.

[4] The hermeneutic image is functionally equivalent to the understanding of a black hole in astro-physics, with a point of light at its depth. The attraction, or should we say attunement, of Islamic philosophical consciousness to the mystical mathematics of the Greek philosophers and their Indian roots is evident.

emanating from the Void, located in the Sphere of Hanging Forms carved and chiseled from the hyletic substance of cosmic divine Light and Sound that drips and streams to form the Sphere. The Sphere, despite naïve appraisal as static substance and matter, is a dense and dynamic world of thickened pulsated Light congealed into form figuration and sound. The aesthetic language and conventions of all Sufi and Islamic sacred art are mindfully tuned to the mystical paradox (*shati'h*) of this self-luminous Light that lights all other lights and creates all sounds and form figuration. Let us begin from there.

> Allah is the Light of the Heavens and the Earth. The similitude of His Light is as it were a Niche wherein is a Lamp: the Lamp within a Glass: the Glass as it were a pearly star. From a tree right blessed is it lit, an Olive-tree neither of the East nor of the West, the Oil whereof were well-nigh luminous though fire touched it not: Light upon Light! [5]

The 100th Name is of the Unseen realm (*alam i-gharb.*) Its Light is not manifest to the ordinary senses, but only to the extraordinary esoteric seeing acquired by deep love of God transformed into Sufi

[5] *The Light Verse*, trans. Pickthall, S.24.35. For a more literal translation, with explanations, see the translation by Muhammad Asad. Asad rightly inflects *similitude* with the conceptual gloss of a *parable*, noting well that the complexity of some truths requires the specialized analogy and metaphor of a parable. We would wish that the aesthetic form of the parable (and parabolic meaning), of which Isa/Jesus as Word and Spirit was a Master, be more fully explained, for its allegorical meaning requires a grounding in several poles the most important and essential of which for sacred aesthetics is the supra-conscious (mystical) experience of God. Indeed the surrounding verses in the 'fenced in' meaning of this Surah refer to persons who are not guided by truth. That is, they are not grounded in this important Pole which is godly in the extreme. Such persons are as those who mistake a mirage of water in the desert for real water, and are those to whom the Darkness Verse (S.35.40) applies. Such persons are not guided out of the desert in their lives, nor again do they appreciate the goodness and abundance of nature and creation. They see only billow upon billow of darkness and cloud amassing until they are blinded in the darkness, unable to perceive that God is ever present and all-pervading. Asad's translation leaves in play the possibility of persons to turn from darkness into light and seek the help of a merciful God to do so, desisting from their contribution to and as the billows of darkness, or indeed suffer the consequences of a swift reckoning beyond their ability to fathom (S.35.39.)

God-intoxication, mostly guided in its highest stages by the authentic Islamic Sheikh, Pir or Mursid.[6] The reality of divine Light pervades all levels of the cosmos, ultimately more an experience than ever a name, a form or an image, each of these a limitation expressing only a facet of the massive and incomprehensive full prism and Unity (*tawhid*) of the Godhead. The other 99 Names are projected into Lettered Sound and Light and appear in the visible world (*al-mulkh*) in the coordinated oral and written forms of calligraphy and language where they create meditative conditions through which humans may enter the Qur'an's *mercy and consolation.*[7] The Lettered Light of Calligraphy, the Sounded Light of Sufi Sama', the divinely grounded Voice of Arabic in the Qur'an, light reflecting pigments, the architecturally lightened maghribi arch, and more are discussed in this context in Chapters III, V, II and IV, respectively, as both aesthetic and meditative demonstrations of cosmological truths.[8]

---

[6] As in any other mystical tradition, no less Islam, God may guide whom God wills. Grace may fall on a person for what the Irish call 'second sight' according to intense love, perseverance, and the high state of the person. By Indian accounts, the high state is in fact what allows the *barakah* (spiritualizing initiatic transformation) facilitated by a Master, Guru or Pir to take effect at all, albeit acquired over a journey that traverses many lifetimes. In all traditions, this *barakah* is administered by God's guiding permission, and is not a business commodity for sale.

[7] The constantly recurring sacred iconic message of the Qur'an as itself the ultimate icon or standing miracle of Islamic revelation is *consolation and mercy.* The sacred message of Indian sacred icons is *bounty and encouragement* for humans. The Indian message occurs mostly in carved and sculpted icons in the symbolic language of vehicles, arms, coordinated hands, weapons and objects held in hands, gestures and more, even sacred dance in which dancers pantomime the impossibly complex poses of the icons by balancing each other in expressive unities formed by as many as three dancers freezing and holding the expressive pose as if one. Thus each pose of sculpted figure must be read, reading for example the coordinated sacred sentence in two of the 4 coordinated hands of a Shiva icon expressing Lord of the (Cosmic) Dance (Shiva Nataraj), we have the sacred message that the Elephant Hand is pointing to what is most important, namely, the foot held in freedom representing the Soul coordinated in the sacred symbol sentence with a hand in the 'Fear Not' gesture; all this *encouragement* given *bountifully* to humans despite the appearance of danger in a dance of life that takes place inside an inherently temporary circle of flames.

[8] Extreme aversion to idol worship continues to eclipse the learned ability to discuss, without socio-political and metaphysical tensions, authentic functional distinctions between icons and idols.

Not everyone is finely tuned to the Light. We explore a certain spiritual iconography that emerges around Light and Ibliss, the personal name of the leader of the non-god-fearing Jin that forms an army of Shaytans/Satans. The distinction in the Qur'an between Jin/Shaytans, Angels and Humans as diverse species surfaces philosophical issues not articulated in Judaism or Christianity[9] pointing to a wider dimension of Ibliss as the ultimate keeper of the last gate. The Darkness Verse follows the Light Verse and is revealed for those of the human species who are lead away from the Light by Ibliss. His ability to tempt humans is made easier by the oft-repeated Qur'anic reminder that *the human species is by nature disputatious and contentious*, favoring argument and rational dispute, thus easily susceptible to the constant whispering (*waswasa*) of Ibliss across the hearts and minds of persons. Important clarifications and tensions among species contribute a didactic aesthetic language and symbolism in Sufi philosophical tales. The Qur'an repeats throughout that *Satan (Ibliss) to the human species is an open enemy,* leader of an army of Jinn of a particular class, not at all a fallen Angel, bearing within himself extreme intelligence, intimate shared knowledge of the universe, free will, the desire for revenge characteristic of a scorned lover, and arrogance in abundance. Yet he provides somewhere a hidden service as he is not destroyed by God. Made of smokeless fire, as all Jin, Ibliss has a deep flaw despite his great intelligence and intimacy with the Godhead. This flaw is his inability to penetrate surfaces and discern deeper realities, and again, his inability to love beneath the surfaces, nor again, to subdue anger with love. Chapter VII treats the sacred story of Ibliss as an icon of meaning manifesting in sacred aesthetic conventions that advance the complex mystical paradox (*shat'h*) of Ibliss, and the theme of the rehabilitation of Ibliss, plus other *shat'h* used in Sufi teaching tales.

[9] The Qur'an distinguishes and clarifies three created species, Jin, Angels, and Humans. The modern Christian view does not distinguish the Jin, though they are understood by Jews and Muslims in common parlance. No one except modern Christians considers Satan a fallen 'Angel', thus obfuscating the terms of discourse of even very ordinary language and learned communication. Careful scholarship is needed to sort through the origins, probably Andalusian prior to the Grand Inquisition, for even such Angelologies as the one by Thomas Aquinas, which remains essentially unfounded in the official versions of the Old and New Testament.

The Void and its 100th Name occupy the zone where only mystics, godfriends, prophets, and saints venture well. It accounts for the rigorous so-called *aniconism* of Islam in the land of its birth originally intended to counter the thriving business model of idol worship in use in the Near East at that time. The ways in which an educated and well-traveled Islam has been called to expand its original comprehension concerning idol worship and to appraise the authentic aesthetic difference between an idol and an icon are examined repeatedly in what follows. Only icons have sacred spiritual grounding and bear meditative forms not of the ordinary world of the senses. We shall examine this axiom of consciousness in every chapter, mindful that all revelations come from a divine source to humans in a particular culture and community at a particular time and place of understanding in human history. A symbolic language arises that points conspicuously to universal norms of a Void that grounds multiple world traditions. The Islamic revelation is still in process of acquiring adjusted understanding of its revealed meanings achieved in, for example, Islam's encounters with both the sacred aesthetics of Persian art and icons, and after great and bloody initial conflict, with diverse strands within the Indian tradition where an active worship employs a sophisticated sacred symbology parsed among numerous sacred icons loosely resembling human form, but in no way intending human form.[10] Descriptive values are completed in normative meanings, transcending physical forms.

The paradox of the Void is the grounding aesthetic image for Islamic and Sufi cosmology and all sacred arts throughout the world *'ummah*. The Void cannot be separated from Light. The *mystical paradox* (*shati'h*) of a *black light*[11] or a *supreme blackness*[12] is a Luminous Black Light that lies at the heart of the universe in the invisible locus of a cosmic cave that is beyond all image and form figuration. It parallels distinctions preserved in Indian traditions that clarify and distinguish

[10] One of the best phenomenological accounts of the differences between sacred icons and secular idols is the one by Ananda K. Coomaraswamy in his *Transformation of Nature in Art*. He follows Benedetto Croce, who in turn followed Plotinus' distinctions. Another fellow of this learned circle in Islamic aesthetics is Professor Sayyed Hosein Nasr, a student of Coomaraswamy's.

[11] Persian *nur i-siyah*

[12] Classical, Arabic *sawad a'zam*

phases in the evolution of sacred Sound and Light from a similarly cosmic Formlessness, though the Islamic Sufi tradition offers the important condition of Black Light as a complement in light for the Indian Unstruck Sound (*Anahata*), both of which describe the mystical experience of persons in high state mystical awareness of the Godhead as Void. The Islamic-Sufi *people of proximity* (nearness) are the Indian equivalents of those in *savikalpa* or *nirvikalpa* states and *samadhi* (enlightenment and communion) described authoritatively by Patanjali in the Yoga Sutras (Aphorisms.) Both sets of godfriends, a Sufi term, experience Light and Sound of a different and exalted order, though it would be safe to say that the Islamic tradition lays greater emphasis on Light while the Yoga tradition places greater emphasis on Sound. We may discern that the two phenomena, Light and Sound, are not so easily separated in either tradition, nor in modern science, and that the boat of Yoga sails as well on the Islamic magic carpet as on the sacred Zephyr (West Wind) of the Greeks. The Qur'anic Void foretells the black light and nutrinos of modern science, while the Indian cosmology conserves collateral verification fitting this sacred cosmology into the organically holistic systems models of post-Einsteinean relativity, other emerging paradigms, string theory and the process philosophies that work out theoretical issues and implications of the shifted interactive perspective. Mathematical physics is ever on the cusp of a sacred mystic embrace of cosmology and metaphysics, as it has always been across traditions from ancient times. All aspects of human life, indeed ethics, politics and all else, converge on the Void.

The Indian tradition conserves meticulous distinctions regarding the spiritual evolutions of mystical states in the fluid continuum between Light and Sound in its distinctions of *para*, *pasyanti*, *madhyama*, *vaikhari* and *shabda* (*sakti*) that capture the evolution of Unmanifest Sound (*para* or *supreme* vibration) into an elongation and crystallization into vector directions (*dik*), designs and luminous sound (seeing sound), contrast and duality of forms, a many from a One, so dense that it appears to the senses as solid. This image is carried forward into its philosophical implications about the form figuration in Arabic Calligraphy, discussed in Chapter III, and indeed all form figuration visible to the senses in the physical appearing creation. The Indian didactic philosophical image is highly compatible with the Qur'anic image of a universe made of Allah's Light as its hyletic substance, sometimes called Mohammedan Light.[13] The appearing world (*alam al-mulk*) is in essence the lowest of Seven Spheres, the Sphere of Hanging Forms carved and chiseled from this Light. The entire cosmos is constituted by what Ibn 'Arabi has called the *cosmic dust* (*al-haba'*), the Mohammedan Light (*Nur Mohammad*),[14] which pours from the Void. Indeed the first creation in the cosmology of the Qur'an is Light, created from the Luminous Black Light of the Void, thus beginning the seeming duality of the cosmos, its evolution from a Non-Dual One into a created many, just as the Supreme (*Para*) Siva-Sakti pendulum vibration launches the Indian cosmology into subtle and yet still unmanifest parallel evolutions in Sound and Light proceeding from a Non-Dual Oneness. Broadly, this also reflects the Tao's less detailed picture of an Invisible and Unmanifest Tao that can never be named which never fully *shows* its Infinity, but only its existentiated *te*, the playful and partial manifestation of Itself projected into the appearance

[13] We may speculate intelligently with a small group of scholars that the two traditions, Indian and Islamo-Sufi, were formerly unified in some way and at, in my view, and exceedingly ancient period. The resemblances in the linguistic form alone of using roots, mostly triliteral, elevation of lettered sound over other sound, doctrines of meaning (*sphota-vada* and *mana'*, respectively), and even the inherent spiritual meaning of certain letters and sounds as the literal sound and light body of the godhead are striking, but neglected domains of study and correctives to the merely linguistic division of languages into 'different' families. This is a separate topic and vastly instructive topic. The Qur'an not only recommends travel and study, even naming one destination (China) while excluding none, but it allows that Allah has never abandoned humanity and has in all times, places and situations opened the Invisible Book to people. While Mohammad *pbuh* is considered the seal of Prophets, this in no way precludes the reality of other authentic revelations laid down by Allah. Key is the word authentic. Perhaps one of the best systematizations of tests of authenticity is the one laid down by the Nyaya-Vaisheshika school of Indian logicians who extended their inquiry, unlike modern Anglo-analytic traditions, to supra-conscious reality and the godhead, contributing a decent and careful checklist for the wary and for the sincere seekers. It does not appear to contradict Islam.

[14] The *Nur Mohammad* is not intended to make the Prophet the source of the cosmos, or a 'partner' with God. It is rather a metaphor to explain that everything is *existentiated* or created of Light. Mohammad *pbuh* is manufactured by Allah from a column of Light in the horizontal position, the position of submission. It is not possible for him to become insolent (vertical.) This is explored in the discussions of the prayer Carpet and Ibliss (Shaytan/Satan.)

of a world on a lighted screen that the Qur'an would describe as carved and chiseled from cosmic Light then rolled into Sound. The Qur'anic domain of the earthly Garden as also the entire appearing cosmos is hanging, suspended, chiseled, carved and pervaded by this Light breath of life. We will revisit the abiding didactic image of Light and Void in each Islamic sacred art that follows, with accompanying illustrations.

Allah is One God. No plurality, divisions, rivals, or idol partners. In a philosophical word, Allah is a radical position on Unity (*Tawhid*) and Oneness pervading and constituting the cosmos. To style Islam a monotheism eclipses its even greater merit as a mystical embrace of Allah as the Void, a conception on par with the Formlessness captured in the Indian Brahman, *Sanatana Dharma* or Aleik traditions. It applies a technical and radical philosophical monism where all distinctions are in a real sense suspended as a temporary *mirage* that resembles the Indian concept of dream levels exposed in *Maya*/*maya*.[15] The Sufi tradition forces its awareness of Unity, Indivisibility and monism in *Allah* with emphasis on its composition as two sound syllables of two phonemes[16],

[15] The analogy, though correct, has for the most part been imperfectly applied. A very full understanding of Maya is required beyond a simple translation as *illusion* or temporary *appearance*. Part of the axiom remains missing so that the uses of *Maya*/*maya* remain mostly confined, especially in sacred arts, to mirrors or reflection, meaning the world as a reflection of Allah, often expressed artistically with pieces of mirrored glass on fabrics, mosaic tiles and other surfaces. Without the axiomatic pieces of Yoga and the direct awareness of *Cit* (Cosmic Consciousness) as the ultimate atomic building block and dream projection along the simple lines expressed in the Mandukhya Upanisad, the idea of a *reflection* throughout a consciousness which is indeed cosmic in dimension, transcending ordinary boundaries of space and time, remains incomplete and confined. The hierarchical projection of the Islamic Spheres remains less easy to grasp without the continuous projection of Maya, in parallel evolutions of Sound and Light, from Supreme to subtle to gross (physical) appearance. When *Cit* is united with both the Light of the Islamic Void and the Unstruck (*Anahata*) Sound of the Mantra and Tantra Shastras, the result is powerful and more faithfully comprehensive of the experience of mystical union (Yoga) in high states of spiritual communion with the Godhead across traditions. Black luminous light absorbs all other light in the zone where sound is unstruck, both pointing to the nearness (proximity) to the Void, which can only be experienced non-discursively. Both traditions point to an antecedent systemic unity of an exceedingly ancient provenance, a speculative hidden Tantra uniting both.

[16] Read *phoneme* as a *discrete sound sounding*. A phoneme is a vibratory reality, a discrete sound body.

a letter and a vowel, inflected, ordered, repeated and sequentially fixed the only Arabic root which has *no other form* throughout the language.[17] Its resemblance to the familiar *laptap* sound of the heart heard through the chest and augmented by a stethoscope is noted.[18] It has no masculine, feminine or plural forms. It cannot be added, multiplied, subtracted, divided or deformed in any way.[19] Its Formlessness grounds all number and created series in its aniconic conjunction of Infinity and Zero, both linguistically and mathematically. The Allah carved in Light, Sound, Creatures and 99 Names points, in the way of a sacred symbolic grammatical preposition, to Absolute Formlessness, Non-Duality[20] and Oneness beyond space, time, form, articulation and ordinary mind. That there is no physical image for Allah is more a full address of the inherent approachability of Allah as a mystically internal experience than ever can be implied by the reproaches of idol worship and monotheism.[21]

---

[17] Other sacred dimensions of the letters are discussed in the section on Calligraphy.

[18] Not the best analogy in a created word, albeit the one frequently heard in verbal usage by some modern medical professionals. So we introduce it that way here. In deep meditation the sound can be captured and followed supra-sensibly, and penetrated insofar as its internal echo like any true mantra, here a natural mantra of sacred sound. Such internal acoustic and supra-sensible hearing is not possible for worldly people attached to gross physical sound vibration. The Sufi musical concert (Sama') is in its deepest audition a sacred symphony which, for worldly people, ends as soon as the esoteric music is stopped. For mystics, the concert continues. In fact, there is no need for musical instruments.

[19] As, for example, the patterns of deformation for colors and other adjectives in classical Arabic. Inability to deform the sacred syllable Allah is an index of its primordial sacred meaning and radical Unity. All the hermeneutic word strings we could use to convey this meaning converge on the decoding of the Void (Unity, Formlessness, 100th Name, Invisible, One, without a partner, no image, and more.)

[20] The typically Islamic way to discuss Non-Duality is to use the terminology without partners, a choice of terms which, given the context of the revelation, points discussants back to idols, idol worship and a worldly address of biological form figuration. Too often the functional metaphysical competence of the terminology is turned back from flight to oneness to sink into the fundamentalism and literalism of a worldly view. This fuels the difficulty of persons unable to manage sacred distinctions of idols and icons.

[21] It is no accident that the Islamic traditions and early educated Christian mystics of the Near East conserved the Neo-Platonism of the Greeks and Plotinus. We should not forget that Porphyry, Plotinus' trusted inner circle disciple, was from Tyr. The deeper understanding of the issues and import of Neo-Platonism by Muslim intellectual and

Allah is a sacred syllable that can neither be multiplied, increased, decreased nor inflected by any application of any available grammatical rule of Arabic. It is a classically single, radical unity that remains distinctively *neutral*, resisting further limitation as either masculine or feminine in just the way that *To* remains the neutral but still definite article of Classical Greek and Neo-Platonism. It is a grounding function for all later articulation, differentiation and emergence of plurality from Unity. The *To On* (mystic *One*) so favored, appreciated and conserved by ancient and medieval Muslim philosophers, whose libraries were in effect the caretakers of vast Greek and Mediterranean mysticism and culture, discovers a classically compatible, neutral and formless Unity that understands the clinical difference between numerical or arithmetic one and the mystic Unity (*Tawhid*) of the One, a mystical paradox of conjunction of Infinity and Zero quite characteristic of all genuine mysticisms and developed spirituality, always contemplatively complementary to Allah. This mystic awareness is clearly diffuse in the Near and Middle East, discernible in pre-Islamic Arabia in the diffuse mystical practices of the Hanifi, in whose company we may rightly place the pre-Islamic Mohammad when he is found by the Angel Jibril in his usual silent worship of Allah in the solitude of a cave, in basic refuge from the lawlessness, idol worship, merely religious rivalry and ritualism of his time and place.[22] Though orphaned, we know Mohammad's father's name is *Abdullah*, literally the *Slave of Allah*, pre-dating the formal revelation of Jibril to Mohammad, and his progressively ripening contemplative appreciation of the ancient desert awareness of *Allah*.

Pre-Islamic awareness of Allah stood in mystic contrast to the lawlessness of the desert and the worship of Jinn (genies) as mischievous desert spirits manipulated through black and white magic, rivaling each other's power, invoking one magic over another. The Prophet's Companions and the Prophet Muhammad himself were contemplatives well within the diffuse strain of desert contemplatives, surfacing deep Sufi roots in a widespread desert culture of spiritual purification.

---

spiritual cultures is neglected in the scanty sentences it receives in most Euro-centered texts.

[22] We always distinguish between *religious* and *spiritual*, one exoteric and the other esoteric, respectively. What is religious is not necessarily spiritual, and vice versa.

The warm welcome of the desert contemplative abiding in Silence persists even today across all world cultures in the warm welcome of the authentic Masters and high state mystics. Sufism exists prior to Islam, part of a penetrating net over all world spiritual cultures, more persisting than emerging throughout Islamic history. We find it easily in its sophisticated form in the heavily fused mystical traditions of Afghani and Indo-Greek meditative cultures.[23] We find it wherever there are sacred caves in alluvial mountains. This well accounts for the stubborn association of Sufi to the root *Safa* for *Purity* despite attempts to confine it to *wool*, to woolen and natural fabric weaves, indeed even burlap or sack cloth[24], in the habits of Middle and Near Eastern saints. The more recent famed Sufi cloak, all patched rags and tatters on the outside to show a poor *faqir* (beggar) to the world, is secretly rich on the inside that is never shown to the world. The spirit of the realized godfriend, Master or Saint is worn on the inside. The real Sufi cloak is the worldly body, a temporary garment that everyone gets, a thing ending in tatters in the clay of the earth for all concerned, but which nevertheless hides an unimpeachable jewel of eternal Lighted Spirit on its hidden side for the one who can find and polish it in the temple within. We will discuss this gemstone in Chapter IV related to the mysticism of architectural structures.

The role of the binary divinely lighted sound (Allah) is functionally indistinguishable from the role of a high sacred Mantrum, a spiritually saving and mystically tuned sound, resonating across several well-developed world spiritual cultures. We recognize it easily in the well-conserved details and parallel explanations in the Indian Mantra and Tantra Shastras and throughout the Sanskrit and Indian philosophico-religious tradition of Sanatana Dharma and Yoga (Meditative Union) with God. Both Arabic and Sanskrit claim revealed status as sacred languages. They bear striking similarities to each other much beyond any cited here, forming a vastly informative and neglected topic addressed peripherally in the section on the spiritual dimensions of Calligraphy, and in more depth elsewhere. Both are cultures of *polish*

[23] Quite possibly its true origin as an Afghani phenomenon.

[24] As famously worn by the Egyptian mystic, teacher of both Plotinus and Origen, whose personal name was lost to the sack cloth he wore (Amonious Sacchus).

(*adab)* and *refinement*, Sanskrit itself being the culture and the language of the semi-divine devas (*shining and lighted ones)*, each tradition conserving a self-understanding of the respective sacred meanings embedded in its linguistic roots and vibrations as *Alphabet* (*Lettered*) sound. Not everything is Alphabet (Lettered) Sound, a peculiar human phenomenon hardly noticed by anyone apart from a few modern professions, including speech therapists and the music business, and occasional serious scholars, and mystics.

We will suggest to anyone interested that the supremely healing Word of Isa/Jesus is none other than a meditative conjunction of the *shati'h* of Sufi Black Luminous Light and the Yoga of *Anahatta* (Unstruck) Sound occurring in the mystical Heart of Love and Compassion that founds all reality. It is an Unspoken Word, more a state anchored in Silence than a word at all. We have written elsewhere of the analogies of AUM and the Greek resonance *Pi.*[25] Here, we elaborate briefly in Chapter III on mystical dimensions of the Calligraphy of the Points, Dots and Wands of written Arabic, largely following Ibn 'Arabi's exposition in his classic *Meccan Revelations*, and consider them well treated as authentic high Yantra (sacred design) coordinated with the spiritual musical resonance of Classical Arabic as a high Mantra in Qur'anic recitation. The aesthetic coordination of Mantra and Yantra, of course, raises the classic sacred temple in Indian sacred aesthetics from invisibility into architectural visibility. Here, we must consider how the coordination and purification in sacred Sound and Light raises the temple within the human person as a piece of living architecture. Other short chapters on sacred Sufi Music and Poetry add complementary dimensions to the mystical experiences of Sound and Light in Islamic sacred aesthetics that are transferable across many world sacred traditions. The transition from Light to Sound is indeed a sacred bolt, a bolt of ancient lightning and thunder, unifying many traditions.

In sum, the Void is the high sacred aesthetic symbol of Sufi and Islamic sacred aesthetics expressing the radical Non-Duality and Awesome Reality of the cosmic source of all creation locked in the symbolism and aesthetic language of its *shati'h* (mystical paradox) of

---

[25] See Barbara A. Amodio, "The World Made of Sound," *Journal of Dharma*, XVII/3 (1992).

Light. Black Luminous Light absorbs all other light in the Zero-Infinity zone where sound is Unstruck, both paradoxes pointing to extreme nearness (proximity) to the Void in its Unmanifest situation marked by total absence of duality, duality against which either light or sound may be struck, played against, contrasted, outlined or defined. No paired meanings exist and thus no contrast is achieved in this non-discursive zone of unified inarticulation. The Sufi Sama' or Spiritual Concert links Islamic mysticism to the non-ordinary hearing of sacred Sound occurring at or near this nearly unstruck and subtle realm of mystical hearing, while the poetic singing recitation of the Qur'an coalesces this esoteric music into elegantly audible tones. The direct esoteric connection to Sound is made more apparent in the written mystical traditions of India and in the training by Masters, Indian in particular and Sufi alike. The mystical paradoxes of Black Light and Unstruck Sound remain sacred aesthetic conventions poised on the necessary mystical experience of Non-Duality. No duality, no contrast, no otherness, no plurality, not a many, only a One. The Sama' is discussed in Chapter V, and Black achieves special sacred aesthetic meaning in both the Persian Miniature and the Prayer Carpet with its sacred ecology discussed in Chapters II and VIII, respectively.

Such non-duality as this requires the total annihilation of distinctions including personal identity and ego, merging and fusing into the non-discursive oneness of the Godhead. Mystical fusion is infinitely more understandable, more culturally acceptable and far less dangerous in the Yoga meditation of the Indian tradition, authoritatively conserved by Patanjali, than in the Islamic Sufi tradition where it has led to hasty trials and executions of high state Sufis mistaken as idol worshippers.[26] The Void as such, let us never forget, is an experience, a spiritual state, not a logical proposition. It is the classic non-dual experience of the mystical embrace wherein all personal identity and ego simply disappear into uninterrupted love and merger with the Godhead. This is what is intended by the Bliss (*Ananda*) of Yoga Enlightenment and the ecstatic states of the high Sufi in Union (*Jam'*), Annihilation (*Fana'*) and even

[26] The celebrated case of al-Hallaj. On coming out of the mystical fusion with the Godhead his ecstatic utterances were mistaken as assertions that he was the "I" of the Godhead. He was exonerated after death.

the extreme fusion and loss of personal identity of the Annihilation of the Annihilation (*Fana' al-Fana'*.) Such experience may only be told in ordinary words off the parabolic curve of technical symbols and philosophical versification in sacred story rendered as didactic tale or poetry, discussed in Chapters VI and VII where sacred story, Sufi versification and teaching tales are discussed as forms of sacred aesthetic icon in both proto- and full philosophical form.

References

01. 'Arabi, Ibn, *The Bezels of Wisdom (Fusus al-hikam)*, Classics of Western Spirituality, trans. R.W.J. Austin, New Jersey: Paulist Press,1980.
02. 'Arabi, Ibn, *The Meccan Revelations, (al-Futuhat al-Makkiya)*, vols. 1-2, ed. James W. Morris, New York: Pir Press, 2004.
03. 'Arabi, Ibn, *The Ringstones of Wisdom (Fusus al-hikam)*, trans. Caner K. Dagli, Chicago: Publications Inc., 2004.
04. Amodio, Barbara A., *Symbols of the Sacred at the Ether in the Heart: The Perfected Human Form As Living Aesthetic Experience (Rasasvadana), Aesthetic Symbol (Paroksa-Priya), and Taste of God (Brahmasvada-sahodarah) in the Universal Aesthetic Experience of Indian Aesthetics,* Kolkata: SIPR, 2009.
05. Amodio, Barbara A., *Unveiling the Heart Locus and Expanding the Gemstone in the Ocean of Consciousness: Unifying Islamic and Indian Tradition Perspectives on the Inner Way,* London: Ibn 'Arabi Society, 2008.
06. Arberry, A.J., *The Koran* Asad, Mohammad. *Interpretation of the Qur'an,* Pickthall, Marmaduke.
07. Barry, Michael, *Figurative Art in Medieval Islam and the Riddle of Bihzad of Herat (1465-1535)*, Paris: Flammarion, 2004.
08. Ghazzali, *The Niche for Lights (Mishkat Al-Anwar)*, trans. W.H.T. Gairdner, New Delhi: Islamic Book Service, 1997.
09. Kersten, Holger, *Jesus Lived in India: His Unknown Life Before and After the Crucifixion,* London: Element Books, Ltd., 1991.
10. Khalili, Nasser D., *Islamic Art and Culture: A Visual History,* New York: Overlook Press, 2006.
11. Muqaddasi, Sheikh Izzidin, The *Book of the Revelation of the Secrets of the Birds and Flowers by the Learned Sheikh Izzidin Al-Muqaddasi (d.1280): From Four Manuscripts*, ed. J.H. Garcin de Tassy, London: Octagon Press, 1980.
12. Nasr, Sayeed Hossein, *Islamic Art and Spirituality*, Albany, NY: SUNY Press, 1987.

13. San'ai, Hakim, *The Walled Garden of Truth (The Hadiqa)*, trans. D.L. Pendlebury, London: Octagon Press, 1974.
14. Sells, Michael, *Early Islamic Mysticism: Sufi, Qur'an, Mi'raj, Poetic and Theological Writings,* New York: Paulist Press, 1996.
15. Shah, Idries, *The Sufis,* New York: Random House/Anchor, 1971.
16. Sze, Mai-mai, *The Way of Chinese Painting: Its Ideas and Technique with Selections from the Seventeenth Century Mustard Seed Garden Manual of Painting,* New York: Random House, 1959.

5

Sufi Inspired Devotional Islam in Egypt

Dr. Emilio Giuseppe Platti
Professor Emeritus of Faculty of Theology
Katholieke Universiteit Leuven, Leuven, Belgium

1. Diversity in Egyptian Islam

Egyptian Islam is often identified with the traditional Sunni institution of Al-Azhar, the famous University, on the one hand, and the militant organisation of the Muslim Brothers on the other hand. There are, however, many other aspects of Egyptian Islam, and one of them is until now very popular, even if the political authorities are mostly reluctant to support the activities linked to it[1]. It is the devotional Islam connected with the tombs of saints who are spread all over Egypt: 1° in the Northern Delta and Alexandria, 2° in the land South of Cairo, called "*al-Sa'îd*", where one will find also very important Christian festivities, and 3° in the Cairo area, with the Eastern and Southern *Qarafa*, the necropolis extended over more than 12 kilometres[2].

These Cairo cemeteries, this "*City of the Dead*", has been "as a Magnet for *tasawwuf*" (mysticism), according to the expression used

[1] Catherine Mayeur-Jaouen, « Pèlerinages et politique en islam égyptien », in MIDEO 28 (2010), 101-125.

[2] Galila El Kadi & Alain Bonnamy, *La Cité des morts. Le Caire*, Paris-Liège/Sprimont: IRD-Mardaga, 2001.

recently by Tetsuya Ohtoshi[3]. Tombs of saints, mausoleums, *zâwiya*s and *khânqâ*s, buildings and institutions for gatherings of Sufi brotherhoods and places for spiritual retreat, were attracting pious visitors and brotherhoods' practices. Some of them are still very much active centres of contemporary devotion. Modern research has shown how much the *ziyâra*, the visit of these places of devotion, was, and is still, practised by many Egyptian Muslims.

2. Popular Devotions Challenged

Attracting my attention recently in the Qarâfa area were the headquarters of the Shâdhiliyya brotherhood in the Northern Qarâfa and the tomb of *Ibn 'Atâ' Allâh* al-Iskandarî (or Sikandarî, d. 1309), the second successor and biographer of Abû l-Hasan al-Shâdhilî. Abû l-Hasan, born in Morocco, was the founder of the Shâdhiliyya brotherhood, and died in 1258 in Humaytharâ, in the Eastern desert of Egypt, while he was on his way to the pilgrimage in Mecca[4]. His shrine there in the desert is highly venerated; the Shâdhiliyya being one of the most popular *tarîqa*s (plur. *turuq*), brotherhoods, in Egypt. The importance of *Ibn 'Atâ' Allâh cannot be underestimated, as he was directly involved in the attacks against Ibn Taymiyya (d. 1328), the Hanbalî jurisconsult who condemned directly certain doctrines held by the Sufis and in particular Ibn 'Atâ' Allâh himself.*

The condemnation of the devotion linked to the shrines of Muslim saints has been repeatedly expressed in modern times, sometimes with explicit references to Ibn Taymiyya. That is certainly the case for Muhammad Ibn 'Abd al-Wahhâb (d. 1792) and the following Wahhabi-Sa'ûdî tradition who has a considerable influence on modern militant Sunnism. It should be kept in mind that the monstrous terrorist attack in

---

[3] Tetsuya Ohtoshi, "Tasawwuf as Reflected in Ziyâra Books and the Cairo Cemeteries", in Richard Mc Gregor & Adam Sabra (ed.), *Le développement du soufisme en Égypte à l'époque mamelouke – The Development of Sufism in Mamluk Egypt*, Le Caire: IFAO, 2006, 299-330 ; see also May Al-Ibrashy, « Cairo's Qarafa as Described in the Ziyâra Literature », in Id., 269-297 ; Muhammad Abû l-'Amâyim, « Mantiqat Masjid Gâhin al-Khalwatî, mantiqat tasawwuf qadîma », in Id., 1-31 (pg.ar.).

[4] Denis Gril, « La stèle funéraire d'Abû l-Hasan al-Shâdhilî à Humaytharâ », in Éric Geoffroy (ed.), *Une voie soufie dans le monde: la Shâdhiliyya*, Paris: Maisonneuve & Larose, 2005, 503-511.

Lahore on July 1, 2010, on the shrine of Abû l-Hasan al-Ghaznawî al-Hujwayrî *(d. 1074), author of one of the most famous and earliest books on Sufism, Kashf al-Mahjûb*[5]*, has been influenced by militant anti-Sufi contemporary movements such as Wahhabism or Salafism.*

3. The German Scholar Ernst Bannerth (1895-1976)

It was Vienna emeritus-professor Ernst Bannerth (d. Cairo, 1976), a member of the Dominican Institute in Cairo (*IDEO*), who introduced me as a student (1972-1976) to the very much diversified Egyptian Islamic devotional world. His articles on the Shâdhiliyya-brotherhood and *Ibn 'Atâ' Allâh made me aware of their importance for contemporary Egyptian Sufism*[6]. He was my first guide while visiting tombs of saints, explaining to me how important it is for pilgrims to visit these shrines, distinguishing the different types of saints, and the brotherhoods, still very active in Egypt, their processions, "*mawlid*s" (the celebration at the birthday of the saint) and "*dhikr*" (the particular prayer sessions of Sufi-brotherhoods). His book written in German, "*Islamische Wallfahrtsstätten Kairos*"[7], was the first I knew on this subject. It introduced me to this world, mostly ignored by foreign visitors. Ernst Bannerth also mentioned Ibn Taymiyya condemning the *ziyârât*, the visiting of tombs of saints[8].

4. Diverse Categories of Muslim Saints

4.1. Scholars in Islamic Law

By visiting tombs of saints in Cairo, mostly in the Qarâfa area, one will realize very soon that there are several "types" of saints in Egypt. And in the first place, there are the famous medieval Muslim scholars, such as al-Imâm Layth (d. 791) and, more famous, al-Imâm al-Shâfi'î

[5] Reynold A. Nicholson (ed.), *The Kashf al-Mahjub. The oldest Persian treatise on Sufism by 'Alî b. 'Uthmân al-Jullâbî al-Hujwîrî*, Karachi: Darul-Ishaat, 1990 (new edition).

[6] Ernst Bannerth, "Aspects humains de la Shadhiliyya en Égypte", in *MIDEO* 11 (1972), 237-250; Id., "Dhikr and Khalwa d'après Ibn 'Atâ' Allâh", in *MIDEO* 12 (1974), 65-90.

[7] Ernst Bannerth, *Islamische Wallfahrtsstätten Kairos* (*Pilgrimsplaces in Cairo*), Kairo: Österreichisches Kulturinstitut, 1973.

[8] Id., 90-93: *Anhang. Aus der Kontroverse um die Heiligenverehrung.*

(d. 820), the founder of the renowned Sunni school of Law. Whenever one is visiting his mausoleum, he will find devotees praying, reading the Qur'ân, or writing a prayer-intention which is left on the carpet inside the wooden enclosure, called *al-maqsûra*. It is obvious that al-Imâm al-Shâfi'î as well as al-Imâm Layth are considered saints. This is however not the case for the also famous contemporary scholars, 'Abd al-Rahmân Ibn al-Qâsim (d. 191 AH./806 AD.) and al-Imâm Ashhab (d. 204 AH./819 AD.). They belonged to the Mâlikî school of Law and were buried in a small and now desolate mosque, together with several others, in that time renowned medieval scholars.

It was with professor Bannerth that I attended the prayers of a brotherhood at the Sayyidnâ al-Husayn square, the night of the *Mawlid al-Nabî*, the birthday of Prophet Muhammad, with sermons, *dhikr* and recitations until dawn. It is however only much later that I realised how two very different devotional traditions are intertwined, in such an extent that devotional Islam in Egypt has a very specific character, compared to other Islamic countries.

4.2. Members of the Family of the Prophet

I attended Sufi ritual prayers not only in tents on al-Husayn square, but also inside the al-Husayn mosque, in the Sayyida Zaynab mosque and the Zayn al-'Âbidîn mosque. These saints are all members of the so-called "*Ahl al-Bayt*", or "*Âl al-Bayt*"[9], members of the family of Prophet Muhammad, whose devotion was established in Egypt by the Fatimids (969-1171), an Ismâ'îlî dynasty, a branch of the Shî'a traditions. The three mosques mentioned are the most popular shrines, centres of daily devotion towards members of Muhammad's family, 1° his grandson, al-Husayn, son of his cousin 'Alî and his daughter Fâtima, 2° his granddaughter, al-Sayyida Zaynab, and 3° his great grandson 'Alî Zayn al-'Âbidîn[10], son of al-Husayn.

---

[9] Gino Schallenbergh, "Ibn Taymīya of the 'Ahl al-Bayt", in U. Vermeulen & J. Van Steenbergen, *Egypt and Syria in the Fatimid, Ayyubid and Mamluk Eras, 3*, Leuven: Peeters, 2001, 407-420; see, Taha 'Abd al-Ra'ûf Sa'd, *Âl Bayt al-Rasûl al-ashrâf. Âl Bayt al-Nabî*, (Silsillat Âl Bayt al-Nabî), Cairo: Maktabat 'Ilm al-Islâmiyya, n.d.

[10] Taha 'Abd al-Ra'ûf Sa'd, *Al-Husayn. Ibn Bint al-Nabî, Sayyid Shabâb Ahl al-Janna. al-Sayyida Zaynab, 'Aqîlat Banî Hâshim. Zayn al-'Âbidîn. 'Alî Ibn al-Husayn. Al-*

According to the tradition, two verses of the Qur'ân are to be applied to the members of the Family of the Prophet; the first verse is Qur'ân 33, 33: "*And obey God and His Apostle. And God only wishes to remove all abomination from you, ye Members of the Family ("Ahl al-Bayt": litt." the People of the House"), and to make you pure and spotless*"[11]; the other verse is written at the side door of the al-Husayn mosque, Qur'ân 11, 73: "*The grace of God and His blessings on you, o ye People of the House! For He is indeed worthy of praise, full of all glory!*"[12]

When the Fatimids took power in Egypt, coming from North-West Africa, they founded their own new city in 970, called Misr al-Qâhira, *Egypt, the Victorious*. Very soon they brought to the city the relics of several members of Muhammad's family, and in particular the relic of al-Husayn, and built several mausoleums, but not only for the three saints already mentioned.

In Taha 'Abd al-Ra'ûf Sa'd's collection, thirteen saints of Muhammad's family are presented, whose shrine is still very much visited by pilgrims. But we discovered others, sometimes ignored even by the most detailed inventory of holy shrines in Egypt[13], such as the small tomb of Sayyida Fâtima, Umm al-Ghulâm, daughter of al-Hasan,

---

Hasan, Ibn Bint al-Nabî (Silsillat Âl Bayt al-Nabî), Cairo: Maktabat 'Ilm al-Islâmiyya, n.d.

[11] Yusuf Ali, in his commentary, includes "*besides the Consorts, the whole Family*": "*Hadrat Fâtima, the daughter, Hadrat 'Alî, the son-in-law, and their sons Hasan and Husain, the beloved grandsons of the Prophet*": the verse of the Qur'ân is referred to in the famous prophetic Tradition where Muhammad is wrapping 'Alî, Fâtima, Hasan and Husayn under a striped cloak of the black camel's hair (*Sahîh* Muslim and *Musnad* Ahmad).

[12] Another Prophetic Tradition (*hadîth al-thaqalayn*) is mentioned by Muslim in his *Sahîh*, where "Allah's Messenger is saying: "I am leaving among you two weighty things: the one being the Book of Allah [...]. The second are the members of my household (Ahl Baytî)"; the tradition goes on quoting Zaid: "*His (i.e. Muhammad) wives are the members of his family [...]; and 'Alî and the offspring of 'Alî, 'Aqîl's ('Alî's brother) offspring, Ja'far's ('Alî's brother) offspring and 'Abbâs' (Muhammad's uncle) offspring*". Some authors refer also to Qur'ân 3, 61, where Muhammad proposes to bring together his wives and "sons" in the dispute with the Christians of Najrân; some commentators explain this verse by referring to Fâtima and 'Alî and their two sons.

[13] Sa'd Abû al-As'ad, *Nayl al-Khayrât al-malmûsa bi-ziyârat Ahl al-Bayt wa l-Sâlihîn bi-Misr al-mahrûsa*, Cairo: Sharikat al-Fath, 2004.

brother of al-Husayn, in the very neighbourhood of al-Husayn square, Umm al-Ghulâm street. A clear and mysterious reference to the Shî'a Imams is found on the sheet covering the tomb, with the name of Mûsâ al-Kâzim, the seventh imam of the Twelfth Shî'a, and father of Sayyida Ruqayya, whose tomb in Cairo is almost as old as Cairo itself. Another shrine is situated in the southern city of Beni Sueif, al-Sayyida Hurriyya, Zaynab al-Sughrâ, the little Zaynab, another daughter of al-Husayn.

4.3. Sufi Brotherhoods and their Saints

Why mentioning the *Ahl al-Bayt* saints in a context of Islamic mysticism? The answer is that these shrines could probably not survive if there was not a very strong support from Sufi Brotherhoods. Brotherhoods, *turuq sûfiyya* - have their rituals in these mosques, their procession on the *Mawlid al-Nabî* will bring all the devotees to the al-Husayn mosque. They bring together Sufi-saints and *Ahl al-Bayt* in one tradition of *ziyâra*, the visiting of shrines. The detailed inventory of holy shrines in Egypt is written by the secretary of the general office of Sufi Brotherhoods in Egypt, and he brings together saints from both traditions, *Ahl al-Bayt* and Sufism.

5. Sufi Brotherhoods and their Link with Muhammad

If the *Ahl al-Bayt*-shrines are still the most important category of shrines in Egypt, many other revered saints belong to the Sufi-movement and Sufi-Brotherhoods. But in this case also, the link to Muhammad is essential.

5.1. The Genealogy Back to Muhammad

The link to Muhammad is very explicit in the genealogy (the *nasab*) going back to him. I came across at least three complete genealogies of a Sufi master, whose ancestors go back to the Prophet. But there are many more, without the list being completed. And we could add to this list, of course, the text of the epitaph on Abû l-Hasan al-Shâdhilî's tomb, edited by Denis Gril, whose genealogy is going back to al-Hasan, son of 'Alî[14].

---

[14] Denis Gril, « La stèle funéraire d'Abû l-Hasan al-Shâdhilî à Humaytharâ », 508-509.

In one case, and although the Shaykh died only very recently, in 1979, popular devotion has been building and developing the shrine of Imâm Sâlih al-Ja'farî, shaykh of the *Ja'fariyya tarîqa*, the Ja'fariyya brotherhood. And, next to the tomb, they wrote his complete genealogy, going back to the great grandson 'Alî Zayn al-'Âbidîn, the grandson Husayn, his parents 'Alî and Fâtima, and finally the Messenger himself, Muhammad.

Another inscription with the genealogy of Sîdî Abû l-Su'ûd al-Jârihî (d. probably after 1523) was published by Ernst Bannerth[15], and goes back to the fifth Shî'a imam Muhammad al-Bâqir, son of 'Alî Zayn al-'Âbidîn and so back to the Prophet. Al-Jârihî was well-known for his ascetic life, and is mentioned by another Sufi saint, 'Abd al-Wahhâb al-Sha'rânî (d. 1565), whose multiple writings on Sufism (*tasawwuf*) are still very popular. Sha'rânî's genealogy goes also back to the Prophet, according to the inscription in front of his mosque, mentioning Muhammad Ibn al-Hanafiyya, another son of 'Alî. Many other saints' genealogy is said to go back to the Prophet, and indications are sometimes given on inscriptions in their mosque or nearby their tombs, as it is the case for Ibrâhîm al-Dusûqî, whose ancestry goes back to Muhammad's daughter Fâtima, called *al-Zahrâ'*, "*the Shining one*" and her son Husayn.

The third genealogy is mentioned in connection with the family of the Wafâ'iyya, a large group of scholars and saints belonging to the Shâdhiliyya, and buried all together in different tombs in the mosque called *Masjid al-Sâdât al-Wafâ'iyya.*[16] This family originated from al-Maghrib, and in particular from the Tunisian city of Sfax. The first to come to Egypt was Muhammad al-Nijm; he met the Sufi saint Ibrâhîm al-Dusûqî and lived in Alexandria. His grandson, Sîdî Muhammad Wafâ became the pole of his time. He was the son of Muhammad al-Awsat Ibn Muhammad al-Nijm, and is born in Alexandria in 702 AH., where he met the Shâdhilî Sufi master Yâqût al-'Arshî from Alexandria. He died in Cairo in 765 AH., and is buried in the mosque belonging to the

[15] Denis Gril, « La stèle funéraire d'Abû l-Hasan al-Shâdhilî à Humaytharâ », 122-123.

[16] Muhammad Fathî Abû Bakr, *Dhayl Kitâb Murshid al-Zuwâr ilâ qubûr al-abrâr. Al-Musammâ al-Durr al-munazzam fî ziyârat al-Jabal al-Muqattam*, al-Qâhira: al-Dâr al-Misrî al-Lubnânî, 1995, 39.

brotherhood, not far from the tomb of Ibn 'Atâ' Allâh al-Iskandarî, nearby the Muqattam hill. By time, many other members, more than twenty, of the *Sâdât al-tarîqa al-Wafâ'iyya*, some called "*aqtâb*" - *Illuminating Poles* -, scholars and sufis, were buried inside this mosque, making it a very exceptional concentration of tombs.

5.2. The Square of the Mosques in Alexandria

As recently said, Shâdhiliyya is the most celebrated Sufi order in Egypt and in the Maghreb. Its branches amount around 90 in Egypt alone. Each one of these branches has his own shaykh who caused quite a qualitative change in this or that branch, or in Sufi words, each one of those shaykhs was "one illuminating station along the road". In spite of this, these branches are all ultimately ascribed to shaykh Abû l-Hasan al-Shâdhilî, and all of them commenced in Alexandria.[17] This fact is symbolised by the concentration of mosques around the mausoleum of the first successor of Abû l-Hasan, Abû l-'Abbâs al-Mursî (d. 1287). The beautiful mosque, rebuilt in 1928-1935 by the Italian architects Eugenio Valzania and Mario Rossi, containing his tomb, is indeed surrounded by other mosques and mausoleums, each of them containing the tomb of a Sufi saint. All together they form a wide square known as "*Midân al-Masâjid*", or the "*Square of Mosques*" covering some 43,200 square meters. The Mosque of Abû l-'Abbâs al-Mursî is the focal point and center of this square, and it is surrounded by five other mosques, among which is that of Muhammad Maqîn al-Dîn al-Asmar (d. 692 AH.), disciple of al-Shâdhilî and source of inspiration for Ibn 'Atâ' Allâh, Yâqût al-Iskandarî al-'Arshî (d. 732 AH./1317 AD.), Sharaf al-Dîn al-Bûsîrî (d. 1294 AD.), - author of the famous so-called "*al-Burda*", Poem of the Mantle -, the *qâdî al-qudât* Muhammad Nâsir al-Dîn Ibn Salâma al-Shâdhilî (d. 777 AH.). In the park we find other tombs of saints belonging to the family of Ibrâhîm al-Dusûqî (1287), such as the aunt of Ibrâhîm, al-Sayyida Mandara Abû l-Majd al-Qurashî and his uncle, 'Alî Abû l-Fath.

---

17 Youssef Ziedan, "The Legacy of the Shâdhiliyya in Alexandria: Buildings and Manuscripts", in Éric Geoffrey, ed., *Une voie soufie dans le monde: la Shâdhiliyya*, Paris: Maisonneuve & Larose, 2005, 63 (63-71).

5.3. The Reference to the Muhammadian Light

Ibrâhîm b. 'Abd al-'Azîz al-Dusûqî, who died in 1287 in Dasûq, a city on the Rashîd branch of the Niledelta, is the founder of one of the larger Egyptian Sufi brotherhoods, the Burhâmiyya or Burhâniyya. When he died at the age of 43 years, his brother Mûsâ became his successor. Both brothers are buried in the same mausoleum in Dasûq. The celebrations at the *Mawlid* al-Dusûqî are still very popular, but the most popular *Mawlid* outside Cairo is without doubt the *Mawlid* of al-Sayyid Ahmad al-Badawî at Tanta, the city in the middle of the Delta.

Ibrâhîm was a great Sufi master, and is called *al-Qutb al-Nûrânî* (*the illuminating pole, or pinnacle*). Three contemporary Egyptian Sufi saints, Al-Dusûqî, al-Sayyid al-Badawî (d. 1276) and Abû l-'Abbâs al-Mursî (d. 1287), are sometimes mentioned together with the famous 'Abd al-Qâdir al-Jîlânî (d. 1166), who gave his name to the Qâdiriyya brotherhood, and who is venerated in Iraq. They are considered the four most excellent spiritual leaders, the highest in the hierarchy of saints and friends of God, who assist in the order of the universe, with Muhammad himself being the highest in rank. His pre-eternal light, *al-Nûr al-Muhammadî*, is reflecting God's Holy Spirit and universal Intellect. According to the Qur'anic perspective, the prophetic reality finds its final expression in the Seal of the Prophecy, Muhammad. In the Sufi interpretation, Islamic saints receive inspiration only through the mediation of his Muhammadan Light (*Nûr Muhammadî*). This doctrine has been expressed in the Shâdhiliyya doctrine and in particular by Ibn 'Atâ' Allâh, according which "*Muhammad is the first and unique mediator to the divine wisdom and love*"[18].

6. Saints, *Awliyâ'* in the Koran

The Quranic verse mostly quoted in connection with the saints, the *Awliyâ'* or "Friends of God", and written on the *Maqsûra* (the enclosure surrounding the tomb), of many of the saints' tombs, are the verses 62-64 from Sûrat Yûnus: "*Behold, verily on the friends of Allah (Awliyâ'*

[18] Geneviève Gobillot, « Présence d'al-Hakîm al-Tirmidhî dans la pensée shâdhilî », in Éric Geoffrey, ed., *Une voie soufie dans le monde: la Shâdhiliyya*, 49 (31-52); cf. Denis Gril, «L'enseignement d'Ibn 'Atâ' Allâh al-Iskandarî, d'après le témoignage de son disciple Râfî' Ibn Shâfi'", in Id., 93-106.

Allâh) there is no fear, nor shall they grieve; those who believe and (constantly) guard against evil – for them are glad tidings, in the life of the present and in the Hereafter; no change can there be in the Words of God (Kalimât Allâh). This is indeed the supreme felicity".

7. *Mawâlid*, Processions, *Dhikr* and Litanies

The birthday anniversary of a saint, his *mawlid* (plural *mawâlid*)[19], is the most apparent and clear sign of the vitality of a brotherhood and the devotion to a particular saint[20]. *Mawâlid* are not only Islamic, Christians have there own *mawlids*, festivities and anniversaries of saints (*mouled*, in the Egyptian dialect). In the whole of hundreds of *mawâlids*, it appears to me that four of those are the most popular, the first being, of course, the *Mawlid al-Nabawî*, the birthday of the Prophet himself, the 12th of *Rabi'al-awwal*, the third month in the Islamic calendar; then the *mawlid* of his grandson Husayn, then the *mawlid* of Sayyida Zaynab, both in Cairo; and surely the *mawlid* of Sayyid Badawî in the city of Tanta in the Delta region of Egypt[21]. We could add to these the important *mawlid* of Ibrâhîm in the city of Dusûq.

It is on the occasion of these *mawlids* that we can attend processions of the brotherhoods. We can see them in particular, in Cairo, on the occasion of the *mawlid* of the Prophet. The Burhâmiyya, Rifâ'iyya[22], Shâdhiliyya, Khalwatiyya and Bayyûmiyya are the brotherhoods best represented in the contemporary procession on the occasion of the *Mawlid*. We attended the procession in the seventies and nineties, and also in the new century: it became obvious for us that the authorities were restricting more and more the space reserved for the procession. In the seventies, the tradition prevailed that the starting point of the procession

[19] Nicolaas Biegman, *Living Sufism: Sufi rituals in the Middle East and the Balkans*, Cairo: American University in Cairo Press, 2009.

[20] Rashida Shih, *Le soufisme au quotidien: confréries d'Égypte au XXe siècle*, Arles: Actes Sud, 2000.

[21] Catherine Mayeur-Jaouen, *Al-Sayyid Ahmad al-Badawī: un grand saint de l'islam égyptien*, Le Caire: Institut français d'archéologie orientale (IFAO), 1994 ; Id., *Histoire d'un pélerinage légendaire en Islam: le Mouled de Tantā du XIIIe siècle à nos jours*, Paris: Aubier, 2004.

[22] Ernst Bannerth, « La Rifa'iyya en Égyte », in *MIDEO* 10 (1970), 1-35; Id., « La Khalwatiyya en Egypte: Quelques aspects de la vie d'une confrérie », in *MIDEO* 8 (1964-66), 1-74.

was the mosque of al-Rifâ'î, facing the citadel, and approximately five kilometres away from the mosque of al-Husayn, where the brotherhoods entered the numerous tents prepared for their *dhikr*-prayers. Now the procession has been reduced to a 500 meter walk, starting at the mosque of Imâm Sâlih al-Ja'farî towards al-Husayn. The number of tents prepared is also considerably reduced. The attendance however is still considerable; thousands of pilgrims from towns and villages are attending, and are proud to show their flags from the local section of one of the brotherhoods.

On the days of *mawlids*, one can attend the *dhikr*-prayers in and outside the mosque of al-Husayn, just like in so many other mosques of Egypt. *Dhikr* is a devotional rite, involving the whole of the human body, with repetition of religious poems of the brotherhood concerned, with prayers and supplications, sometimes with the repetition of God's 99 beautiful names, or the names of Prophet Muhammad. We came across the litany of the names of Prophet Muhammad, *Asmâ' al-Habîb al-Mustafâ*, the Names of the Beloved, the Chosen, according to the *Tarîqa* Ahmadiyya Idrîsiyya in the mosque of 'Alî Zayn al-'Âbidîn, where weekly *dhikr*-sessions are organized.

8. The Sufi Poet Ibn al-Fârid

Since the time of professor Bannerth, I visited hundreds of tombs in Egypt, not mentioning the pharaoh's pyramids! We passed by tombs of "secular" people being buried, like the emirs and sultans who built gracious minarets and domes, and who were sometimes far from being saints, or pashas and eminent scholars, like Taha Husayn (d. 1973), or eminent sheikhs, sometimes imams of al-Azhar, like Muhammad 'Abduh (d. 1905). Between the thousands of tombs of saints, we had to distinguish the shrines of saints classified as *Ahl al-Bayt*, eminent scholars in Islamic Law, Sufis or initiators of brotherhoods.

Among the Sufis, one is to be mentioned in a particular way is the famous Sufi poet 'Umar ibn 'Alî ibn al-Fârid (1181-1235), called the *Sultân al-'âshiqîn*, the Prince of lovers. His collection of poems, his *diwân* has recently been published by a member of our IDEO Institute[23],

[23] Giuseppe Scattolin, "A Critical Edition of Ibn al-Fârid's Dîwân", in B. Michalak-Pikulski & A. Pikulski, ed., *Authority, Privacy and Public Order in Islam* (OLA, 148),

Giuseppe Scattolin. His shrine, his *maqâm*, at the foot of the hills of the Muqattam, is still considered that of the most outstanding mystical poet of the Islamic Egyptian Sufi-culture.

To underline his vision, let me quote what Giuseppe Scattolin wrote some years ago, in a text in which two crucial terms appear, that of "the perfection of sainthood", actualized in the "pole" (*qutb*), and the illumination inherent to the "*Muhammadan Reality*":

> The Sufi who has reached a complete identification with such eternal 'Muhammadan Reality' will become the true 'Perfect man' (al-insân al-kâmil), realizing the perfection of sainthood, i.e. the absolute unity of the pre-eternal covenant. The concept of 'Muhammadan Reality' indeed "designated in the Sufi literature the 'Islamic Logos', the eternal principle and goal of all creation, the perfect manifestation of the Divine qualities, operating and manifesting itself in the whole universe, and in particular, in the history of prophets and saints'. This is what is meant by the pre-eternal covenant. "Ibn al-Fârid seems to make explicit reference to that 'Muhammadan Reality' with which he, in his mystical ascension, has come to identify himself.[24]

References

01. 'Abd al-Hâdî al-Qasabî (Shaykh al-Mashâ'ih), « Bâyi'û Rasûl Allâh 'alâ al-sam' wa l-tâ'a », in *al-Tasawwuf al-islâmî*, 21 (2010), n° 276, 4-10.

02. Al-Sayed el-Aswad, "Spiritual Genealogy: Sufism and Saintly Places in the Nile Delta", in *International Journal of Middle East Studies* 38 (2006), 501-518.

03. Catherine Mayeur-Jaouen, « Pèlerinages et politique en Islam égypti*en* », in *Mélanges de l'institut Dominicain d'Études Orientales du Caire* (MIDEO) 28 (2010), 101-125.

Louvain: Peeters, 2006, 203-216; *The Dîwân of Ibn al-Fârid*, a critical Edition by Giuseppe Scattolin, Cairo: IFAO, 2004.

[24] Giuseppe Scattolin, "New Researches on the Egyptian Sufi Poet 'Umar ibn al-Fārid (576-632/1181-1235) : A Contribution towards a new Understanding of his Sufi and poetic Experience", in U. Vermeulen and D. de Smet, ed., *Philosophy and Arts in the Islamic World* (OLA, 87), Louvain: Peeters, 1998, 39 (27-40).

04. Éric Geoffroy, éd., *Une voie soufie dans le monde : la Shâdhiliyya*, Paris : Maisonneuve & Larose, 2005.

05. Frederick De Jong, *Turuq and turuq-linked institutions in nineteenth century Egypt: a historical study in organizational dimensions of Islamic mysticism*. Leiden: Brill, 1978.

06. John Renard, ed., *Tales of God's Friends*, Berkeley-London: University of California Press, 2009.

07. John Renard, *Friends of God. Islamic Images of Piety, Commitment and Servanthood*, Berkeley-London: University of California Press, 2008.

08. Muhammad Fathî Abû Bakr, *Dhayl kitâb « Murshid al-zuwwâr ilâ qubûr al-abrâr »*, Cairo: Dâr al-Masriyya-al-Lubanâniyya, 1994.

09. Pierre-Jean Luizard, « Le soufisme égyptien contemporain », in *Égypte/Monde arabe* I/2 (1990), 36-94.

10. Rachida Chich & Catherine Mayeur-Jaouen, *Le soufisme à l'époque ottomane – Sufism in the Ottoman Era*, Cairo: Ifao, 2010.

11. Rachida Chich & Denis Gril (éd.), *Le saint et son milieu ou comment lire les sources hagiographiques*, Cairo: Ifao, 2000.

12. Rachida Chich, *Le soufisme au quotidien. Confréries d'Égypte au XXe siècle*, Paris: Sindbad, 2000.

13. Richard Mc Gregor & Adam Sabra, *Le développement du soufisme en Égypte à l'époque mamelouke. The Development of Sufism in Mamluk Egypt* (*Cahier des Annales islamologiques*, 27), Cairo: IFAO, 2006.

14. Sa'd Hasan Muhammad, *Ahl al-Bayt fî Masr*, Gizeh: Al-Nâfidha, 2003.

15. Sa'îd Abû l-As'âd, *Nayl al-khayrât al-malmûsa bi-ziyârat Ahl al-Bayt wa l-sâlihîn b-Masr al-mahrûsa*, Cairo: Sharikat al-Fath, 2004.

16. Safwat Jawdat Ahmad, ed., *Fadl Ahl al-Bayt fî l-Qur'ân al-Karîm wa l-Sunna al-nabawiyya*, Cairo: Dâr al-Sundus, 2008.

17. Taha 'Abd al-Ra'ûf Sa'd & Sa'd Hasan Muhammad, *Al-Husayn, Ibn Bint al-Nabî. Sayyid shabâb Ahl al-Janna*, Cairo: Maktabat al-'Ilm al-islâmiyya, 2002.

18. Valérie J. Hoffman-Ladd, "Devotion to the Prophet and His Family in Egyptian Sufism," in *International Journal of Middle East Studies* 24 (1992), 615-637.

6

The Place of the Word of God in Mystical Experience

Dr. Luke Emehiele Ijezie
Catholic Institute of West Africa, Port Harcourt, Nigeria

1. Introduction

Mysticism has a variety of meanings for different authors and traditions. Basically, the phenomenon of mysticism expresses an intense communion between the human world and the supernatural world. Majority of the diverse interpretations of mysticism borders on the dynamics of this communion. The biblical understanding of the divine-human relationship is that it is always and every where a mediated relationship. The human being has no direct access to the divine. This is equally the case both in the Old Testament and in the New Testament. In both traditions, the medium of divine communion is the word of God. This is the central element of the biblical revelation. But the gnawing question is whether one can bypass the word of God and enter into a direct relationship with God. Many forms of Christian spirituality, ancient and modern, seem to underscore this, but the issue remains very problematic.

The argument of this paper is that mystical union within the biblical context is better understood as a union effected through the encounter with the divine word. In other words, the word of God is the medium of mystical experience. This word is fully revealed in sacred scripture but it can also be encountered in different contexts, all relating to the biblical revelation.

2. The Problem of Defining Mysticism

There is hardly any religious tradition that does not have some sort of relationship with the divine or the supernatural. Because the divine-human relationship can be explained from diverse perspectives, the understanding of mysticism becomes a matter of how one defines the relationship. The question is, 'What type of relationship with the supernatural qualifies as a mystic relationship?' One's answer to the question determines to what extent one can attribute mysticism to any religious or cultural tradition. In some quarters, people are very hesitant about talking of mysticism. The reason is that when mysticism is interpreted as a direct experience of the divine, the question arises on the capacity of the human person to have such direct experience. Thus, one reckons with much controversy built around what mystics are purported to experience. This makes it imperative to search for a balanced understanding of the phenomenon of mysticism.

What is called a religious experience in one religious tradition may qualify as ordinary profane experience in another tradition. Much depends on the type of phenomena which a particular culture regards as religious or as having religious significance. Within the social sciences, one encounters nuances in the interpretation of the sacred. Emile Durkheim interprets the experienced world as divided between the sacred and the profane, with the society as the determining factor. Durkheim puts it thus: "This division of the world into two domains, the one containing all that is sacred, the other all that is profane, is the distinctive trait of religious thought; the beliefs, myths, dogmas and legends are either representations or systems of representations which express the nature of sacred things, the virtues and powers which are attributed to them, or their relations with each other and with profane things."[1] According to Durkheim, the sacred is not limited to the personal beings, called Gods, but to anything or object which the society considers as having a special religious significance, such as a rock, a tree, a spring, a pebble, a piece

[1] Emile Durkheim, *The Elementary Forms of Religious Life*, Original 1912; New York, 1961, 52.

of wood, a house, in a word, anything at all.[2] In a similar way, Mircea Eliade considers the sacred and the profane as the two modes of being in the world, but he distinguishes between the sacred, which is a reality wholly different, and its manifestations in different contexts.[3] Eliade describes every manifestation of the sacred as a *hierophany*, and points out that such manifestation could be present in any reality such as a stone, a tree, a human reality, etc.[4] The *hierophany* remains unchanged in its profane appearance, but its sacrality is recognized only by those who regard it as a sacred sphere, and to such a group the whole cosmos can also become a *hierophany*.[5] But from another perspective, Rudolf Otto considers the "sacred" as a reality completely out of the ordinary or "wholly other" (*ganz andere*), and he identifies it as "Numinous" (a combination of the Latin *numen* and *omen*), as it awakens a "numinous state of mind". According to Otto, the numinous reality is perceived both as a *mysterium tremendum* ("dreadful mystery"), and a *mysterium fascinans* ("fascinating mystery"), and thus paradoxically, there is always both the fear of approaching it and the desire to cling to it.[6]

---

[2] Durkheim, *The Elementary Forms of Religious Life*, 52. According to Durkheim, the simplest form of primitive religion is totemism which considers an animal, a plant or any other object as sacred. The clan or community considers itself as sacred in relation to the totem and in fact the totem represents the clan, and every clan is identified with its totem. Durkheim considers the totem a symbol which expresses the force behind it and worship is directed to this force which gets personalized in a god. Thus the totem becomes a symbolic representation of both the clan and the god, two realities which in the context merge into one as both the god and the clan are one and the same thing (235-255).

[3] M. Eliade, *The Sacred and the Profane. The Nature of Religion*, London 1957, 8-213.

[4] M. Eliade *The Sacred and the Profane*, 11-12.

[5] M. Eliade, *The Sacred and the Profane*, 12-13. According to Eliade (23), "Revelation of a sacred space makes it possible to obtain a fixed point and hence to acquire orientation in the chaos of homogeneity, to 'found the world' and to live in a real sense. The profane experience, on the contrary, maintains the homogeneity and hence the relativity of space."

[6] R. Otto, *The Idea of the Holy*, London 1923, 5-49. For a more elaborate critical evaluation of Otto's views, see the recent discussion in T. A. Gooch, *The Numinous and Modernity: An Interpretation of Rudolf Otto's Philosophy of Religion*, BZAW 293; Berlin: 2000.

In the Western tradition, the phenomenon of mysticism goes back to the Greek mystery cults whereby the initiates were required to keep secret the knowledge acquired in the initiation process. This knowledge is called mystical knowledge (= hidden or secret knowledge) while the initiates are called mystics.

In the Jewish tradition, Philo is known to have reinterpreted the idea of mystical knowledge as the knowledge derived from the word of God rather than knowledge derived from the mystery cults. For Philo, the word of God possesses a hidden meaning and knowledge of such is mystical knowledge. Philo thus bridges the gap between the Greek and Jewish understandings of mysticism.[7] The central element here is the idea of knowledge as the means of mystical union.

This aspect of knowledge in the mystical experience is central to Rudolph Otto's exposition of the similarity between the basic ideas of Eastern mysticism and those of Western mysticism, which he does by comparing the ideas of the great Indian philosopher, Acharya Sankara, and the great German mystical theologian, Meister Eckhart.[8] In both thinkers, mystical experience is understood both ontologically and epistemologically. From the ontological perspective, mysticism is based on the radical unity of all things in the being of the one and only Being, the Absolute. From the epistemological perspective, this unity is consciously realized through a continuous quest for knowledge of the Absolute Being. In both thinkers, however, this quest for knowledge is not merely theoretical but oriented towards salvation.[9] Otto argues that "in mysticism there are indeed strong primal impulses working in the human soul which as such are completely unaffected by differences of climate, of geographical position or of race."[10]

3. Word of God in the Christian Understanding of Mystical Experience

The divine-human relationship is made possible by the initial divine invitation. This is the Christian perspective. It is not the human being

---

[7] See Harvey D. Egan, *An Anthology of Christian Mysticism*, Collegeville, Minnesota: Liturgical Press, ^{2}1996, xx.

[8] Rudolph Otto, *Mysticism East and West: A Comparative Analysis of the Nature of Mysticism*, New York: Macmillan, Original 1932, Present Paperback 1970, 19-55.

[9] Rudolph Otto, *Mysticism East and West,* 19-55.

[10] Rudolph Otto, *Mysticism East and West*, 14.

who sets out first to search for God. Rather, it is God himself who takes the initiative to invite humanity into communion. The invitation is through God's word. This is the point Bernard Lonergan stresses when he says, "The divine initiative is not just creation. It is not just God's gift of his love. There is a personal entrance of God himself into history, a communication of God to his people, the advent of God's word into the world of religious expression. Such was the religion of Israel. Such was Christianity."[11] The point that Lonergan is making is that both the Jewish religion and the Christian religion owe their existence to the word of God. Each of these religions is a response to God's word which is God's self-disclosure. Since the word is the medium of God's self-disclosure, the human response to God is fundamentally a response to God's word. All religious practices of the Judaeo-Christian tradition are responses to the divine word. It is within this response that one locates all forms of religious experience, including mysticism.

The mystic is, over and above all, preoccupied with the word. In this context, one has to understand the word both in its spoken and unspoken forms. The word by its nature is a spiritual reality. It is the mental construct of things which are either visible or invisible. But there arises the problem of how the mind can construct an idea of what is invisible. This is the power of the human imagination. In the case of religious or mystical experience, the matter becomes a little complex. But however the experience takes place it is always through the agency of the word. The invisible reality gets incarnated in the mind's constructs. The revealed word is thus the incarnation of the divine reality in the human mind. The mystical experience is the mind's experience of this incarnated word. One may call it introspection. But from the Christian perspective, the mind is enabled to do this by the action of God's own Spirit. Here lies the relationship between the divine word and the divine Spirit. The human mind is capacitated by the divine Spirit to receive the divine word.

---

[11] Bernard J. F. Lonergan, *Method in Theology*, Toronto: University Press, 1990, 119.

4. Mysticism and the Word of God in the Old Testament/Jewish Tradition

The Old Testament presents a very complex picture of religious experience, and the place of mystical experience within that picture is a matter of interpretation. For the sake of coherence, the mystical dimension will be examined in this paper from two domains, the domain of wisdom which centres on God's presence in creation and the domain of prophecy. The common denominator in both domains is the presence of God as the source of mystical experience. The Hebrew word for "presence" is *pānîm* (= "face"). God's presence is represented as the face of God. To be in the presence of God is, thus, expressed metaphorically as to see the face of God. The idea that Moses saw God "face to face" (*pānîm el pānîm*) may be understood in this light. One aspect of this divine face is the word through which God permeates the universe.

4.1. God's Presence in Creation

The Old Testament presents the created world as originally good, and this goodness is as a result of God's presence in creation. A noteworthy fact is that the presence of God in the created world is made manifest through his word. The psalmist puts it in a colourful way:

> The heavens tell (*mesapprim*) the glory of God, the vault of heaven proclaims (*maggid*) his handiwork; day discourses of it to day, night to night hands on the knowledge. No utterance at all, no speech, not a sound to be heard, but from the entire earth the design stands out, this message reaches the whole world (Ps 19:1-4).

The irony in this poem is that the heavens are said to be telling and proclaiming the divine glory and yet there is no word and no speech.[12] The word "glory" (*kabod*) here expresses God's majesty and the radiance

[12] According to J. Ross Wagner, "From the Heavens to the Heart: The Dynamics of Psalm 19 as Prayer," *CBQ* 61 [1999], 250. There is a logical contradiction here even though poetically the text makes perfect sense. Cf. H.-J. Kraus, *Psalms 1-59*, Minneapolis: Fortress, 1993, 267-269.

of his presence.[13] These heavenly bodies function as witnesses to God's presence. Thus, they reveal the face of God. What this text is saying is that through these works of creation, one comes to hear the voice of God. This point is brought out powerfully in the Final Document of the recent Synod on the word of God, which, quoting this text of Psalm 19, says, "Thus, a first 'cosmic' revelation is found which makes creation similar to an immense page opened up before all of humanity, in which a message from the Creator can be read."[14]

Many texts of the Bible see the whole creation as the voice of God. For instance, the roar of thunder is regarded as the voice of God (Ps 68:34; Sir 46:17). In the texts of the wisdom literature, the divine word is identified as wisdom (*hokmāh*) which is derived from reflection on creation. In Proverbs 8, wisdom is personified as a lady (Lady Wisdom), and she functions as the subtle voice of God present in all the ordinary affairs of life. Roland E. Murphy aptly describes Lady Wisdom as a divine communication given to human beings through creation.[15] From this perspective, many theologians describe creation as grace, as through creation God reaches out to all humanity.[16] According to Ps 139:6-18, God's presence so permeates creation that nobody can ever run away from him. Where can I flee from your presence (139:6)? The Hebrew word for presence here is *pānîm* (face). Interestingly, the word *pānîm* is used in synonymous parallelism with the word *ruah* (spirit), showing that the face of God (= his presence) is not clearly distinguished from the Spirit of God. One then reckons with three semantically related ideas, Face of God, Spirit of God and Word of God, all in denoting the same presence of God.

In Sir 24:3-21, wisdom is presented as an emanation of God's mouth, and who, as the divine word, has reigned over the whole universe and finally established herself in Jacob, more precisely, on the temple mount in Zion. In this text, wisdom is not only identified as the word of God but also as the Torah. From the foregoing, it becomes clear that the

---

[13] See Wagner, "From the Heavens to the Heart," 249.

[14] "The Word of God in the life and mission of the Church", Final Document, XIIth General Assembly of the Synod of Bishops, Vatican 25 October, 2008, no. 1.

[15] Roland E. Murphy, "Introduction to Wisdom Literature," *NJBC*, 450.

[16] See John Goldingay, *Theological Diversity and the Authority of the Old Testament*, Grand Rapids: Eerdmans, 1987, 220.

word is the medium of God's presence in creation. It must be pointed out that this centrality of the word of God in the identification of God's presence has not always been properly emphasized. Sometimes, there is the tendency to present God's presence as if it were something that appears purely in material terms. Of course, there is always the danger of idolatry when created things or persons are posited as representations of the Deity. It is instructive that the Synod Fathers make this point, in the light of the experience of Moses and the Israelites in the desert: "The Lord presented himself not as an image or an effigy or a statue similar to a golden calf, but with 'a voice of words'. It is a voice which entered the scene at the very beginning of creation, when it tore through the silence of nothingness."[17] Thus God is present in the world as word, and this word needs to be interpreted and reinterpreted in every age and context.

Since the presence of God is perceived through the medium of his word in creation, the consciousness of that presence depends to a great extent on the reflective power of the human mind. This is the great gift of wisdom. Through wisdom, which employs the human intellect, one is able to commune with God in creation. Stories of great mystics on this level abound. In saying this, one does not exaggerate the powers of the human mind, as it has many limitations. In fact, the Israelite sages recognized this and stressed the point that the wise person is one who is guided by the fear of the Lord (cf. Prov. 1:7; 9:10, Job 28:28; Sir 1:14; Ps 111:10).[18]

4.2. Mysticism and Prophecy

Another means of encounter with the word of God is prophecy which has very much in common with wisdom. Prophecy is commonly understood as a phenomenon of intermediation between the human world and

---

[17] Synod's Final Document, no. 1

[18] As von Rad, in *Wisdom in Israel*, 108-109, puts it, "The fear of God not only enabled a man to acquire knowledge, but also had a predominantly critical function in that it kept awake in the person acquiring the knowledge the awareness that his intellect was directed towards a world in which mystery predominated. This fear of God has trained him to openness, to readiness for an encounter even with the inscrutable and the imponderable, that is, it has taught him that the sphere in which definite, verifiable orders can be discerned is a very limited one."

the divine sphere. In the biblical tradition, the common means of this intermediation is the divine word which the prophet possesses. It is the very fact of the possession of this word that makes the prophet to be considered as one in communion with the divine. The prophet is thus believed to enjoy a privileged relationship with the divine sphere. He is regarded as the mouthpiece of the divine. The divine word can be obtained through diverse means but the fact that it is the divine word makes the possessor a mystic. Such phenomena as inspiration, ecstasy, visions, dreams, auditions, etc., can be considered as different ways of obtaining the divine word or message.

Some scholars, however, are doubtful whether mysticism can really be attributed to the prophetic phenomenon. For instance, Helmer Ringgren argues that the biblical text does not give any information regarding the mental state of the prophets and they are never described as introspective but are shown to be conscious of the distance between them and YHWH.[19] One needs not stretch the argument too far since the same biblical text underlines the prophet's awareness of himself as a possessor of the divine word. The point of the present argument is that the possession of the divine word makes it possible to qualify the prophet as a mystic. In other words, a true prophet is necessarily a mystic.

In many instances, the word of God is said "to come" to a person, thus, equipping him or her with the responsibility to speak in God's name (Gen 15:1,4; 1 Sam 15:10; 2 Sam 7:4; 24:11; 1 Kgs 6:11; 12:22; 13:20; 16:1; 17:2,8; 18:1,31; 19:9; 21:17,28; 2 Kgs 20:4; 1 Chron 17:3; 22:8; 2 Chron 11:2; 12:7; Isa 38:4; Jer 1:2,4,13; 2:1; 7:1; 11:1; Ezek 1:3; 3:16; Hos 1:1; Joel 1:1; Jonah 1:1; 3:1; Mic 1:1; Zeph 1:1; Hag 1:1,3; Zech 1:1; 8:1,18; etc.). These recipients of the word of God (among whom are Abraham, Samuel, Nathan, Gad, David, Solomon, Shemaiah, Elijah, Jehu, Isaiah, Jeremiah, etc.) are all regarded as prophets, especially, in the Jewish tradition.

5. Mysticism and the Word of God in the New Testament

The New Testament continues the tradition of the Old Testament but with a new interpretation. The hermeneutic of this new interpretation is Jesus himself who is regarded as the word made flesh, otherwise

[19] Helmer Ringgren, "Mysticism," *ABD* 4, 945.

called the incarnate word. The mystical experience, thus, acquires a new dimension as it becomes an encounter with the word of God now made visible and concrete in the person and message of Jesus Christ.

5.1. Mysticism in John's Gospel

The Prologue of John's Gospel makes it clear that God is not known to any human being. Only the incarnate word of God makes him known. This unique role of the *Logos* is summed up in John 1:18: "No one has ever seen God; it is the only Son, who is close to the Father's heart, who has made him known (*exēgēsato*)." This verse brings to a climax the whole argument of the Prologue. The first clause makes it clear that no one has ever had a direct vision of God. This calls to question all the purported visions of God in the Old Testament. In other words, neither Moses nor any other human figure of the Old Testament could have had a direct vision of God. The only one who has seen God is the only Son who is also identified with God. Thus, only what is of the same nature as God sees God. The logical conclusion is that only the one who sees God can truly make him known. The Greek word used here is *exēgēsato*, which is aorist indicative middle of *exēgeomai* meaning "to explain, make known, interpret." The word "exegesis" is derived from this verb. The point then is that only the Logos, Son of God, can do the exegesis of God, that is, make him known or interpret him. This point underlies many of the discourses in the Gospel.[20] Jesus, the incarnate word, is presented continuously as the unique revealer of God.[21] Union with God is achieved through the acceptance of the revelation brought about by Jesus. This is well articulated in John 14:23: "If anyone loves Me, he will keep My word; and My Father will love him, and We will come to him and make Our abode with him." The possession of the word not only endows one with prophetic identity but more and above all it brings one into direct communion with the divine nature.

---

[20] As R. Alan Culpepper, *The Gospel and Letters of John* [IBT], Nashville: Abingdon Press, 1998, 120, points out, "All that follows in the Gospel's account of what Jesus does and says serves to confirm the prologue's declaration that 'the Word became flesh and lived among us' [1:14]."

[21] See R. Alan Culpepper, *The Gospel and Letters of John*, 92-94.

Just as in the Old Testament, the writers of the New Testament also express the prophetic possession of the word in the sense of the word of God "coming" to a person (Luke 3:2; John 10:35). This expression is given a more exalted significance in John 10:35-36 where Jesus is quoted as saying, "If those to whom the word of God came were called 'gods' – and the scripture cannot be annulled – can you say that the one whom the Father has sanctified and sent into the world is blaspheming because I said, 'I am God's Son'?" This statement comes as a response to the Jews who are accusing Jesus of equating himself with God. The response of Jesus is actually taken from Ps 82:6 directed against the unjust judges of Israel who because of their sacred function of giving judgement are likened to the divine being.[22] A reading of the full text of Ps 82:6-7 brings out this nuance: "You are gods, children of the Most High, all of you; nevertheless, you shall fall like mortals and die like any prince." The psalm is, however, interpreted by the rabbis, in the Jewish Haggadah, as addressed to the Israelites who received the word of God at Sinai and yet died (cf. 1 Kgs 18:31).[23] Jesus employs this rabbinic exegesis to respond to his Jewish interlocutors.

5.2. Mysticism in Pauline Theology

The Pauline writings provide another important ground for the understanding of the New Testament perspective on mysticism. Harvey D. Egan considers Pauline mysticism as summarized in the phrase "in Christ."[24] For Paul, to be "in Christ" is to be a new creation (2 Cor 5:17; Gal 5:15), and the phrase, thus, denotes the "mystical ambience" within which Paul lived his new life.[25] In a similar way, Celia Kourie has in a recent study highlighted the centrality of the expression "in Christ" in Paul's writings and how it exposes the Pauline understanding of mysticism.[26] She argues that the term, "in Christ," which occurs 164

---

[22] Raymond E. Brown, *The Gospel According to John [I-XII]. A New Translation with Introduction and Commentary*, Anchor Bible 29; New York: Doubleday, 1966, 408-411.

[23] See Nils Alstrup Dahl, "The Johannine Church and History," in *Current Issues in New Testament Interpretation*, ed. W. Klassen, New York: G. F. Snyder 1962, 133.

[24] Egan, *An Anthology of Christian Mysticism*, 9.

[25] Egan, *Anthology*, 11.

[26] Celia Kourie, "A Mystical Reading of Paul," *Scriptura* 101 (2009), 235-245.

times in Paul, provides a crucial hermeneutical principle for reading the whole Pauline theology and for understanding his other teachings on such themes as reconciliation, salvation, eschatology, ecclesiology, etc.[27] According to Kourie, the very idea of living in Christ summarizes Paul's understanding of mysticism: "I live no longer I, but Christ lives in me" (Gal 2:20).[28] What this means is a "dynamic union" rather than an "undifferentiated absorption" into Christ.[29] It denotes a way of life influenced by the Spirit of Christ and, thus, a life in conformity with Christ.[30] The constituent element of this new life is "freedom from the old life of law and sin and a new sense of belonging to an utterly different locale of existence [Col 3:3]; the believer is a member of a new race of redeemed women and men, whose life is characterized by the fruit of the Spirit [Gal 5:22-23]; faith (Eph 1:12); wisdom and strength [1 Cor 4:10]; and truthfulness [Rom 9:1]."[31]

However, one important thing that could be added to Kourie's analysis is the role of the word of God in Pauline mysticism. While the phrase, "in Christ", highlights adequately the Pauline understanding of mysticism, this is better understood in the light of the central role of the word of God. In Col 1:25, Paul mentions the word of God as the very centre of his missionary apostolate: "I became its servant according to God's commission that was given to me for you, to make the word of God fully known." According to Paul, this word is the very mystery hidden through the ages but now revealed to God's chosen ones (Col 1:26). Paul makes it even clearer in Col 1:28-29: "This is the Christ we are proclaiming, admonishing and instructing everyone in all wisdom, to make everyone perfect in Christ. And it is for this reason that I labour, striving with his energy which works in me mightily." In this way, Paul's mission can be understood in the light of the mission of Jesus Christ as presented in the Prologue of John's Gospel. Just as Jesus, the incarnate Word (*Logos*), functions as the unique revealer of God (John 1:18), in like manner, Paul functions as the privileged revealer of the incarnate

[27] Celia Kourie, "A Mystical Reading of Paul," 241.
[28] Celia Kourie, "A Mystical Reading of Paul," 241.
[29] Celia Kourie, "A Mystical Reading of Paul," 240-242.
[30] Celia Kourie, "A Mystical Reading of Paul," 240-242.
[31] Celia Kourie, "A Mystical Reading of Paul," 241.

word. It is through this revealed word that people come into union with God. The mystical union is thus a reception of the word of God now revealed in Christ.

In Eph 6:17, Paul regards the word of God as "the helmet of salvation" and "the sword of the Spirit". This metaphorical expression can be interpreted on diverse levels. The helmet is a head covering used mostly for defense while the sword is a weapon of war. So both the helmet and the sword can be understood as instruments of war, the helmet for protection and the sword for fighting. In this context of the letter to the Ephesians, Paul presents the Christian life as a spiritual warfare. The word serves as the instrument with which the Spirit pierces everything and also defends everyone. What this means is that the word is both the instrument for union with God (salvation) and the weapon to defend oneself against enemy attack. For Paul, Salvation is the unfolding of God's plan which is to make all things one in Christ. In this process, the icon (image) is Christ and all are being molded in the image of Christ. To become saved is to become like Christ and this is the goal of all creation. Christ is the sphere of God's presence and the whole process of recreation, which is central to Pauline thought, is a process of conforming all things to this sphere. Reconciliation with God is automatically effected by entry into this spiritual sphere called Christ, being in Christ, which actually means, patterning one's life on that of Christ.

Another name for this spiritual sphere is the Body of Christ. All believers in Christ form a network of God's presence which in Pauline language is called the Body of Christ. It is a mystical union of all believers in Christ. To be "in Christ" implies being a member of the mystical Body. The risen Christ is the very embodiment of God's glory, which is his presence. The baptized Christian enters into this sphere of divine presence. This is what Paul calls the new creation. The concept of new creation is linked to the concept of reconciliation. Reconciliation is a change of status: from enmity to friendship, and it takes place in Christ since in him God reconciles all things to himself (2 Cor 5:16-21). Paul interprets the Christian mission as a service of reconciliation (2 Cor 5:18), which means bringing all humanity and all creation to this mystical union in Christ. Such a service is a great challenge to all missionaries, and it has both human and cosmic dimensions. The principle of union is love, and the service of reconciliation is, thus, a service of love.

One recognizes the problem of summarizing Paul's thought, given its complexity. But one important dimension of his theology is the centrality of Christ in the union with God. From this perspective the argument of this essay remains valid. Since Christ is experienced as the incarnate word of God, it follows that the centrality of Christ in the mystical union is actually the centrality of the word.

6. Mysticism in African Traditional Religion: The Igbo Perspective

There are many currents in African Traditional Religion (ATR), and any talk of mysticism must take into consideration the nuances in the concept of the divine being within these currents. This makes it impossible to speak of mysticism for the whole of ATR. Right sense demands that one concentrate on a single current whose ideas are more connected. Because of this, the present discussion will be focused on the Igbo Traditional Religion in Nigeria, which is incidentally the cultural tradition to which the presenter of this paper belongs.

One peculiarity of Igbo Traditional Religion is the belief that every human person has a unique creator god, called *chi*, and which is different for every individual.[32] So there are as many *chi* as there are individuals. This personalized god or *chi* is distinguished from the Supreme Deity called *Chukwu* (a contraction of *Chi-ukwu* = great *Chi*). The idea of every individual having a personal creator god needs not sound too strange because the traditional Igbo concept of creating (*okike*) is a bit different from the inherited Judaeo-Christian understanding of the term. In the Igbo understanding, creating is represented by the verb root *ke* which expresses the sense of dividing or apportioning. Within this semantic field, the act of creating is equivalent to assigning destiny or lot. The individual is marked out by his or her destiny and this is the work of the personal *chi*. The belief is that the Supreme Being (*Chukwu*) delegated this act of creating to the *chi* and this makes every individual very

[32] See Chinua Achebe, "'Chi' in Igbo Cosmology" in *African Cosmology. An Anthology*, ed. Emmanuel Chukwudi Eze; Malden, MA: Blackwell Publishers, 1998, 67-72; P.E. Aligwekwe, *The Continuity of Traditional Values in the African Society. The Igbo of Nigeria*, Owerri: Totan Publishers, 1991, 173-174.

unique. According to the Igbo, the destiny of every person is a result of a primordial negotiation between the individual and his *chi*.[33] Because of this central role of the "demiurge" *chi*, one's character is defined by one's *chi*. Thus the full personality is never complete without the role of this invisible personal deity. The religion postulates a primordial and ongoing interior bond between the *chi* and the individual. This interior bond comes to expression in the popular terminology *mu-na-chim* (= I and my *chi*), which expresses the interior self as a union of the *ego* and the *chi*. One's personal decision is often expressed as the judgement of "myself and my *chi*".

What may be considered here as a very prominent aspect of Igbo mysticism finds expression in this interior communion between the individual and his *chi*, the personal deity. This does not exclude other forms of mystical experience within the complex world of Igbo Traditional Religion. For instance, Gabriel E. Adibe discusses Igbo mysticism elaborately but from a different perspective.[34] He focuses mainly on the traditional religious experts and the rituals that enable them to penetrate the world of the spirits. In the present paper, on the other hand, the focus is on the personal divine entity *chi* which establishes an interior bond between the individual and the divine world. The interior communion between the individual and his *chi* is believed to be ongoing, and one's fortunes can always change as long as one enters into agreement with the personal *chi*.

The *chi*, however, is not part of the individual's substance. It remains a separate entity but having a continual mystical communion with the individual. The *chi* is believed to live in the divine world but the communion with the individual is symbolically represented in the shrine which is erected for every individual as soon as he reaches the age of having such a shrine.[35] The erecting of this shrine is an elaborate ritual called *ima chi*.[36] Through it one comes to a more conscious knowledge of one's *chi*. This shrine remains until one's death, but the traditional

---

33 See Achebe, "'Chi' in Igbo Cosmology," 69.

34 See Gabriel E. Adibe, *Igbo Mysticism: The Power of Igbo Traditional Religion and Society*, Onitsha: 2008.

35 See Achebe, "'Chi' in Igbo Cosmology," 69.

36 See Simeon O. Eboh, *The Gospel of Christ and African Culture. Ozo Title Institution in Igboland [Nigeria]*, African University Studies; Munich-Kinshasa: 1993, 55.

belief is not so clear here on what happens with the personal *chi* at the individual's death. However, the Igbo are traditional believers in reincarnation. When one dies after living a miserable life, a traditional rite of purification, called *Inishi arisi*, is performed over his corpse to rid him of the sinister influences of his *chi*.[37] This rite is aimed at securing for the individual a smooth reincarnation.[38]

The belief is that the *chi* acts as a guardian spirit over the individual. For instance, when the individual survives a great misfortune, the Igbo spontaneously exclaim, *chi ya mu anya* (= his *chi* is awake). But it must be pointed out that the *chi* is more than just a guardian angel. In fact many aspects of the belief in *chi* remain obscure. One interesting facet of the belief, however, is that *chi* functions as a mediating deity between the individual and the Supreme Being. In a similar way, the relationship between the individual and the divine forces of the Earth and the underworld are all controlled and defined by the role of the individual's *chi*. No force can harm or influence the individual unless his *chi* allows it.[39] In this way the Igbo mystical experience with the divine world can be said to be mediated by the *chi*. This resembles the mediating role of the *logos* (word) in the Judaeo-Christian religious tradition.

7. Conclusion

This paper has consistently argued the point that the word of God is the medium of mystical experience. This word is the mode of God's presence in creation, and it is interpreted through wisdom and prophecy. Both the Old Testament and the New Testament witnesses bear testimony to this centrality and mediatory role of the word. Based on this biblical portrait, one finds it difficult to argue for a direct communion with God without this intermediate function of the word.

---

[37] See Francis A. Arinze, *Sacrifice in Igbo Religion*, Ibadan: University Press, 1970, 18; Oliver O. Onwubiko, *African Thought Religion and Culture*, Christian Mission and Culture in Africa, Vol. 1, Enugu: 1991, 92.

[38] See Onwubiko, *African Thought*, 92-94.

[39] This point is epitomized in a famous Igbo proverb quoted by Achebe, "'Chi' in Igbo Cosmology," 69: "No matter how many divinities sit in together to plot a man's ruin, it will come to nothing unless his chi is there among them."

The argument is pushed further on the cultural level where the Igbo Traditional Religion in Nigeria presents a similar picture of a mediated mystical experience. The divine agent *chi* in Igbo religious thought functions as the mediator between the individual and the divine world and also as the basis for the individual's continuing communion with the divine world.

7

Buddhist Epistemology of *Vipassana* and its Meaning

Dr. Hoang Thi Tho
Head of Department of Oriental Philosophy
Institute of Philosophy, Hanoi, Vietnam

'Inward-thinking' of Buddhism was a particular outcome of Indian history of thought during Primeval and Mediaeval ages, it should be considered as a remarkable feature of Eastern thinking. Buddhism was founded when Indian thought had developed its own philosophy and religion through a long history of more than 1500 years before A.D., and was moving to the third period of thought. That means Indian thought had passed over two periods of thought of (i) Legendary thought, (ii) Theocratic thought, and has just entered the third period of De-theocratical thought. In other words, Buddhism was established in the beginning of the stage of thought of humanities, when Indian thinking tended to diminish theocracy power and came to consider human as the center.

Thus, right at the beginning, "primitive" Buddhism was not at all as a primeval system of thought in term of the beginning of human civilization. Further, it is possible to say that Buddhism had got its philosophical thought even before accomplishing its religious thought. Owing to this fact, Buddhist inward-thinking (Pali: Vipassana) was not at the low level, but at the level higher than the simple level of perceptual or sensible perception. So, what is the essence of Buddhist Vipassana? Vietnam, one of the countries where Buddhism was introduced since the ancient times, also adopted Buddhist Vipassana. How about the influences of Buddhist Vipassana on the Vietnamese thinking and their way of life in history and today are?

1. Buddhist Vipassana (Inward-Thinking)

In Buddhist classic scriptures, especially in Buddhology and Zen studies Vipassana is a term relating to "inward" thinking, feeling, mind, looking and introspection, which had been used by Indian religions in Buddha's time. Buddha inherited this term and the model of inward-thinking from Brahmanism, a theocratic religion of India. Now a days, this model of inward-thinking is still utilized and taught in religious training courses on meditation or in Buddhist essays on meditation (Pali: *Dhyana*; English: *Zen, Ch'an*). We also can find it in *Yoga Sutras* which was compiled by Patanjali in the 2nd century A.D. Other religions in the East also know this model of thinking and applied it in their religious cultivation, such as esoteric Taoism and Tantric Buddhism in Tibet and China.

Vipassana is described systematically in Buddhist scriptures. It is possible to say that the entire Buddhist teaching is a "complete systematic works" of human as a perfect whole of inward-thinking/introspection. Firstly, the Buddhist teaching conceives human as suffering-being defined by mentality and physiology internally (including craving, ignorance). Thus, in order to eliminate suffering it is to look inward to get rid of its root in each person by oneself. The Four Noble Truths consist in the decided direction of inward-thinking of the whole system of Buddhist teaching, it is of internal human. In this system of Buddhist thought the nature of universe is closely associated with human nature by general categories such as: Dependent-Origination (*Pratitya-samutpada*), Impermanent (*Anitya*), No self (*Anatman*).

These three categories together describe the origin, the essence and the law of Nothingness and No self (they are dependent-Origination, Impermanent) of human being in the stream of movement. *Nothingness* does not mean vacuum or emptiness, but it means there are not any distinct things or attributes that are separate or unchanged. Because things only can be present independently in the world as a true thing through impermanent relations (Dependent-arising) caused by factors which constitute them. Because the universe's as the same as the human's presence are in process of forming, changing and shifting, replacing in complex relations. So that they do not have unchanged attribute, thus they are permanent Nothingness and No self (*Anatman*). According to this theory, Buddhism affirms that human's essence is *Nothingness*; that is, *No self*; as it is the permanent aggregation of (material and spirit) elements in relations and under (incidental, requisite, sufficient) conditions. Owing to this, the initial cause of suffering of sentient being is the ignorance (*avidyā*) of universal truth, the nature of sentient being within their relations and in movement and changes (the impermanence), and they believe that there is a real Ego (Self) existing for ever. For religious meaning, whenever humans get enlightenment of the essence of impermanence of the universe and the being, as well as about the no self of their ego, it is the moment they realize the root of suffering and since then they will emancipate themselves from suffering consciously, initiatively.

The Four Noble Truths (*Catvāri āryasatyāni*) consists of four important parts connecting to suffering, they are: The Nature of Suffering (*Dukkha Ariya Acca*); The Suffering's Origin (*Dukkha Samudaya*); The Suffering's Cessation (*Dukkha Niroddha*); The Way Leading to the Cessation of Suffering (*Dukkha Nirodha Gamini Patipada Magga*). First, The Nature of Suffering explains all kinds of suffering (*dukha*), as conditioned ones such as: the natural or ordinary suffering that defined by the impermanent aggregation of human being as body pain (*dukkha-dukkha*): birth (*jāti*), old age (*jarā*), illness (*byādhi*), death (*marana*); the suffering caused by limitations of mental, physiology or consciousness, that defined by human sociality, such as: separation from the pleasance (*piyehi vippayogo*), not receiving what they wants (*yampiccham na labhati tampi*); association with the un-pleasance (*appiyehi sampayogo*); the suffering caused by nature of the conditioned arising of five aggregate[1] (*pañcupādānakkhandha*). According to the Truth of suffering all living beings are equal in every way of suffering. Inasmuch as sentient being

[1] The five aggregates are: material form (*rūpa*), feeling (*vedanā*), perception (*saññā, samjñā*), mental formations (*saṅkhāra, samskāra*), and consciousness (*viññāṇa, vijñāna*).

certainly clings to suffering, without exception of caste, of birth or ethnics. It is the internally conditioned suffering, so that when human try to look outwards to affirm his self (ego), the more suffering he gets, in other words, the more human try to satisfying their cravings (as sorrow (*soka*), lamentation (*parideva*), grief (*domanassa*), despair (*upāyāsā*)) the more they get onto trouble. Therefore, in order to eliminate suffering absolutely to attain to the state of freedom, extrication and no trouble human need to turn inwards (inward-looking, introspection) of each oneself.

Second, the Suffering's Origin explains that its initial cause of sentient being depends on their very thinking and thought clinging onto external phenomenon which makes human deviate and do not realize their true nature as no self (*Anatman*). Because of the clinging onto external phenomenon humans often have misconception, ignorance (*avidyā*) and think that there is a true self. Whenever clinging onto external appearance that is the moment they produce *karmas* (volitional action) as bodily acts (body), verbal acts (speech), mental acts (mind; *manas*) which consequently generate a chain of causes of continuous suffering. This chain of causes of suffering is named "Twelve Links of Causality."[2]

Third, the Suffering's Cessation teaches how to look inwards to destroy the root of suffering by elimination of ignorance and craving in one's mind and thought. Having done this is final salvation.

Fourth, consequently, the Way Leading to the Cessation of Suffering analyses the way of inward-looking, as possible and wise one to lead people to ultimate salvation. It is the combination of Threefold Training (*Sikkhā*[3]) through uninterrupted eight steps of introspection, namely, *The Noble Eightfold Path.*[4] This is an inward system which

[2] Twelve Links of Causality: Ignorance (*avijjā*, *avidyā*), Volitional formations (*saṅkhāra, saṃskāra*), Consciousness (*viññāṇa, vijñāna*), Name and form (*nāmarūpa),* Six sense bases (*saḷāyatana, ṣaḍāyatana*), Contact (*phassa, sparśa*), Feeling (*vedanā*), Craving (*taṇhā, tṛṣṇā*), Clinging (*upādāna*), Becoming (*bhava*), Old age, and death (*jarāmaraṇa*).

[3] Threefold Training (Sikkhā) means, the training in the higher moral discipline (*adhisīla-sikkhā*), the training in the higher mind (*adhicitta-sikkhā*), the training in the higher wisdom (*adhipaññā-sikkhā*).

[4] The Noble Eightfold Path (Ashtangika-Marga), namely, right view, right intention, right speech, right action, right livelihood, right effort, right mindfulness, right concentration.

combines closely the cultivation of physical body with the cultivation of mind, ethics and belief as a process of returning *inward*, coming back to the origin of everything; it is the direction towards the *No self*, the *Nothingness*.

It is possible to say that Buddhist concept of emancipation is a consistent way of inward-thinking. On this way each one turns inwards to perceive or realize his own level, abilities and capacities to go by himself without any blessing or salvific offer from any Super Being. Whenever have enlightened the true nature of themselves human will consciously stay aloof from craving, lust and all other sources which cause retribution of karma and the eternal cycle of birth. That is the final goal of the way to salvation of Buddhism.

Buddhist teaching of emancipation relies on the epistemological doctrine of two truths (*satya*) and two ways of perception of truth. Buddhism teaches that there are two ways of perception: outward and inward ones which lead to two different truths: Conventional truth (*samvrtisatya*) and Ultimate truth (*paramārthasatya*). The former one is the outward way of conventional perception, which commonly depends on experiences and concepts of external and phenomenal world. However, according to the truth of impermanency, by conventional perception human being only can perceive the unlimited asymptote of reality, and only can get the relative truth.

On the contrary, the latter way is the inward-perception which turns inwards to calm the mind and conscious of oneself until having no consciousness of body, no sense consciousness, no ideation consciousness, no manas ideation consciousness, and all of them rest in tranquil state, that is the contemplation on emptiness (*suññatanupassana*). This technique of controlling the stream of consciousness of oneself is named *Vipassana*. For Buddhist epistemology, at this moment intuition will brighten up and it can insight directly the ultimate truth. Buddhism especially realizes that the separation between the subject and the object in process of perception by conventional way does kill the reality; so that it is impossible to perceive the reality as that it is, in other words, as the reality "when the universe has not yet formed by the dichotomies."[5]

[5] Daisets Teitaro Suzuki, *Zen* (Vietnamese: *Thiền*), English-Vietnamese translation of Thuần Bạch, Ho Chi Minh City: Publishing House, 2000, 234.

Buddhism believes that Vipassana is the most feasible mode to make the mind tranquil. "Thanks to tranquil mind things should be seen as it is being [...] if mind is tranquil all the craving or greed caused by the world objectively can not affect the mind."[6] It is the situation of enlightenment, or Buddhist salvation.

Buddhist Vipassana had been continuously developed by two schools of Buddhist philosophy, they are Madhyamika school founded by Nagarjuna (about 3rd century A.D.), and Yogācāra school (or Consciousness-Only school; in Sanskrit: *Vijñapti-mātratā*) founded by Asanga (about 4th century A.D.) and Vashubandhu (320-400). For them Vipassana was considered as fundamental issue on the nature, the way and the object of consciousness. The school of Consciousness-Only explained the primitive nature of consciousness and emptiness-consciousness[7] by means of the doctrine of *Independent Origination* through the "Twelve Links of Causality" proposed by Buddha. Consequently, consciousness is also permanent aggregation of elements under certain condition or because of the *Law of Cause and Effect* (*pratītyasamutpāda*).

Yogācāra School considered *ālāyavijñāna* (*Store-house consciousness*) as its central concept. For this school the object of perception is *ālāyavijñāna*, meaning the emptiness of consciousness or the unconscious. The way to perceive *ālāyavijñāna* is not to look out, but to turn back to the inside of the subject. Accordingly, this school developed particular method of introspection, which was inherited from Yoga, just for the aim of training capability of intuition by practicing inward-mediation; in other words, turning back to *ālāyavijñāna.*

Madhyamika School concentrated to develop the issue on the way and capability to grasp the truth. Also, depending on the doctrine of Dependent Origination, this school consisted that, in order to grasp the ultimate nature of Nothingness, meaning the true reality, human beings have to break out of the practice of outward-perception, and stop

---

[6] *Digha-Nikaya* (Vietnamese: *Trường Bộ Kinh*), *Thich Minh Chau,* Sai Gon: Vạn Hạnh Institute Press, 1972, 66-67.

[7] According to the doctrine of Alaija vijnana (Storehouse of consciousness) of Yogācāra School, Alaija vijnana is the store of potential consciousness for all other 7 vijnanas of human (5 sense organs, vijnana, and Manovijnana). In other word, Alaija vijana contains all germs of spiritual phenomenon and being. It means that every thing happening in this world would have its origin in Alaija vijnana.

depending on speech, concept and experience, but have to turn inwards to get the tranquil unconsciousness, from where intuition or (wisdom, *prajñā*) will suddenly insight the true reality. This school further asserted that there are two levels of truth: *Firstly*, the conventional level of truth which only can reflect the reality through its external phenomenon. But, form and phenomenon are what always move and change according to the law of impermanence. So that it fails to reflect correctly the true, the absolute nature of reality; *Secondly*, the absolute level of truth should grasp the true reality behind phenomenon by intuition (*prajñā*). The way of intuition is the direct one, does not depend on form, speech and reason, but does move upstream of process of consciousness, towards thoughtlessness, and unconsciousness. In short, this way of perception is to retrace back the stream of consciousness, as in an eastern proverb "*to learn until unlearned situation*!"

Achievement of Buddhist Vipassana was described vigorously by Cha'n sect of Mahayana Buddhism in China. That was the complex application of both Madhyamika school with Yogacara one of Indian Buddhism, and simultaneously combined with Taoism and Zhuang Zi's doctrine in producing an unique principle of inward-perception as it was termed as: "*no clinging to*", "*no insisting on*" or "*no dwelling on*" in Buddhist monks' or Zen Buddhist masters' thinking and in their way of life.

In conclusion, from aspect of history of thought Buddhist doctrine of Vipassana (inward-thinking) has been contributing its part in promoting particular values of Buddhism, on be half as a school of philosophy in the East. Buddhist epistemology of Vipassana is the very doctrine of intuition (*prajñā*) which was developed much by Zen sect, and belong to Mahayana Buddhism. It did not only contribute its part to enrich the category of intuition in Western epistemology, but also did open a new way for applying this human capability of thinking, and training it from as a talent capability to as a ready and powerful internal energy. It is possible to evaluate Buddhist doctrine of Vipassana on some fundamental issues of modern epistemology as follows:

Firstly, according to the Buddhist doctrine of Nothingness, Vipassana is a special kind of perception; it is *prajñā* (intuition) (which is higher than simple instinct perceptibility and abstractive reason). It is a mode of perceiving the object directly, not through any intermediary, and with special characters such as: 1) direct; 2) concrete, unusual; 3) without language; 4) can train this capability by practicing Buddhist technique of meditation.

Secondly, Buddhist Vipassana should enrich the content of the category of intuition in Western epistemology in particular, and in human kind's knowledge of thinking, in general. There are different kinds of intuitions. However, now *Prajñā* of Zen Buddhism is considered as on the same level as, or even higher than transcendental intuition. This level of intuition has been being investigated and verified by modern sciences.

Thirdly, the nature of present (particular) reality grasped by intuition is often true and correct. However, under the intervention of reason or imagination or illusion intuition will be not correct.

Fourthly, intuition should play its active and feasible role in ordinary and scientific perception, in two aspects in general: 1) Intuition should contribute to discover and invent new thoughts; 2) Intuition is the chain of series of notions which suddenly burst out. This capability should be trained by practicing meditation or high concentration while studying or research.

From the aspect of the issue of relativeness of perception the Buddhist criticism on limitation of outward-perception (ordinary one) is rational and logical in certain level. From this basic point, Buddhism has explored and built its method of inward-perception. Generally speaking, Buddhology and Zen studies has applied Vipassana into its process of combining elements of spirit, psychology, physiology in training skill of controlling stream of thought, even stop it, in order to exploit and develop the capability of intuition in each person individually. Until now, this question has been being an unique and interesting issue of Buddhology and Zen studies, as well as practice of Buddhist meditation concerning in Chinese, Japanese, Korean and Vietnam.

2. How did the Vietnamese Adopt Buddhist Vipassana?

Buddhism was introduced into Vietnam by different ways and at different times, however, the earliest and direct introduction was from India, it was even earlier than from China. So that the influence of Buddhist thinking on the Vietnamese should be not the same as it was on the

Chinese. This adoption did not happened in single way and in one time, but it was complex and connecting with the process of adoption and applying Confucianism and Taoism in Vietnam. And, especially, for the Vietnamese all of them were foreign systems of thought. So, it is not easy to discuss Buddhist thinking or thought of the Vietnamese separately from other systems of thought absolutely. It would be better and easier if we abstract it relatively by researching Buddhist thinking and thought through some famous thinkers' writings in historical periods.

The First Period: Buddhism was introduced into Vietnam when the Vietnamese thought was in the period of *legend* and *myth* and came to enter the period of *theocracy*. Therefore, as mentioned above, in Vietnam the adoption of Buddhism, which had been founded in India in the period of de-theocracy, had deep influence on the way of thinking of the Vietnamese. This first adoption had made an open precedent for the later adoptions of foreign religions and new thoughts as Confucianism, Zen Buddhism from China, or Marxism from the West, etc.

Now we do not have enough materials to analyze the way of thinking of the ancient people in Vietnam to know how did it change after the first introduction of *Bụt-Buddhism*[8] from India and then the later ones of *Phật-Buddhism*[9] from China. However, definitely, Buddhism with the symbol of "*Bụt*" of compassion together with its profound philosophy and doctrines of impermanence, suffering, emancipation, cycle of birth [...], and ethical lessons teach human how to control the lust of oneself and cultivate good, avoid bad conduct, accumulate good works for their next life [...], was accepted by local belief and then preserved in myth, legend, mysterious history, as well as in rituals of water-rice festivals of the Vietnamese.[10] Under Tran dynasty, king Tran Nhan Tong still used the term "*Bụt*" frequently in his writings, such as in *Way of Happiness*

[8] The term "*Bụt-Buddhism*" is used to denote the first imported Buddhism direct from India into Vietnam before Chinese domination period in Vietnam. "*Bụt*" is the name "*Buddha*" in Hindi pronunciation changed into native pronunciation.

[9] The term "*Phật-Buddhism*" means Buddhism imported indirect from China in later period, from Chinese domination period in Vietnam. "*Phật*" is also the name of "*Buddha*" in Chinese changed into pronunciation and character of the Vietnamese.

[10] *Tấm Cám Story*, *Story of Mosquito*, "Narrative of Man Nương," in *Báo Cực Truyện* and *Lĩnh Nam Chích Quái* or Buddhist Legend *Cổ Châu Pháp Vân Bản Hạnh*, etc.

in Worldly Life (in Vietnamese: *Cư Trần Lạc Đạo*),[11] perhaps "*Bụt*" had become Vietnamese Buddhism.

Buddhist writings and translations in Vietnam during this period had introduced fundamental contents of Buddhist teaching and they had impressive influence on the Vietnamese's thinking and their way of life, such as: Mouzi's Li Huo Lun (Vietnamese: *Lý Hoặc Luận*; *Six Paramitas Sutras* (Vietnamese: *Lục Độ Tập kinh*); *Astasahasrika Sutra* (Vietnamese: *Bát Thiên Tụng Bát Nhã*·; *Ānāpānasati* (Pali: *ānāpānasmati*; Vietnamese: *An Ban Thủ Ý*; Chinese: *Anbanshu Y Ching).*[12] In those writings Vipassana was one of the contents which were introduced and accepted through Buddhology in this period.

(a) Mouzi's *Li Huo Lun* introduced Buddhist fundamental conception in comparing with Confucianism and Taoism in order to highlight Buddhist eminent points on how human being could emancipate themselves by inward approach. Many Buddhist categories were introduced, such as: Impermanent, Way (Tao), Extremely Enlightenment, To become Buddha, Human being, Five Precepts, Keeping Buddhist precepts, Vegetarian food, Giving charity, Inaction (in Chinese: *Wu-wei*), Emancipation, Nirvana (Vietnamese: *Nê Viên*). They brought the Vietnamese a new and interesting vision on good and evil, on human being and their birth and death ect.

(b) The *Six Paramita Sutras* introduced Buddhist concepts of universe and human being. It tended to interpret human internal feelings, and teach them to practice Ch'an (Zen) meditation and obey the precepts, and believe that it is the possible way to reach the goal of enlightenment, such as: original nature; cycle of innumerable lives; tree worlds; exterior images; nothingness; still existence; charity; no breach of precepts; resignedness; five precepts; Bodhisatva-hood; assisting and preserving human being; Three treasures; Taking refuge in the Buddha, the Dharma and the Sangha; Tathagàtha; Four elements, Four stage meditation, etc.

(c) The *Astasahasrika Sutra* belongs to system of Prajñā scriptures, which presented the doctrine of Nothingness - an important thought of Mahayana Buddhism. It was especially developed in China and

[11] See, *Ly Tran Dynasties' Literature*, The Literature Publishing House, 506.

[12] Nguyen Tai Thu, ed., *History of Buddhism in Vietnam*, Hanoi: Social Sciences Publishing House, 1998, 67.

considered as the basic doctrine which provided the tendency of inward-thinking of Chinese Zen Buddhism. This tendency also had influenced much on Zen studies in Vietnam in particular, and on Vietnamese Buddhism as the whole in general, and especially on Buddhism under Ly, Tran dynasties."[13]

(d) The *Ānāpānasati* is one of Buddhist sutras on meditation (*dhyana*) which teach the technique of counting in-and-out breath in order to control and concentrate the mind. They are the basic techniques of introspection.[14]

The Second Period: After the first Buddhist introduction, most of the later ones into Vietnam were Mahayana sects and via from China, namely Vinitaruci (Vietnamese: Tỳ Ni Đa Lưu Chi, Wu Yantong (Vietnamese: Vô Ngôn Thông, Thao Duong (Vietnamese: Thảo Đường).[15] They were mainly introduced through intellectual circles, royal families and court mandarins, and especially by the Chinese immigrants. That was why the second introduction had constructed a Buddhist scholarly culture of Vietnam with its height of Truc Lam Yen Tu sect under Tran dynasty. However, common or popular Buddhism, which developed in mixing with agricultural rituals and festivals of working people in the countryside, did not vanish, but many of its elements even influenced on the scholar Buddhist sects and then they together made characters of Vietnamese Buddhism.

(a) Vinitaruci sect is the first Zen one in Vietnam introduced by an Indian bonze. This sect paid special attention on practice of meditation in order to develop one's own inward intuition (*prajñā*) and other internal miraculous power by depending on Madhyamika's philosophical doctrine of *Nothingness*. This Zen sect proposed the transcendental-language thinking, in according with "no clinging", that means neither

---

[13] Nguyen Tai Thu, ed., *History of Buddhism in Vietnam*, 68.

[14] Nguyen Tai Thu, ed., *History of Buddhism in Vietnam*, 68.

[15] Vinitaruci was an Indian nomadic monk who came to Vietnam in the year of Canh Ty (680) from China and lived in Phap Van Pagoda. He was considered as the first patriarch of this Zen sect in Vietnam; Wu Yantong was a Chinese bonze, who transmitted Hui Neng's (Vietnamese: Huệ Năng), Zen sect. He came to Kien So Pagoda in North Vietnam and founded Vô Ngôn Thông sect -- the second Zen sect of Vietnam; The third Zen sect of Vietnam was Thảo Đường sect, which was founded by Van Mon (Vietnamese: Van Môn), around the 9th century.

clinging to "yes" nor "no", as well as neither dwelling in "yes" nor "no." It is the situation of super meditation which is high above language, document and conceptual thinking." This doctrine influenced much on Vinitaruci sects follow generations. For example, Buddhist king Ly Thai Tong (7th generation), Ven. Dao Hanh (12th generation) and Ven. Hue Sinh (13th generation), who much promoted this Buddhist epistemology.

(b) Wu Yantong sect, the second Zen one introduced into Vietnam. It was the religious name of a famous Chinese Zen master. This sect's fundamental thought is about practice of meditation, aiming at attaining the statute of the unconscious or emptiness of consciousness. It is "the very tranquil innermost feeling" while the non-stop, wandering, disorder stream of thought is ceased. At that moment man's potential wisdom which is hind by ignorance (*avidya*) will suddenly arise obviously. "It is the Enlightenment and Salvation. It is Nirvana."[16] The later generations of this sect as Ven. Cam Thanh (2nd patriarch), Ven. Thien Hoi (3rd patriarch) continuously affirmed that, "The final truth is not far, but just at present, just inside of each person, however it only can be perceived directly, [...] every analysis should destroy the enlightenment of the truth (situation of enlighten mind or Eternal truth)"[17].

(c) Thao Duong sect is the third one of Vietnamese Buddhism, founded by Thao Duong, a Chinese bonze, under Ly dynasty. It was transmitted to King Ly Thanh Tong (1st Vietnamese generation), then to King Ly Anh Tong (5th generation). We see that this sect mainly developed in powerful royal family and aristocrat circle in that period. So that, it certainly affected their way of thinking in their political line and policies directly.

(d) Truc Lam Yen Tu sect was a typical Vietnamese Zen one founded under Tran dynasty by King Tran Nhan Tong. It was outcome of a long process of Buddhist collective inheritance from all three former sects. It is often considered as the first unification of Vietnam Buddhist sangha, "without former sects which were of foreign origin."[18] Most of Truc Lam Yen Tu sect's thinkers were Kings, Lords, Royal family, etc., who took great responsibilities of the state and simultaneously as

[16] Nguyen Tai Thu, ed., *History of Buddhism in Vietnam*, 110.
[17] Nguyen Tai Thu, ed., *History of Buddhism in Vietnam*, 114, 182.
[18] Nguyen Tai Thu, ed., *History of Buddhism in Vietnam*, 215.

great heroes of the nation. Many of their writings which had presented Buddhist thought of this period. From aspect of philosophy, those most remarkable writings were the ones discussing the issues as: nature of nothingness, inward-thinking."

"Remarkable character of Buddhism in Tran dynasty period was that the Zen thinkers were so interested in practice Vipassana and also advised other to practice introspection to cultivate the innermost mind of oneself to realize one's own nature", "to turn inwards the innermost," and "the realization of one's own nature" was termed in Vietnamese as "the returning"; so that "no one could transmit the mind to [...] if one's own nature is not realized by oneself." It means that everyone has to do this by themselves!"[19] In the forewords of *Thien Tong Chi Nam,* King Tran Thai Tong had appreciated the role of Buddhist thought, especially as in his line of governing state: "[...] as means leading dark mind to bright way to perceive the truth of birth and death it is the very Buddhist teaching. Proposing norm and criterion for future of human being as model for the future are heavy responsibilities of the Holy Spirits [...]. So why don't I as a king take these holy responsibilities, and consider Buddhist teaching as my own ones!"[20] As far as said, it is clear that Buddhist inward-thinking was applied flexibly in socio-politic actions in Vietnam during feudal time.

Generally speaking, up to this time the process of Buddhist introduction from abroad had stopped, then Vietnamese Buddhism had affirmed its independent direction and characters by its marvelous contribution to the nation. From aspect of thought, many concepts about inward-thinking of scholar Buddhism were explained by Buddhologists and Zen masters through their Vietnamese spirit, and that made them more familiar with various social ranks. For example, Chinese Zen sect's terms as "no clinging to", "no insisting on", "no dwelling on" were explained and interpreted by common language in Vietnamese and they became easy to understand, such as "direct entering", "no thinking", "no words", "turn inward", "turn home", "open heart", [...]. Most of intelligentsia, especially Mandarins and Kings in royal court had good

[19] Nguyen Tai Thu, ed., *History of Buddhism in Vietnam*, 220-222.

[20] *History of Vietnamese Thoughts – Collection*, vol 2, Hanoi: National Political Press, 2004, 10.

knowledge of Buddhology or Zen studies, and they had good utilization of them in diplomatic, cultural policies in relation with China – a great neighbor which also has long Buddhist tradition.

For common working people in Vietnam, Buddhism is considered as a traditional religion, although it is not perceived as high as scholar Buddhism (Buddhology and Zen Buddhist studies), its humane philosophizing was presented flexibly through their plain belief and way of life. In other words, the transcendent Vipassana of Buddhism penetrated into common people when it was normalized, popularized, and colloquialized. We can say that in popular Buddhism Vipassana was not mentioned as the topics of Final truth, Nature, Buddhahood, Nothingness, Wisdom (*Prajñā*), *Tathagath*a, no words or no clinging, etc. […], but it was much more paid attention as matters of cultivation of individual moral by inward principle: "Buddhahood is just in mind." So, the evaluation of right or wrong moral conducts should not be some thing done by the other, but must be frankly done by oneself, or in other words "one suffers what was done by oneself." For the Vietnamese self evaluation is always clearly defined: the moral aspect of inner mind is more important than the talent which can display to the others. People always remind themselves that "mind is three times precious than talent", and in every day life they practice the motto of "extermination of three poisons" (greed, hatred, craziness) in order to avoid bad actions which should cause evil karmas (love, hate, joy, anger); at the same time it is also the way to build up and cultivate lofty and beautiful actions (mercy, altruism, humane) for accumulating good karmas.

Nowadays, when Buddhist contribution to philosophy, in general, as the same as its contribution to the nation in accordance with the main purpose of "religion is to be with the nation" should be effective, this mode of Vipassana closely combines with the general requests of the nation and religion according to the motto of "Dharma – Nation – Socialism" stated by the National Buddhist Sangha. From the aspect of thinking, it is possible to say that, for Vietnamese scholar Buddhism Vipassana mode was accepted and then presented dominantly in the following features: 1) Generalized human's internal life and religious ethics (suffering or salvation is decided by oneself from inside); 2) Mode of Vipassana, particularly the intuition (*prajñā*) of Buddhist Zen sect; 3) the principle of transcending concept, experience and language, that opens the mind, and comes to be more flexible to accept other foreign system of thoughts.

At the same time, scholar Buddhism continued to concentrate on the character of innermost human by affirming the doctrine of Impermanent, No self in order to overcome "the serious unbalance between material life and spiritual one."[21] It would be effective way to perfect the typical standard of inward personality of traditional Buddhist believers in combination with requirements of national religion in modern time; that means, to contribute to "preserve the traditional ethic frame and avoid law-breaking, avert bad foreign miscellaneity [...]."[22] Accordingly, the effective means to realize this aim must be done just by the every self. It means, "to help human to perceive the truth of oneself, the truth of the universe where he is living with his own obvious future, and to take responsibility for his own activity", "aiming at a perfect and all-round human with humanity and wisdom"[23] 'Vipassana' is also an important issue of Buddhist studies, specially with the Consciousness-Only school, because this school "pays great attention to analyze the innermost mind and feeling, in combination with practice of meditation."[24] In fact, Buddhist Sangha has actively built and opened many Zen monasteries, Meditation centers or Institute of Zen studies in Vietnam with the aim to introduce the good technique of meditation, especially the skill of Vipassana which is effective to cultivate the inner mind and to attain "incisive intuition."[25]

The influence of Vipassana on popular Buddhism was mainly under the guideline of scholar Buddhism and indirectly through the Zen masters' and Buddhologists' teachings or their writings that guide common working Buddhists with their activity of belief such as: chant prayers and rituals or Buddhist festival either in pagoda or at home; or adjust their moral behavior and thinking gradually.

Generally speaking, Buddhist Vipassana (inward-thinking) has contributed to improving the particular characters in thought and way

---

[21] See, Vietnam Institute of Buddhology, *The Proceedings of Seminar on "Buddhist Education in Modern Time,"* Ho Chi Minh City: Publishing House, 2001, 13.

[22] Vietnam Institute of Buddhology, *The Proceedings of Seminar,* 215.

[23] Vietnam Institute of Buddhology, *The Proceedings of Seminar,* 63, 67.

[24] Vietnam Institute of Buddhology, *The Proceedings of Seminar,* 92.

[25] Vietnam Institute of Buddhology, *The Proceedings of Seminar,* 221.

of life of the Vietnamese. It is possible to say that the vital force of Buddhism, somewhat, is just strengthened by the exchange, balance and harmony between academic Buddhism and popular Buddhism through the process of practice of Buddhist Vipassana in their cultivation of humane moral principles of the Vietnamese nation. At present, Buddhist Vipassana continuously promotes its high and unique value of humanity. For example, Buddhist inward-thinking should be so effective and realizable for those aims as: to train personal moral from innermost mind and feeling, or to control one's emotion, to relax or unwind absolutely, to adjust the stream of consciousness or to contemplate completely by avoiding all external impacts. These achievements of Vipassana has been tested and proved by modern (western) physiology and psychology, and nowadays people in the world, including the Buddhists and the non-Buddhists learn it and practice it.

8

Mysticism without Bounds

Islamic Perspective

Dr. Gnanapragasam Lazar, SVD
Research and Cultural Centre, Hyderabad, India

1. Introduction

Mysticism, as we normally understand is an immediate, direct, intuitive knowledge of God or of ultimate reality attained through personal religious experience. It is a practical spiritual discipline based on the insight of illuminated seekers after truth. Wide variations are found in both the form and the intensity of mystical experience.

One of the most pervasive trends in Islamic Philosophy has been mysticism (Kilic, 1996; Nasr, 1996). From its origins to the Prophet Muhammad, and the Qur'anic revelation, the mystical trend among Muslims has played an extraordinary role in every sphere of Islamic faith. This mystical movement within Islam which is called Sufism arose as an organized movement after the death of Muhammad (AD 632), among different groups who found orthodox Islam to be spiritually stifling. Sufism according to its adherence is the inner, mystical dimension of Islam. It is 'a science whose objective is reparation of the heart and turning it away from all else but God' or "a science through which one can know how to travel into the presence of the Divine, purify one's inner self from passing things, and beautify it with a variety of praise worthy traits". The concept of Sufism was therefore, to focus the mystic power on the spiritual dimension of Islam with a view to shield the believers from the outwardly and unrealistic dogma of the faith.

The mystic is right to emphasize his closeness to God in the sense that everything is close to God, since there is really one God yet it is a slippery slope from here to identify with the deity in such a way that one fails to appreciate the immense gap that exist between us and God. This contrast between the transcendence and immanence of God is a familiar problem in many religions, of course, but particularly so in Islam, with its explicit rules against idolatry. The mystic tries to resolve this difficulty in a satisfactory way. But can the mystic succeed? How does the Sufi solve this problem in his mystical journey is the objective of this essay.

2. Sufism – Origin and Basic Creed

Islamic mysticism is called Sufism or *tasawwuf.* Sufism, as a form of mysticism, became very important in Islamic philosophy, sometimes as an alternative to other kinds of philosophy, and sometimes as an accompaniment (Nasr, 1996c; Kilic, 1996). In its early stages of development, Sufism effectively referred to nothing more than the internalization of Islam. According to one perspective, it is directly from the Qur'an, constantly recited, meditated, and experienced, that Sufism proceeded, in its origin and its development. Others have held that Sufism is the strict emulation of the way of Muhammad, through which the heart's connection to the Divine is strengthened.

The word Sufism (read - *tasawwuf*) is popularly used for centuries and is often discussed in various meanings.[1] The word "tasawwuf" or Sufism is considered to derive from 3 Arabic letters; *sa*, *wa* and, *fa.* There are several opinions about the origin and the meaning of the word *sufi* that are: 1) It is taken from the word *'safa'* which means purity. 2) It is taken from the word "*safw*" which means chosen. 3) It is taken from the word "*saff*", which means line referring to the Moslems who stand in the first line in *salat* and in war. 4) It is taken from the word "*suffah*" which means low verandah made of clay and heightened above

[1] Carl Ernst argues convincingly that the current preference for the word "Sufism" has much to do with the nineteenth-century perception of Islam by British Orientalists. See his *Shambhala Guide to Sufism*, Boston: Shambhala, 1997.

the ground outside the prophet Muhammad is Medina, where poor but good hearted people gathered to follow him. 5) It is taken from the word *'suf"* which means sheep fur showing that someone who is tended to study mental knowledge does not care about the outside performance of his and often only uses one cloth made of sheep fur the whole year.[2] Mystical love and oneness with God (*tawhid*) form the basic tenets of the Sufi faith. The difficulty arises in defining Sufism, rooted on the essence of Sufism as a mental experience which is almost impossible to explain exactly through speech. Difficulty in defining Sufism is also caused by the infinitive and subjective characteristics of Sufism and historical factor in the growth and development of Sufism which has been through many segments and in the area of different cultures. However, there is one agreed principle of Sufism, that is, a morality based on Islam. It means Sufism has moral meaning and Islamic spirit, because basically Islamic teaching is the principles of moral.

Al-Ghazali's (1111) greatest treatises, the "Revival of Religious Sciences" and the "Alchemy of Happiness," argued that Sufism originated from the Qur'an and was thus, compatible with mainstream Islamic thought, and did not in any way contradict Islamic Law – being instead necessary to its complete fulfillment. This became the mainstream position among Islamic scholars for centuries, challenged only recently on the basis of selective use of a limited body of texts. However, its systematization was really initiated by Ibn al-Arabi (1164-1240). The whole point of mysticism is to provide a taste (*dhawq*) of ultimate reality, and there has been a wide variety of accounts of how to do this. Webster's second definition of mysticism tells us that it can mean "the doctrine or belief that direct knowledge of God, of spiritual truth, or ultimate reality [...] is attainable through immediate intuition, insight, or illumination and in a way differing from ordinary sense perception or rationalization." This doctrine is certainly characteristic of the Sufi approach to understanding God and the world. However, they held that this direct knowledge – which they typically called "unveiling" (*kashf*) – must be rooted in the Qur'an and the Sunnah of Muhammad. Many of

[2] R.A. Nicholson, *The Mystic of Islam,* London: Kegan Paul Ltd., 1966, 3, dapat juga dibaca dalam Syekh Fadhlalla Haeri , Dasar-dasar Tasawuf, Pustaka Sufi, Yogyakarta, 2002, 3-4.

them also had a good deal of respect for the various rational approaches to knowledge. They maintained, however, that despite the opinions of the philosophers, reason alone is not sufficient to attain knowledge of God, and despite the opinions of the theologians, a merely rational understanding of the Qur'an is also inadequate.[3]

The basic principle of Sufism is a manifestation of human spiritual consciousness about himself as God's creature, and it is an effort to understand the existence of Allah by forgetting all the things connected to the joy of the world. Sufism is an effort to fill the heart by only remembering God as the basic of loving God's teaching. Sufis were differentiated from ordinary Muslims not so much by what they did, but rather by their single minded dedication to actualizing their spirits and living in the presence of God. One of the most characteristic methods they employed in the attempt to keep God constantly in mind is known as "the remembrance of God" (*dhikr Allah*). They held that anyone who can forget himself and remember God will overcome the forgetfulness inherited from Adam. Then one will be given access to spiritual reality and real being, just as Muhammad was given access to them.

As we have discussed, the origin of Sufism is traced back to the revelation of the Word to Prophet Muhammad. This revelation is said to be twofold – the one embodied in the contents of Qur'an that is meant for all, and which constitutes the doctrinal teaching of the *ulema* and is called *ilm-i-safina;* and that which was revealed to the Prophet's heart, called *ilm-i-sina,* transmitted by him to the chosen few, which is strictly esoteric and which forms the mystical teachings of the Sufis – the *auliyas,* dervishes, and *faqirs.* The early characteristics of Sufism were the esoteric path to truth and salvation through the *ils-i-Azam* (the great Name), piety, renunciation, love of God, turning away from all worldly goods and vanities, physical pleasures, wealth and power, recitation of Name, contemplation, all leading to ecstasy and vision. Their creed was: *taliban-i-duniya maqhoor und; traliban-i-uqba; mazdoor und; taliban-i-Maula masroor und*; (seekers of the world are doomed; seekers of

[3] For an excellent overview of the teachings and literature of Sufism, see Annemarie Schimmel, *Mystical Dimensions of Islam*, Chapel Hill: University of North Carolina Press, 1975. For a more historical approach, see Alexander Knysh, *Islamic Mysticism: A Short History*, Leiden: Bill, 2000. For a thematic approach, see W.C. Chittick, *Sufism: A Short Introduction*, Oxford: One world, 2000.

paradise are mercenary; and seekers of the Supreme Being are blessed). Rabia (717-831), the Sufi woman-saint, put it thus: "God, if I worship Thee in fear of hell, burn me in hell! If I worship Thee in the hope of paradise, exclude me from paradise! But if I worship Thee for Thine own sake, withhold not Thy everlasting beauty!."[4] The basic theme here is that "*data* (giver) is greater than the *data* (gift); the creator is preferable to things created." Two central Sufi concepts are *tawakkul,* the total reliance on God, and *dhikr,* the remembrance of God). The Sufi observes *faqr,* or "pious poverty," and is therefore known as *faqir*. He follows a path, or *tariqa,* to divine knowledge (gnosis) reading, study, prayer, and most especially the *dhikr* (the endless repetition of God's holy name) – which may lead to self-hypnosis like repeating a mantra. Prayer beads, similar to rosaries, also are used.

The following of the Sufi Path to enlightened love entails a life time, since there is no single moment when true union with God, the vision of the face of God as described in the Qur'an, has occurred. It is the belief of the Sufis that humankind has always been one with God, and that the traveling of the Path serves as a remembrance of this realization. Al-Ghazali talks of "God's 70,000 veils of light and darkness." In seeking to have union with God, the human spirit has to pass through seven stages – service of God, love, *zuhd* or renunciation, gnosis or knowledge, ecstasy, *fana* or destruction of self, *baqa* or bliss. The Absolute, having completely realized itself in human nature, returns to itself through the medium of human nature, and man becomes perfect in the Perfect Man, that is, the Saint. His function as a mediator between man and God corresponds with his metaphysical function as

[4] Rabia was seen one day running through the streets carrying fire in one hand and water in the other. She said, "I am going to light a fire in Paradise and pour water on Hell so that the servants of God may see him without any object of hope or motive of fear." Perhaps her most famous verse is that which describes two types of love: "I have loved thee with two loves, a selfish love and a love that is worthy. As for the love which is selfish, I occupy myself therein with remembrance of thee to the exclusion of all others. As for that which is worthy of thee, therein thou raisest the veil that I may see thee." See M. Smith, *Rabia the Mystic*, 28, 30, 102. Attat of Nishsapur (died 1230) was biographer of Rabia, and himself a mystic, wrote: "In Love no longer 'thou' and 'I' exist. For Self has passed away in the Beloved [...]. He who would know the secret of both worlds will find the secret of them both is Love." See M. Smith, *The Persian Mystics*, Attar, 93.

the unifying principle by means of which the opposed terms of reality and appearance are harmonized. Hence, is the upward movement of the Absolute from the sphere of manifestation back to the un-manifested! Death does not stop the *faqir*'s spiritual communication and training but is only another stage of development. According to Grand Sheikh Idries Shan, the Sufi makes four journeys:

a. *Fana*, or annihilation: At this stage the Sufi becomes harmonized with objective reality and seeks the unification of his consciousness. He is intoxicated with divine love.
b. *Baqa*, or permanency: Here the Sufi becomes a teacher or *qutub*; the magnet to which all turn for wisdom. He has stabilized his objective knowledge and becomes the Perfect Man. Rather than uniting with God, the Perfect Man has subordinated his will to God and lives in and through God (Traditionally, Sufi teachers are male).
c. Sufi attaining the third Journey becomes spiritual guides for all in accordance with their abilities, whereas State Two teachers work only in their local areas.
d. In the fourth journey, the Perfect Man guides others in the transition at death from physical life to another stage of development invisible to ordinary people. Few attain this plateau of wisdom.

3. Union with God

The objective of Sufism, as of all mysticism, is to attain union with God. Mysticism seeks for an immediate experience of the divine reality through the suppression of the ego. The method for attaining this most coveted experience, however, demands insight into a special and hidden branch of knowledge. Sufi doctrine teaches that, beside the usual rules for religious life, set out in the revelation and the prophetic *Sunnah,* there is another and deeper level of spiritual meaning, which the prophet shared with only a few of his chosen companions. The revelation, thus, wears two faces, one open and obvious, and the there only to be seen by those who have been instructed in secrets. The relation between the exoteric and esoteric levels of religious knowledge is symbolic, with every command, or rule of *sharia,* pointing to a higher truth that marks one of the stages or stations on the path (*tariqah*) to God. Knowledge of the *tariqah* has been passed down from the prophet through an unbroken chain (*silsila*) of saints (*walis*), each of whom has chosen his successor and instructed him in the secret knowledge of the way to union with God. The point of Sufism teaching is directly connected to Allah and stands in front of him without barrier. *Khasyful hijab* (the opening of curtain) between God and human is the main purpose of all Sufism activities in revealing the secrets of universe. If this purpose is reached, then human can directly comprehend the occultism and *marifat* with Allah, to know and to be united with him.

4. The Search for the Divine

Sufism is basically a spiritual journey to Allah, the almighty. It shows the world view specified into divinity. Therefore, despite containing axiological, Sufism also has epistemology and ontology aspects. The goal of the Sufi's long journey along the way (*tariqa*) is the achievement of *fana,* or extinction of the individuality in the reality of the divine. Fana consists in turning away from the world so that one sees only God. According to al-Huwiri, "the Sufi is the one who has nothing in his possession nor is he possessed by anything. This denotes the essence of annihilation." Fana is a state of ecstasy in which all human attributes have been left aside, and for many it beings the joy of intoxication in the divine love. For others, however, there is a stage beyond even annihilation. In their view, the greater value for the Sufi is to achieve subsistence (*baqa*) in God, so subordinating will and humanity to the divine that, passing beyond ecstasy, that person lives continually in and through God. Fana may be temporary; a climactic experience to be enjoyed at most a few times in the course of human life, but *baqa* is an enduring condition of complete human in-dwelling in God. These goals are not attained by all who strive in the path, but for those who can attain them is the *summum bonum* of human life.

> The perfect human being, says the Sufi, must not only die into God in ecstasy (*fana*), but abide in and with Him (*baqa*), manifesting His truth in the world of time. He or she is called

> to a life more active, because more contemplative, than that of other people: to fulfill the monastic ideal of balanced career of work and prayer.[5]

5. The Impossibility of the Real: The Paradox of God's Transcendence and Immanence

We cannot honestly say that there is any wide difference between the Brahman, Sufi or Christian mystic at their best. They are far more like each other than they are like the average believer in their several creeds. What is essential is the way mystics feel about their Deity, and about their own relation with it. In the following analysis we shall see how the paradox of Deity as transcendent and immanent in the Islamic mysticism.

In Islamic terms, the "cosmos" (*al-alam*) is defined as "everything other than God", so the term has no spatial or temporal limitations. The relationship of God to everything other than God is described from two basic points of view. In one respect, God is infinitely beyond the cosmos. Here, the theological term is *tanzih* which means "to declare God incomparable" with everything that exists. In this respect God is completely inaccessible to His creatures and beyond their understanding. This point of view is the classical position of "Kalam" (Islamic dogmatic theology). Many verses could be cited to show how the Qur'an takes this point of view, such as "Glory to be God, the Lord of Inaccessibility, above everything that they describe" (37:180) or in simpler terms, "Nothing is like Him" (42:11). Tanzih also means "to declare something pure and free of something else." It is to assert that God is pure and free of all the defects and imperfection of creatures. In the perspective of *tanzih,* God is so holy and pure that he cannot be compared to any created thing, including concepts; since all ideas are also created. The Qur'anic verse that expresses *tanzih* most clearly is "Nothing is like Him" (42:11). Divine names that are taken as expressing *tanzih* are the names of God's essence such as Holy, Glorious, Independent, and Transcendent.

[5] This aspect of contemplation and action of a mystic is further explained by Evelyn Underhill, *The Essentials of Mysticism*, Oxford: Oneworld Publications, 2007, 34.

In this respect, God is an impersonal reality far beyond human concerns. He is the God of negative theology. Though the proponents of Kalam emphasized the incomparability and transcendence, they represented only a small number of intellectuals who had relatively little influence on the Muslim masses. There is also a second point of view which is clearly supported by many Qur'anic verses and which is stressed in popular Islam and the spiritual tradition of Sufi. The God of the theologians, as Ebno I-Arabi remarked, was a God whom no one could possibly love, since He was too remote and incomprehensible (Ebno'I-Arabi n.d. Vol II. P.326, line 13). But the God of Qur'an, the Prophet, and the spiritual authorities of Islam is a God who is supremely lovable, since He is dominated by concern for His creatures. As the Qur'an puts it, "He loves them, and they love Him (5:54)." God's love for creation produces in the creatures love for God. This God of compassion and love can be grasped and understood.

To use the theological term, He must be "declared similar" (*tashbih*) in some mysterious fashion to His creation. We can rightly conceive of Him in human attributes. It is to assert that God must have some sort of similarity with his creatures. God's signs within the cosmos and scriptures designate this attributes, such as love, knowledge, desire, power, and mercy. All divine names suggest some sort of *tashbih* because they allow us to think that God is such and such. For example, as soon as we hear that God is compassionate, we think of God in terms of our understanding of compassion. This is the point of view of God's immanence in all things, and it is clearly supported by such Qur'anic verses as "Wherever you turn, there is the face of God" (2:115) and "We are nearer to man than the jugular vein" (50:16). Qur'an does describe God, as we saw before as "The Hearing, The Seeing." But even further, the Qur'an describes God's speech, His hands, His eyes, His feet and describes God sitting on a throne. The Qur'an also asserts that God blew His spirit into Adam and that Adam was made in God's image. Qur'an presents a God who communicates. God spoke the Qur'an. God is unique and unlike anything in creation, While God is also immanent in all of creation and creation is – when truly perceived – a system of signs and symbols revealing God's nature. Thus in that spirit – perhaps even taking the idea to the extreme – the Indian Sufi saint Hazrat 'Inayat Khan

(1882-1927) said, "There is only one scripture: the sacred manuscript of nature." In this respect, God is a personal God.

Thus, *tashbih* is where "God as He appears to us in created being. His being appears to us in a being which is not His but it appears to us [...]. He makes Himself known in His creatures. Not merely by argument from cause to effect." The Sufis are very definite about the fact that every creature manifests God's love...doesn't manifest God's essence but manifests His love, is a manifestation of love. Everything manifests love. Everything comes from love and is a manifestation of love.[6] Furthermore, a Sufi teacher like Ibn'Arabi declares "that if it were not for this love, the world would never have appeared in its concrete existence. In this sense the movement of the world toward existence was a movement of love which brought it into existence. The great thing in Sufism is love." The Creative Love and Compassion of God, according to Ibn'Arabi, "the Sufis are able to experience in themselves, this sort of a creative ferment that is going on, to realize themselves, as it were. tingling with this light which is being shot through them at every moment by the power of God."

6. The Debate

In Islamic tradition, the Muslim theologians (*mutakallimun*) fought vigorously to defend the transcendence of God (*tanzih*) against the danger of anthropomorphism (*tashbih*). The Mu'tazilites in particular were adamant in safeguarding God's absolute transcendence to the point of explaining *away* His names and qualities in terms of the various modes and states of His Essence. Yet, emphasizing the pole of transcendence at all costs is not without its perils. Presenting God as the utterly other runs the risk of cutting Him off from the world He has created. An absolutely transcendent God with no relation to this world can easily become a 'regulatory principle' rather than a divine being to whom we pray, whom we love, and whose friendship we seek. What this means is that pure negation is never sufficient. To use the symbolism of the Islamic testimony which says *la ilaha illa Allah* (there is no god but God), saying "la" (no) without saying "illa" but does not

[6] Al-Ghazali, *Tahafut al-falasifa* (*Incoherence of the Philosophers*), trans. S.A. Kamali, Lahore: Pakistan Philosophical Congress, 1963, 70.

deliver. A believer says "la" to all false deities to be able to say "illa" to only one God. From this point of view, Derrida seems to be with the station of "la"![7]

Ibn al-'Araabi, the great Sufi metaphysician of the 13th century from Andalusia, has an interesting solution for this. He believes that neither the defenders of transcendence nor the advocates of immanence do justice to God. Taken in itself, each invites metaphysical error and theological impropriety. He further criticizes the defenders of both transcendence and immanence as two opposite poles of a very familiar debate "that of the knowability of God. One pole emphasizes the absolute transcendence of God, the other his immanence, but neither has understood the actual situation" that the Real can actually be both at the same time.

Ibn 'Arabi's insistence on the simultaneity of everything being He/not He (*huwa la huwa*) is an important step. It acknowledges the illusion of the dualism, the fundamental mistake of believing God to be either 'this' or 'that', transcendent or immanent, 'out there' or 'in here'. As long as rational thought conceives of God in terms of binary oppositions, 'opposing the reports brought by the messengers' in order to establish 'true knowledge of God', the 'reflection can only roam in its own specific playing field', which is one of many fields. As a staunch Sufi, Ibn 'Arabi believes in the positive, independent, signification of both transcendence and immanence, and he still believes these meanings to be opposed to one another. However, it is an opposition which is dissolved in the Real. He believes in a God paradoxical enough, all-comprehensive enough, impossible enough to be both immanence and transcendent at the same time.

---

[7] Jacques Derrida was one of the most controversial philosophers of the 20th century. He developed a philosophy of 'deconstruction. This consists of a number of assumptions about language, reality and what occurs at the intersection of the two. How language evades any easy formulations and what this means for us humans is the fundamental given of deconstruction. His contribution is an insight or intuition into the reality of what is constructed through language in the countless forms of novels and poems. He said that a text always evades us. The construction of a text is such that there is always something that is left out, remains unsaid, resists clarity, and forces us to look for what appears to be a mere supplement or footnote to the main text. In a sense, we can only speak in terms of negations.

He resents the dualism because it veils a presence "the presence of a paradox, the ultimate, unthinkable Oneness of God.[8] He proposes the position of what he calls a "true believer". For Ibn al-'Arabi, a true believer is the one who sees God with two eyes (*dhu 'l – 'aynayn*). With one eye, he sees God as utterly transcendent, remote, sublime, and dissimilar. At this level, God is the *mysterium tremendum* and beyond all comprehension, utterance, and description. Here He is the Lord to be worshipped. But the same believer sees God with his other eye as here and now, always present and intimately linked to His creation. Immanence implies transcendence or Beyond Being.[9] At this level, God is "closer to us than our jugular vein". Here He is the supreme friend, the Beloved of all lovers, the centre towards which every thing moves, the light that illuminates the whole cosmos. As we have seen that the transcendence represents the "absolute otherness of God", which is "not able to be expressed in any way, not able to be understood, not able to be manifested," while the latter indicates that God "is able to be understood", that, indeed, "He is manifested in concrete things, and He's in everything." The Sufis "run these two things together and actually the point is that there is no knowledge of God without these. In fact, *tashbih*, is not a question of reasoning; it is a question of symbol. This could be found in the writings of Thomas Merton as he speaks about the understanding of transcendence and immanence in Sufism:

"It is a question of creative imagination, and so, whereas *tanzih* says God cannot be imagined, *tashbih,* says God can be imagined. A God who cannot be imagined does manifest Himself in visible symbols, and the visible symbols are real manifestations of God, and to grasp them one must have imagination and one must see them, and they must be concrete [...] So that the most absurd thing for the Sufis would be simply a ruthless policy of, say, demythologization, just simply demythologize

---

[8] It should be noted here that, Derrida rejects binary oppositions because they veil an absence. For him to believe in a word like 'transcendence' is to believe in a certain absence. 'Transcendence' and 'immanence' are semantic vacuities which can only pretend to meaning through contrast with their opposites 'in other words, the immanent can only be understood as the non-transcendent, the transcendent as the non-immanent. Ibn 'Arabi, however, is not making any such critique of meaning.

[9] "Beyond Being" is also Platonic (*Republic* 7.6.509b), although it is more usually associated with Plotinus (for example, *Enneads* 4.3.17; 6.9.11).

for the sake of demythologizing [...]. (You) have to have both of these things, and they are not arrived at logically...They synthesize. They go together, so that the perfection of one includes the perfection of the other."[10]

For Thomas Merton this represents "a very good point about religious knowledge. A purely logical knowledge doesn't do it. A purely affective knowledge doesn't do it. A purely abstract knowledge doesn't do it [...]. There is a special kind of knowledge which is religious knowledge by which we are able to know God, which is not like other knowledge, and which combines both these things which appear to be opposite."

According to Sufis, it is only by seeing God with two eyes that we can do justice to His transcendence-cum-immanence. Seeing God with two eyes does not lead to duality because we see things with two eyes. Yet what we see is not two but one. In short, *via negative* cannot be our only refuge. An infinite play of deconstructions may offer us some illuminating and even liberating perspectives.

These two basic theological perspectives form two poles between which Islamic thought takes shape. The Sufism strikes a delicate balance between the two positions. Negative and positive theology both plays a role in the understanding of the Divine Reality. Often *tanzih* and *tashbih* are associated with two divine names *batin* (inward or Non-manifest) and *zahir* (outward or Manifest.). Inasmuch as the Real is inward, all outward is unreal, and oneness is found only in the Real himself.

But inasmuch as God is outward, all outwardness is Real. Hence, the universe itself is real through God's realness and one through God's oneness. If God is far, he is also near. Although he is beautiful and stirs up love in the heart because of his beauty, his beauty is not like the beauty of creatures. "Nothing is like Him". In the midst of his nearness he is far, and in the midst of his similarity he is incomparable.

One way to understand the idea of in comparability is to conceive of infinitely vast circle. God is at the centre. He is the dimensionless centre point that serves as the origin of the circle. The world we experience is the periphery, infinitely distant from centre. Only centre point has

---

[10] Merton, T. (Unpublished), *The Mystic Life: a series of talks on Sufism,* given at Gethsemani Monastery. Talk 2.

no dimensions, and "Nothing is like Him". At the same time every concentric circle is similar to every other circle. Created things share the same qualities, but God shares none of their qualities.

In order to picture *tashbih*, we can use the same dimension less point but now we need to imagine that the point has an infinite number of radii extending outward. Each creature in the universe is situated on a radius and is connected directly to the centre, gaining its reality from the central point. The radii suggest God's concern for creation through love, mercy, compassion and kindness.

However, neither *tanzih* nor *tashbih* provides a complete picture of reality. The universe needs to be understood in terms of both perspectives simultaneously (see figure – 3). Then we see that each thing is at once near to God and far from him, at once similar to God and incomparable with him. Each thing is confronted simultaneously with mercy and wrath, gentleness and compassion, life-giving and slaying. This is Tawhid (oneness of God). The two perspectives of *tanzih* and *tashbih*, or God's distance and nearness, are met constantly is in Islamic texts and in the every day life of a Sufi. In short, *tanzih* and *tashbih* represent the two poles of Tawhid. Rumi further expresses the ultimate goal of Islamic transcendence and immanence with these words, "Heaven and earth and I live together, all things and I are one" (Rumi, III 4404, cf. Chitticck, 1983 168).[11]

One can gain a certain grasp of the role these two perspectives have played in Islam by comparing them with the situation found in the Chinese tradition, where the Confucians place emphasis upon yang and the Taoists upon yin. In other words if asked whether the Tao itself is yin or yang, Confucians would more probably answer that the Tao itself is yang, while a Taoist would be more likely to say that it is yin. In the same way the experts in jurisprudence and Kaam that is, those Muslim authorities who defend the outward and legalistic teachings of Islam – lay stress upon God's transcendence. They insist that He is a wrathful

---

[11] Here we can understand the Qur'anic teaching that everyday natural, physical and material phenomena and events are "signs" and "examples" of God's nature. The sense of this is echoed in Einstein's admiration for "...God who reveals Himself in the orderly harmony of what exists..." However, Einstein did not believe in a personal God, whereas Muslims do believe in a personal God with whom one maintains a personal relationship.

God and they constantly warn about hell and the divine punishment. These are the Muslim "Confucians", who see God primarily as yang. In contrast, those authorities who are concerned with Islam's spiritual dimension constantly remind the first group of the prophetic saying, "God's mercy precedes His wrath". They maintain that mercy, love and gentleness are the overriding reality of existence, and that these will win out in the end. In their view, God is primarily yin.

To review what has already been said, the one God is looked upon from two points of view, transcendence and immanence. With respect to God's transcendence and distance, human beings and all other creatures are God's absolute servants who must submit to His will. But with respect to God's immanence and nearness, human beings have another role to play. They were chosen out of all creatures to be God's vicegerents upon the face of the earth. They possess all the divine attributes and can, therefore, act as God's representatives. In gaining correct knowledge of God, one needs to combine the declaration of God's transcendence with understanding of His immanence. In the same way, Islamic anthropology sees a perfect human being as one who combines servanthood with vicegerency. In respect of God's transcendence, man is God's servant, but in respect of His immanence, man is His representative and vicegerent.

The Divine Immanence is, in effect, its own receptacle, in a similar manner to which it might be said that a word is the receptacle of its meaning, while at the same time being identical with it. Divine Immanence, or the Divine Presence, is identical with Being, which is both its own principle and effect. In turn, Being gives rise to the distinction, recognized by Plato among others, between Being and becoming (Timaeus 27d-28a). A simple overview of the station of Immanence in the context of the Transcendence can be expressed thus:

Transcendence = Beyond Being
Immanence = Being
Being 'contains' becoming
Becoming = the play of cosmic existence

The existential world is a mode or level of the Divine Immanence. Immanence is itself "contained" or prefigured by the Divine

Transcendence. The relationship of Transcendence and Immanence is one of identity and distinction. Identity means that the cosmos is not other than God. Thus, in his chapter on Noah, Ibn-al-'Arabi says, "The Reality never withdraws from the forms of the cosmos in any fundamental sense, since, the cosmos, in its reality, is implicit in the definition of the Divinity".[12] According to Al-Ghazali, "That we are conformed to God, made in His image," – this is certain; otherwise we should not exist. That we are contrary to God, this is also certain; otherwise we should not be different from God. Without analogy with God we should be nothing. Without opposition to God we should be nothing. Without opposition to God we should be God."[13] For Ibn-al-'Arabi: "God says, *there is naught like unto Him*, asserting His transcendence, and He says, *He is the Hearing, and the Seeing,*[14] implying comparison (Relativity and Immanence)".[15] 'The Father is greater than I' (Jn.14:28), but, at the same time, "The Father and I are one" (Jn.10.30).[16]

According to Sufism, God's transcendental cannot be separated from his immanent towards human. Thus, in his life, human should always reach God' immanence so it is immanent in his or try to get as close as possible to God, so it opens the curtain between him and God. Human being will get the divinity consciousness through practices of spiritual purification which functions to synthesize God in his life. God includes Himself in human.[17] However, God is not human or it does not mean that human should be the same or can make himself the same as God. As the limitation, human cannot include himself in infinite God. As part of Islamic teaching, Sufism is initially trying to bridge the concept of divinity which is transcendental and immanent. Sufism is aimed at

---

[12] Ibn al-'Arabi, *Fusus,* 1980, 74. St. Augustine, in his *Confessions,* says, "He (God) did not create and depart, but the things that are from Him are in Him" (4.12.18).

[13] Quoted by Schuon in, *Spiritual Perspectives and Human Facts,* 1987, 167.

[14] Qur'an, 42:11.

[15] Ibn al-Arabi, *Fusus al-hikam,* trans. Austin, Mahwah: Paulist Press, 1980, 75.

[16] On the interplay of the hypostases see Schuon, *From the Divine to the Human,* Bloomington: World Wisdom Books, 1982, 41-42.

[17] Schuon cites Ibn al-'Arabi: "He (the Absolute; *Brahman*) sent His ipseity (Self; *atman*) by Himself from Himself to Himself". God (Infinite and Transcendence) sends forth His ipseity (Immanence) by Himself (as a possibility of His Infinitude) from Himself (from the Infinite) to Himself (to the Infinite).*Light on the Ancient Worlds,* London: Perennial Books, 1995, 97, 2.

meeting face to face with the God almighty. With a full consciousness, human continues to train himself/herself and clean his/her soul to get into Allah the almighty. Since Allah the almighty is transcendental and divine, He can only be approached spiritually. The main objective of Sufism can not be possibly reached with religious service alone. For that, Sufist will have to improve himself not only for doing the physical dimension (exoteric), religion makes Sufism starts to avoid the living world and physical religion, so that it is likely making spiritual life as the most important. The phenomena that are seen from the Sufists life are poverty, retardation, and exclusivity.

However, the meaning is the existence of God together with his creatures. God shows his power and adequacy especially through the whole manifestation of his love, existence, creation, and care for what He creates, guidance to what He creates and the acceptance of His creature that is lost wholeheartedly. On the other hand, Immanence of God does not mean that every behaviour from human and nature realistically is done by God, God is not arrival to human producing the effect in nature and God also does not interfere in human working process.[18] Human can erase and eliminate the existence of God in his life and translate those statements into definition which is naturalistically without loosing anything, as long as the facts of the statement is there. God is not a fact among other facts; rather God is more like meaning given to the facts with a new dimension integrating those facts into regularity.[19] What is lost from human by eliminating God in his life is the meaning of regulatory and the meaning of life. God, nature and human are a cause and effect principles with different levels. Nature and human have a direct relationship with God as well as the relationship between God and the universe. God is always there accompanying something and it is He who causes the integrity of something.[20]

The goal of the inward life in Islam is to reach the Divine as both the Transcendent and Immanent. It is to gain a vision of God as the Reality

---

[18] Fazlur Rahman, "The Qur'anic Concept of God, The Universe, and Man," *Islamic Studies*. No 1 vol V, Karachi, 1967, 1-18.

[19] Fazlur Rahman, "Major Themes of Al-Qur'an, *Bibliotheca Islamica,* Chicago, 1982, 3.

[20] Fazlur Rahman, *Islam and Modernity,* The University of Chicago Press, Chicago, 1982, 46.

beyond all determination and at the same time of the world as "plunging in God". It is to see God everywhere.[21] The inward dimension is the key for the understanding of metaphysics and traditional cosmology as well as for the penetration into the essential meaning of religion and of all religions, for at the heart of every authentic religion lies the one Truth which resides also at the heart of all things and most of all of human beings. In Christianity, it is the person of Christ who saves and who washes away the dross of separation and externalization. In Islam, such a function is performed by the supreme expression of the Truth Itself, by the *Shahadah, La illaha ill'llah.* To take refuge in it is to be saved from the debilitating effect of "externalization" and "objectivization" and to be brought back to the Centre, through the inward dimension.

7. New Dimension of Mysticism: The Social Dimension

Fazlur Rahman considers that the absoluteness of transcendence and immanence concept of God cannot give any meaning to religion and cannot bring the concept alive in human life. The relationship between God and human is not to be seen and understood absolutely as something that is transcendent or immanent because this form of relationship will influence the way human impose himself in his life. While understanding God immanently will place human in theme position as God in order that every willingness. Therefore, the neo-sufism proposes a new dimension to the concept of transcendence and immanence of God.[22]

Today Sufism straightens and brings back the mysticism through rules and laws along with practical aspects. Sufism in Al-Ghazali system is viewed as something softer and higher than Islamic Laws and rules (Sharia). In Al-Ghazali's concept, Sufism is put above Sharia with the following order: Sharia, Tariqat, Hakkikat and Makrifat. Conversely, Fazlur Rahman would like to see the Sufism that obeys Sharia, also the communitarian aspect of Sufism that can get closer to Allah, what he calls as Kasyfi comprehension that does not have any absolute truth

---

[21] See F. Schuon, "Seeing God Everywhere", in his *Gnosis, Divine Wisdom,* trans. G.E.H. Palmer, London, 1959, 06 ff.

[22] Fazlur Rahman, "The Impact of Modernity on Islam", Islamic Studies No 1 vol v, Karachi, 1966, 158.

which can only be felt by the Sufist who experienced It,., but still need to be testified by the reality outside.

Modern mysticism stresses on the construction of moral and social aspects of Muslim Society or it can only be defined as *tauhid* or social Sufism. Thus, generally the characteristics of neo Sufism are 'puritan' and activist'.[23] The objective of modern Sufism is the intense emphasis on deep faith based on the Islamic principles and evaluates the human life as having the same importance as the life after the material world.[24] The consequence is that the integration of the world life value with the after life value or the exoteric and esoteric approach. If it is seen from the principle value and the objective, this modern Sufism is not completely new but only tries to bring Sufism back to its root like the one practiced in the prophecy era by adding some modern colours suitable with the present era. This neo-Sufism wants to bring back the Islamic values completely, that is balance between material world-life with the after world's-life.

This *Godness* concept of modern Sufism propounded by philosophers like Fazlur Rahman is transcendent and immanent. Nature is performance of God and God includes Himself in the reality of nature. He created so that all creatures contain the elements of *Godness*. Thus, human should always get himself to God to be able to reach His transcendence in order to become immanent in his life. The concept of *Godness* in Fazlur Rahman's neo Sufism is an effort to bridge God's transcendence and immanence through an action which is contemplative (soul purifying act in human world's activity). It must be noted here that the existence of God cannot be narrowed into the existence of the world. World is an empiric expression of God which is inside everything immanently and transcendently. Therefore, according to Fazlur Rahman in neo Sufism, God is transcendent and at the same time immanent in human life. That makes human can reach God without keeping oneself away from the world. After reaching God, it does not mean that human is the same as God.

---

[23] H.A. Rival Siregar, *Tasawuf,* Rajawali Pers, Jakarta, 1999, 250.

[24] Fazlur Rahman, *Islam,* Weidenfel and Nicholson, London, 1966, 230.

8. Mysticism without Bounds

In this pluralistic world, no theology or philosophy is adequate; the degree of its inadequacy is of secondary importance. Though some creeds have proved more helpful to mystics than others, they are found fully developed in every great religion. We cannot honestly say that there is any wide difference between the Brahman, Sufi or Christian mystic at their best. They are far more like each other than they are like the average believer in their several creeds. What is essential is the way mystics feel about their Deity, and about their own relation with it, for this adoring and all-possessing consciousness of the rich and complete divine life over against the self's life, and of the possible achievement of a level of being, a sublimation of the self, wherein we are perfectly united with it, may fairly be written down as a necessary element of all mystical life. This is the common factor that unites those apparently incompatible views of the universe which have been claimed at one time or another as mystical. Their mystical quality abides wholly in the temper of the self who adopts them.

Mystics may be transcendentalists, but if so, it is because their intuition of the divine is so lofty that it cannot be expressed by means of any intellectual concept, and they are bound to say with Ruysbroeck, "He is neither This nor That." They may not be the believers of animism; but if they are, it is because they find in other people – more, in the whole web of life – that mysterious living essence which is mode of God's existence, and which they love, seek and recognize everywhere. "How shall I find words for the beauty of my Beloved? For He is merged in all beauty" says Kabir. "His colour is in all the pictures of the world, and it bewitches the body and the mind." They may be – often are – sacramentalists, but if so, only because the symbol or the sacrament helps them to touch God. The moment mystics suspect that any of these things are obstacles instead of means; they reject them, to the scandal of those who habitually confuse the image with the reality.

Thus we get the temperamental symbolist, nature-mystic, or transcendentalist. We get Plotinus rapt to the 'bare pure One'; St. Augustine's impassioned communion with Perfect Beauty, Eckhart declaring his achievement of the 'wilderness of God'; Ruysbroeck describing his achievement of 'that way-less abyss of fathomless beatitude where the Trinity of divine persons possess their nature in the essential Unity'; Kabir listening to the rhythmic music of Reality, and seeing the worlds told like beads within the Being of God; Sufis enraptured description of God as the 'Matchless Chalice and the Sovereign Wine'; and the narrow intensity and emotional raptures of contemplatives of the type of Richard Rolle. We cannot refuse the title of mystic to any of these, because in every case their aim is union between God and the soul. This is the one essential of mysticism, and there are as many ways from one term to the other as there are variations in the human spirit.

Al-Ghazali insists on the importance of the mystic being a good Muslim, as does Ibn al-"Arabi. Their argument was that it is only through preparing oneself along the Islamic path that one can find the higher path to experience of the reality that lies behind everything. Yet, there seems to be no reason in principle why the higher path should only be accessible through religion, or even just through Islam. This is the question that was also difficult to answer for the *falasifa* (Islamic Philosophers), since they argued that the highest form of awareness and indeed happiness was available only to the philosophers. Many times it is argued that it is only through communal life that one can influence others, and it is surely better to involve others in one's journey to happiness rather than merely selfishly pursue it by oneself. Then again, for most people it is not possible to reach ultimate happiness by oneself, since one need to work with others to get on the right path in the first place. One needs to be guided in some way, and unless there is someone there to guide, and a community to make sure that one keeps on the right path, there is little likelihood of success. The only people who can pursue this end by themselves are those of extraordinary intelligence and virtue, who have direct help from God; but it is easy for lesser mortal to deceive themselves in this respect.

9. Conclusion

Sufism is the mystical dimension of Islam based on the esoteric, or "inner-meaning" of its scripture, namely the Qur'an. Sufism's central doctrine is based on a verse of the Qur'an in which God says, "I created man and breathed my spirit into him." This "Divine spark" placed into every individual, says the Sufi, must be nurtured and cherished. Furthermore, each individual "spark" or "spirit" separated from the Universal Spirit desires to return and reunite with the Universal spirit. This "returning" is vital and central to the Sufi doctrine Now, the Sufi embarks on a spiritual journey known as the Sufi Path; a path of devotion and love; which leads to none other than God Himself.

The basic creed of Islam is belief in the oneness of God (*tauhid*). This essay has been a debate on the concept of God whether He is transcendent or immanent. Nature is performance of God and God includes Himself in the reality of nature. He created so that all creatures contain the elements of *Godness.* Thus, human should always get himself/herself to God to be able to reach His transcendence in order to become immanent in his life. The concept of *Godness* in Islamic mysticism is an effort to bridge God's transcendence and immanence through an action which is contemplative (soul purifying act in human world's activity). Everything is in God, but never can be same as God. According to this concept, every reality is in God includes Himself in His creation. Nevertheless, the existence of God can not be narrowed into the existence of world. World is an empiric expression of God which is inside everything immanently and transcendently. Therefore, according to Islamic mysticism God is transcendent and at the same time immanent in human life and self-transformation of an individual is achieved through transcendence and immanence. That makes human can reach God without keeping himself away from his world. After reaching God, it does not mean that human is the same as God. It maybe appropriate to conclude our discussion with the words of the Egyptian Sufi Dhu'l-nun who said:

> *"O God, I never hearken to the voices of the beasts or the rustle of the trees, the splashing of waters or the song of birds, the whistling of the wind or the rumble of thunder, but I sense in them a testimony to Thy Unity and a proof of Thy Incomparableness that Thou art All-prevailing, the All-knowing, and All-wise."*[25]

---

[25] A.J. Arbery, *Sufism,* London, 1950, 52-53

References

01. Arbery, A.J., *Sufism*, London: 1950.
02. Chittick, W.C. *The Self-Disclosure of God: Principles of Ibn al-"Arabi's Cosmology*, Albany, New York: State of University of New York Press, 1998.
03. Chittick, W.C., *Sufism: A Short Introduction,* Oxford: Oneworld, 2000.
04. Chittick, W.C., *The Sufi Path of Knowledge: Ibn al-"Arabi's Metaphysics of Imagination*, Albany, New York: State of University of New York Press, 1996.
05. Ernst, Carl, *Sufism*, Boston: Shambhala, 1997.
06. Knysh, Alexander, *Islamic Mysticism: A Short History*, Leiden: Brill, 2000.
07. Merton, T., *The Ascent of Truth*, Tunbridge Wells, Kent: Burns & Oates, 1951.
08. Mott, M., *The Seven Mountains of Thomas Merton*, Boston: Houghton Mifflin, 1984.
09. Murata, Sachko and Chittick, W.C., *The Vision of Islam*, New York: Paragon, 1994.
10. Nasr, H., *Science and Civilization in Islam*, New York, 1970.
11. Nasr, H., *The Interior Life in Islam,* (http://www.al-islam.org/al-serat/interior-nasr.htm).
12. Padwick, *Muslim Devotions: A Study of Prayer-Manuals in Common Use*, London: 1961.
13. Schimmel, Annemarie, *Mystical Dimension of Islam*, Chapel Hill: University of North Carolina Press, 1975.
14. Schuon, F., *Dimensions of Islam*, trans. P. Townsend, London: 1969.
15. Schuon, F., *Esoterism as Principle and as Way*, Middlesex: Perennial Books, 1981.

9

Mysticism and Sociability in Daoism from a Christian Point of View

Dr. Romualdas Dulskis
Vytautas Magnus University, Kaunas, Lithuania

1. Introduction

The image of the heron standing in a body of calm water, which is so well liked in Chinese visual arts, conveys the mystical lifestyle of a Daoist sage. It seems the heron is doing nothing but resting, probably snoozing. The heron's inactivity first refers to the Daoist *wuwei* (non-action) principle. A Daoist sage lives as if engaged in nothing, submerged in silence and devoid of earthly ambitions. Such a contemplative lifestyle could appear similar to idleness. Nonetheless, the existence of the Daoist sage is maximally concentrated, vigilant and purpose-directed. The heron symbolizes absolute calm that is, at the same time, absolute attentiveness of the existing state. A heron does not squander its attention and inner resources: it is not a curiosity seeker and does not glance around at its surroundings. Nonetheless, it observes the surroundings and sees everything that appears important and necessary to it. It is on watch duty. The image of the Daoist heron is reminiscent of the urging in the Gospel to be vigilant. Jesus spoke repeatedly to his disciples about the importance of vigilance, "And what I am saying to you I say to all: Stay awake!" (Mark 13: 37). Vigilance has become a Christian feature, which particularly was practiced in the monastic vocation. The Fathers of the Church and the later Christian spiritual teachers were fond of comparing clear and muddy waters. For muddy water to become clear, it must settle calmly, in the same as a person must achieve peacefulness in the soul, to be able to see God within a now, purified soul. The book of *Wenzi* speaks very similarly, "No one uses flowing water for a mirror, still water is used for a mirror. By keeping thus inwardly, you become still and are not scattered outwardly."[1]

The Daoist lifestyle encourages controlling heated actions and fostering inner peace. The focused and calm sage is able to direct his entire inner energy—*qi*—in the proper direction. Nothing is more important to a heron than catching a fish; nothing is more important to the human than to decipher the mystery of life and to concentrate power on the most important purpose of life.

This article analyzes the essential parameters of mysticism in Daoism and their relationship with social life. The Christian view on Daoist mysticism assists in highlighting the special valuable elements of this teaching and their meanings in the sphere of public life.

2. Spontaneous Effectiveness of Mysticism

The Daoist classics are convinced that mysticism is a necessary condition for a productive life. At first glance, this may seem a paradox. After all Daoist sages do not seek effectiveness, external results or success but rather, unity with Dao. Their fundamental and most important purpose is one – to live by the principles of Dao. In fact the Daoist classics are sure that authentic mysticism cannot remain fruitless. In and of itself, it traces a diverse effectiveness.

> When mountains are high, clouds and rain form on them, when waters are deep, dragons are born in them; when ideal people reach the Way, the richness of virtue flows in them. Those

[1] *Wenzi*, 94. After in 1973 a bamboo manuscript of the *Wenzi* dated to 55 B.C. was found in the tomb of King Huai near Dingzhou in Hebei, Eastern China, the *Wenzi* was re-classified as one of the most important texts of the Daoist philosophical heritage. All citations are from the only existing English translation of *Wenzi* to date: T. Cleary, *Wen-tzu. Understanding the Mysteries: Further Teachings of Lao-tzu*, Boston & London, 1992.

> who have hidden virtues will surely have manifest rewards; those who do good deeds in secret will surely have illustrious reputations.[2]

Wenzi compares the sage to a high mountain and a body of deep waters. Two images that are the opposite of one another are used here. However, they are specifically best at revealing the characteristics of a sage. The Daoist sage is not a one-sided personage. If a sage is able to achieve oneness with Dao, then various, positive features, or as *Wenzi* asserts, the "richness of virtue" manifest in that sage. By his knowledge and wisdom, the sage is similar to a high mountain where its shade offers pleasant refreshment from the sweltering midday heat; and by the sage's goodwill – to the body of deep water, a favorable sphere for the growth and for the development of living beings. *Wenzi* emphasizes that the mountain, as much as the body of water, influences the surroundings. The same way as the clouds, which gather around the mountain, water the parched earth with rain and as the deep waters form the conditions for habitation by the dragon – the symbol of goodwill, power and wisdom – thus,_the sage who lives in oneness with Dao serves society with wisdom and goodwill. Additionally, since a sage has great insight, he/she often gives rise to social initiatives.

Daoism accents the meaningfulness of hidden virtues. These are more important than visible ones because they affect the internal resolve of a person. The person who has inner virtues surely has outward virtues as well, whereas the person who is satisfied with the outward alone (which Daoist tradition considers as inferior) faces the danger of becoming merely superficially virtuous. "Those who possess high virtues do not need [to engage in lower] virtue. Those who possess mundane virtues have to force themselves to be virtuous."[3] It is not difficult to perceive the necessity of inner, hidden action and the power of inner virtues in all the teachings of classical Daoism. Inner action constitutes the foundation of any sort of outward activity. Inner quality creates external results in and of itself whereas, if only external results

---

[2] *Wenzi*, 97.

[3] *Cultivating Stillness: A Taoist Manual for Transforming Body and Mind,* trans. Eva Wong, Boston & London, 1992, 107.

are sought without heed to the quality of inner life, then an unstable and unnecessary product is produced. The Daoist classics often mock outer virtues and point out their negligibility and incapability.

Wenzi chapter 97 unavoidably reminds us of the teachings of Jesus to contribute alms, pray and fast in secret (Cf. Matthew 6: 1–18). Jesus emphasizes that our Heavenly Father shall reward people for such good works. Meanwhile the Daoist tradition highlights the *spontaneous usefulness* of hidden virtues and good works done in secret. *Wenzi* does not assert that Dao shall reward them. Nonetheless, it is to be understood that positive, secret action is in accord with the Way of Dao, thus it will meet with success and recompense.

Good works done in secret and hidden virtues are part of the Daoist sage's day-to-day life. Texts of the Daoist classics do not say whether secret practices take up the greater part of a sage's day. It can be guessed from certain areas in the book of *Laozi* that it depends on circumstances. A sage can devote a great deal of time to internal practices and good works done in secret, so long as duties or life's circumstances do not force the sage to be involved in public activities. On the other hand, he can devote much time and energy to public activities and lessen his secret actions to a minimum. Nevertheless, a sage gives secret practices the priority.

Although a Daoist sage values hidden virtues more than he does public activity, his mysticism is not a purpose in and of itself. The technique of mystical life is not as important to the sage as is the realistic oneness with Dao. Such unity undoubtedly has numerous mystical elements but it is not only a hidden reality. Oneness with Dao encompasses the entire existence of a sage and manifests in the entirety of that sage's life. It is impossible to hide; the same as a city built on a hilltop or a light placed on the lamp-stand (Cf. Matthew 5: 14-15).

3. The Way of Sages: Nothing can Surpass Water

A Daoist sage seeks to live in harmony with nature and its processes. Of its own accord, this encourages the sage to create harmony in the community. Thus the entire essence of the sage is devoted to the needs of the community. He is convinced that harmony in communal life springs from goodwill, which is grounded in a close individual relationship with

Dao. If a sense of duty bases the public activities of a Confucian sage then, for a Daoist sage, it is the mystical unity with Dao. Duty, whether an internal or external obligation, from the perspective of a Daoist sage, is not able to generate stable wellbeing in the life of a community for long. Therefore, the Daoist sage bases his/her social obligations on intensive mystical practices and the pursuit of all-encompassing harmony.

> The way of heaven is to reduce what is much to add to what is little; the way of earth is to decrease what is high to augment what is low. [...] The way of humanity is not to give to those who have much. The way of sages is humility that no one can overmaster.[4]

The way or the task of heaven and earth is to create harmony in nature by adding what nature lacks at this time and reducing what is overabundant. The vocation of people is to create harmony in the community by reducing poverty and social inequality. It is understood in and of itself that a sage performs what is known as the way of all humankind. Despite this, *Wenzi* makes a clear distinction between common people and sages. If all people must have compassion for one another and help each other, then the vocation of a sage is to seek *mysterious humility*. *Wenzi* expresses the conviction that a sage cannot limit his life only to social activity. His vocation lies in the *way of humility*. Here, however, we would greatly delude ourselves if we understood humility in a narrow sense. In Daoism humility associates with water and its uncontrollable force. Water on its way surmounts all obstacles; that is why *Laozi* said about water that "nothing can surpass it."[5] Yet water is a symbol of Dao itself. Thereby, humility, as the way of the sage, implies the dimension of transcendental life. The mystical unity of a sage with Dao lays the groundwork for an exceptional moral and spiritual power to manifest in that sage's life.

Although humility is one of the virtues in Christianity, it takes on special meaning in the writings of distinguished theologians. As Doctor of the Church Isidore of Seville was pointing out the etymological link

---

[4] *Wenzi*, 95.

[5] *Laozi*, 78, trans. D. C. Lau.

of humility (Latin *humilitas*) with earth (Latin *humus*), he came close to identifying humility with the *spiritual fertility* of the entirety of Christian life: the same as the earth sprouts fruit in ripened plants, so humility brings forth matured virtues and successful activity.[6] Thomas Aquinas believed that humility eliminates the obstacles between a human being and God: "Thus humility is, as it were, a disposition to man's untrammeled access to spiritual and divine goods."[7] The *Doctor Angelicus* concluded that "*humilitas facit hominem capacem Dei*" ("humility makes the human receptive to God")[8] and, akin to the tradition of Daoism, stressed that "*humilitas ad sapientiam disponit*" ("humility prepares for wisdom").[9] Thereby, authors both on Daoism and on Christianity agree that humility and wisdom are closely interrelated. These two qualities support one another and lay the premises for a mature mystical experience as much as for the social realization of human vocation.

4. Kenosis and Social Responsibility

Nonetheless, Daoism asserts yet another meaning of humility. To be precise, it would be appropriate to name it as an essential dimension of the virtue of humility. Although it is associated with the image of water, it reaches much further. *Laozi* talks about "being the valley of the world."[10]

> Know glory and keep to humility
> [Or to *disgrace* as per translators J. Legge and D. C. Lau].
> Become the valley of the world.
> Being the valley of the world is eternal power.[11]

The image of the valley identifies with the image of water: a river flows in a valley, the waters of which moisten the earth. The Daoist

---

[6] *Etymologiae*, lib. X, ad litt. H.: "*humilis dicitur quasi humi acclinis*," in: Thomas de Aquino, *Summa Theologiae,* Roma, 1962, II, II, 161, 1.

[7] *Summa Theologiae*, II, II, 161, 5.

[8] Thomas Aquinas, *In Mattheum*, 11, in: Thomas von Aquin, *Sentenzen über Gott und die Welt*, Einsiedeln: Johannes Verlag, 2000, 166.

[9] Thomas Aquinas, *Quaestiones disputatae de malo*, 8, 3, ad 8.

[10] *Laozi*, 28, trans. Sanderson Beck.

[11] *Laozi*, 28, trans. Sanderson Beck.

sage *consciously* decides to be like a valley; this means, to follow Dao and serve people in the noblest manner. Such a decision demands determination and magnanimity because it is the choice for a self-sacrificing lifestyle. The Chinese character □ (rǔ) which, in *Laozi* chapter 28, appears as the antithesis of the character □ (róng), meaning *glory*, is differently translated by various sinologists: as *humility* by Sanderson Beck, *disgrace* by James Legge and D. C. Lau, and *obscurity* by Lin Yutang. Thus, here, *Laozi* talks about the sage's lifestyle that is related to the kenosis of Christ. The Daoist sage is similar to the image of the suffering Servant presented in *The Book of Isaiah*: "I have offered my back to those who struck me, my cheeks to those who plucked my beard; I have not turned my face away from insult and spitting" (Isaiah 50:6).

This idea is expanded even more in *Laozi* chapter 78. The author says that a sage dares to bear the humiliation (or reproach) of the people and to take upon him/herself the calamities (or direful woes or sins) of the society. Those who bear the humiliation (*humiliation* as translated by D. C. Lau or *reproach* by J. Legge) of the people are able to minister to them. "Those who take upon themselves the sins[12] (*direful woes* as translated by J. Legge or *calamities* by D. C. Lau) of the society are able to lead the world."[13]

What is *Laozi* talking about here? Are these vital truths of life or merely poetic, philosophical considerations detached from the reality of the world? How is it possible to take upon him/herself the humiliation of the people and the calamities of the society? And, even if this were possible, what is the meaning of it? The book of *Laozi* does not undertake any comprehensive answer to these questions. It merely underscores that such behavior is very necessary for society and that such persons "are able to lead the world." However, *Laozi* does not explain his view on this. The book merely outlines the most important principles of a sage's life, which often sound paradoxical. Nevertheless, *Laozi* notes that paradoxes specifically reveal the truth of life: "Words of truth seem paradoxical."[14]

---

[12] ⊠⊠ literally is *non-blessing*.

[13] *Laozi*, 78, trans. Sanderson Beck.

[14] *Laozi*, 78, trans. Sanderson Beck.

Certain attitudes of the Daoist classics appear nearly identical to the teaching by the Apostle Paul on the following of Christ. Paul comprehends the humility of Christ as an all encompassing, generous devotion to the Father: "He was humbler yet, even to accepting death, death on a cross" (Philippians 2: 8), and he urges his followers, "Make up your own mind of Christ Jesus" (Philippians 2:5). This sounds much like the urging by *Laozi* to become like a valley and accept the humiliation and the calamities of the world. Paul says, much like *Laozi* does, that Christ knew the glory of His Father but maintained humility: "Who being in the form of God, did not count equality with God as something to be grasped. But he emptied himself, taking the form of slave" (Philippians 2: 6–7). Nonetheless, there is an obvious difference between the two religious traditions on this issue. The New Testament talks about the kenosis of Christ and considers Him as an example for all the faithful, whereas Daoist texts recommend the kenotic lifestyle to all sages appealing to the social fruitfulness of such a choice.

5. Mysticism and Political Insight

Confucianism, as much as Daoism, pays a great deal of attention in its doctrine to the virtuousness of rulers. Both teachings express the conviction that the rule of a country will not be successful if their rulers are not virtuous and noble. However, Daoism goes even further in talking about the vocation of rulers for a mystical life:

> If rulers are not humble to their subjects, the influence of their virtue will not be effective. Therefore, when rulers are humble to their subjects they are lucid and clear, and when they are not humble to their subjects they are blind and deaf.[15]

A wise ruler is "like a river, which is flavorless but endlessly useful."[16] Flavorlessness refers to the rejection of any sort of egoism and harmful ambitions. The river is not concerned about its image; its water simply carries all that is necessary for nature – for plants, for animals, and for people. River waters refresh the earth, sustain life, and ripen the

---

[15] *Wenzi*, 95.

[16] *Wenzi*, 82.

new harvest. That, according to the Daoist classics, how a ruler should be; a ruler should not be making efforts towards self-aggrandizement but upholding good initiatives by the citizens and fostering the nation.[17] Humbleness gives rulers insight because, due to their humbleness, they do not distance themselves from the problems of the common people. The Daoist classics are convinced that, when first and foremost a ruler follows Dao, that ruler understands his vocation to *serve* his country and its people. By being concerned with performing his duties appropriately, the ruler gains insight and wisdom. Otherwise, when a ruler distances himself from Dao, he loses virtues and, by the same token, is no longer capable of concern for true justice and honesty in his own country. Then the harmony of communal life goes askew, and honest officials of the country are forced to withdraw:

> When the sun emerges over the horizon, beings grow; when true leaders preside over the populace, they illumine the virtues of the Way thereby. When the sun goes down below the horizon, beings rest; when petty people preside over the populace, everyone runs and hides.[18]

Isn't Daoism overly naive by accenting a leader's virtuousness and interior, mystical life? Can such a viewpoint be seriously assessed today, when the major roles in ruling democratic countries are played out by laws and transparently operating national institutions? The philosophy of Daoism does not deny the significance of laws but merely emphasizes that a virtuous governmental official is no less necessary to the successful evolvement of a country than is a good base of laws. Social ethics, according to the Daoist classics, cannot rely on itself of its own accord, but must rest on an inner, personal relationship with Dao. If the foundation of social ethics in Confucianism consists of the personally obligating *Tian ming* or Will of Heaven, then in Daoism, it is the mystical unity with Dao that encompasses a person's entire existence.

---

[17] Cf. L. Kohn, *Daoist Mystical Philosophy: The Scripture of Western Ascension*, New York, 2007, 156–158.

[18] *Wenzi*, 95.

Not only a ruler of a country but also each and every person holding a responsible position, has the vocation for a mystical life. If such a person does not live the mystical life, that person lacks insight. It will be difficult for such a person to grasp the true designation of human existence. He/she makes an essential error in life and thereby impoverishes the self. This person in his/her life sets purposes, which does not conform to the way of Dao. Since there is no other reality than that of Dao, such a person begins to live a life of illusions. It will seem to this person that his/her way is "knowledgeable and bright",[19] and such an erroneous, good opinion about the self only deepens his/her life's tragedy. Due to erroneously comprehending the self, such a person also lacks perception in many areas of social life. The Daoist classics emphasize how important it is for a ruler to have sufficient insight for ruling a nation. Such insight, according to them, closely relates to a ruler's experience with a mystical life. So long as a ruler lives in unity with Dao, that ruler is capable of building a country where righteousness and other virtues predominate. The citizens of such a country, as *Wenzi* says, feel satisfied with their duties and the results of their work. "Merchants make their markets convenient, farmers enjoy their fields, officials are secure in their jobs, independent scholars practice their ways and people in general enjoy their work."[20] On the contrary, when virtuousness diminishes in a society, then production and business diminish, taxes rise disproportionately and punishments must be meted out more and more often to maintain order. A faulty situation forms in the country, however it is not permissible to criticize it, critics are punished, and the virtuous are dismissed.[21]

By following the style of discourse by the Daoist classics, which does not avoid paradoxes, it can be stated that the leaders whose *only* concern is the ruling of a country are bad leaders. What should be of greater concern than governing the country is their own relationship with Dao and the practice of their moral and mystical life. Only then will they be capable of governing their country appropriately and successfully.

---

[19] *Laozi*, 20, trans. Sanderson Beck.

[20] *Wenzi*, 75.

[21] *Wenzi*, 75.

6. Conclusion

The Daoist classics talk about mysticism first and foremost as the lifestyle of a sage. Rulers are also obligated to become sages, because the quality of their rule destines the fates of other people. Do the Daoist classics consciously limit themselves to sages and rulers alone? The reality of life testifies that sages are always a minority in society. Some of the places in the texts of *Laozi* actually present a sage as an entirely lonely person. In any case, it would be naive to expect that searching for wisdom would become popular in society. Nonetheless, there is no apparent basis for claiming that the Daoist classics would have narrowed their circle of followers consciously and artificially. A sage does not represent some special class of people but rather each person who yearns to live a life of wisdom and harmony.

In Christianity mysticism closely associates with theological love. In classical Daoism, despite its expansion of mysticism, the topic of love is lacking. Nevertheless, respect for nature and for people is very much pronounced here. It would be absolutely unacceptable to a Daoist sage to harm the harmony in nature or hurt another person. The entire wisdom of Daoism is abundant with subtle attention to others.

An analysis of the mystical aspects of Daoist teaching reveals the elements of this rich doctrine born in ancient China. Some of these elements, albeit, their remaining unique to the culture of Chinese thought, seem to be related to Christian doctrine and the Christian worldview at the same time. Ancient Chinese sages grasped numerous, important factors about human existence and had the ability to explain about them in their writings. These texts, which have survived to our days, were guideposts of life and an inspiration for many generations of humankind. Naturally, over the course of history, they have received various and not only one-sided interpretations. Regardless, today, and especially when looking at them from the Christian perspective, we can find many ideas in the works of the Daoist classics that are "Christian" in their deepest sense. Daoist mysticism does not speak about salvation and a vocation to holiness like Christianity does, but it does extend an invitation for a wise and kenotic lifestyle. Kenotic wisdom maximally approaches what the New Testament refers to as the following of Christ:

"This, in fact, is what you were called to do, because Christ suffered for you and left an example for you to follow in his steps (1 Peter 2: 21)."

A mystical component of human life becomes pronounced in Daoist texts as an imperative that cannot be changed by anything. Authentic mystical experience is not only important to a person of any profession but also essential for that person to be able to perform his/her duties appropriately. It cannot be denied that Daoist sages were critical of social activity that arises from a narrow sense of duty or that harms the harmony of the universe. On the contrary, activity that is based on knowing Dao and has a mature mystical experience, flows naturally into the harmonious process of the world's evolvement and fosters progress.

References

01. Aquinas, Thomas, *Quaestiones disputatae de malo*, trans. Richard Regan, ed. with an introduction and notes by Brian Davies, Oxford /New York: Oxford University Press, 2003.
02. Aquinas, Thomas, *Sentenzen über Gott und die Welt*, Einsiedeln: Johannes Verlag, 2000.
03. Aquinas, Thomas, *Summa Theologiae,* Roma: Editiones Paulinae, 1962.
04. Cleary, T., trans., *Wen-tzu. Understanding the Mysteries: Further Teachings of Lao-tzu*, Boston & London, 1992.
05. Kohn, L., *Daoist Mystical Philosophy: The Scripture of Western Ascension*, New York, 2007.
06. Lau, D.C., trans., *Laozi*, Harmondsworth, England: Penguin Books, 1970.
07. Wong, Eva, trans., *Cultivating Stillness. A Taoist Manual for Transforming Body and Mind*, Boston & London, 1992.

10

In Quest for the Unbound

Sufi Ritual as Sacred and Secular

Dr. Kashshaf Ghani
Doctoral Fellow, Department of History
University of Calcutta, Kolkata, India

1. Introduction

Sufism represents the inner aspect of Islam in its doctrinal sense, while as an experience it is a spiritual journey of the individual – from a limited understanding of his own self towards a limitless quest for the realization of the divine. But this rather simplistic interpretation, over a single sentence, tends to gloss over the nuances of spirituality and belief that underline the life and activities of those who embark on this journey towards the ultimate Truth. It is a journey where the Path is uncharted, the boundary limitless and the goal elusive. In a sense Sufism represents a deep yearning and quest for divine realities, with the ultimate aim of spiritual union with God. But this is just one of the many senses in which we understand Sufism. Or rather, it can be said, we do not understand it at all.

Collating whatever little understanding they have of the subject, scholars have, over the time, tried to interpret Sufism as an interpersonal relation with God, with the ultimate aim of spiritual union through a rigorous practice of meditative exercises, aimed primarily towards the moral and spiritual elevation of an individual by purging the soul of all insidious and materialist tendencies. The state of prolonged austerity bore fruits with the mystic becoming aware of the divine realities, thereby graduating himself from an ascetic to a *Wali* or 'friend of God'. He is then the 'chosen one'- 'honoured above the rest of His worshippers, after His messengers and prophets'.[1]

A sense of intense austerity characterized the mystics of Islam on their path towards purification of the 'inner self' through simultaneous dissociation from pleasure and 'material possessions' that bind him to this world. In course of such practices, Sufis intended to graduate from the external realities (*zahir*) of ones social and religious life to an inner realization (*batin*) of the reality of God. Thus for Sufis the realization of God's existence and beneficence was not limited to an understanding of the rhetoric of Islamic religious norms and regulations alone. Rather while going through the structural modalities of studying Sufism one cannot possibly miss the attempt on part of these mystics to internalize the spiritual realties of Islam, beyond the revealed words of Allah and the recorded words of the Prophet, thereby aiming at a higher station of spiritual maturity.

2. Sufi Rituals

It was this spiritual goal that necessitated, by the thirteenth century, the development of a number of Sufi rituals, together with a simultaneous process of institutionalization of the Islamic mystical tradition. On the latter front we witness the crystallization of mystical orders (*silsila*), formulation of the master-disciple (*pir-muridi*) relation, together with the establishment of numerous, and often finely built, Sufi hospices known as *khanqahs,* and most importantly the codification of mystical doctrines for the spiritual guidance.

However, the most dynamic development, during this period, was the emergence of mystical rituals and exercises. Rituals and practices are the primary means of upholding the individuality of an order – both within the mystical fraternity and beyond it. While it is the ritual of *sama* (listening to mystical poetry and music, with or without musical accompaniments) for the Chishtis, for the Suhrawardis it is the ritual of *zikr* (remembrance and recollection of God). With Islamic mysticism

[1] Al Qushayri, *Al Risala al Qushayriyya fi ilm al-Tasawwuf,* trans. Alexander Knysh, Lebanon: Garnet Publishing Limited, 2007, 20.

making its foray into the Indian subcontinent, these rituals too made their presence felt in the midst of a little known civilization and society. This paper would limit itself to the most influential Sufi order in the subcontinent, the Chishtis, together with an analysis of the most intrinsic spiritual practice of that order – the exercise of audition (*sama*).

3. *Sama* in the Indian Subcontinent

Since most of the first generation Sufi masters who settled in south Asia, had their spiritual training in central Asian and Arab lands, it is little of surprise that *sama* too made its way into the Indian subcontinent through the Sufi orders trained in Iran, Iraq and Khurasan. In its Indian career, *sama* was championed by the earliest Sufi order of south Asia, the Chishtia. An ardent proponent of music and poetry, the Chishtis considered *sama* to be an intrinsic part of their spiritual practice, a way of union with God that must be combined with the strict self discipline and austerity.[2]

The Chishtia belief behind their emphatic advocacy of *sama* lay in the fact that, for them it represented both the ontological and epistemological *sine qua non* of Islamic mysticism.[3] Chishtia Sufis viewed *sama* as an exercise limitless in scope, which if applied in the right spirit of the mystical assembly could transfer the entire spiritual proceeding into a realm of divine experience, facilitating the mystic's journey towards his Beloved.[4] It was this realization that led Chishtia saints to vigorously defend the cause of *sama,* irrespective of their socio-cultural ambience. Therefore it is of little surprise that Khwaja Moinuddin Chishti, the progenitor of the order (*silsila*) in the Indian subcontinent, reveled in such an exercise. Sources attest that Moinuddin frequently used to participate in *sama,* with much passion. So that everyone who attended the assembly (*mehfil*) – including the *ulama* and

---

[2] Carl Ernst, *Eternal Garden: Mysticism, History and Politics at a South Asian Sufi Center,* New Delhi: Oxford University Press, 2004, 147.

[3] Bruce Lawrence, "Early Chishti Approach to Sama", in Milton Israel and N. K. Wagle, eds. *Islamic Society and Culture: Essays in Honour of Professor Aziz Ahmad,* Delhi: Manohar, 1983, 70-71.

[4] Bruce Lawrence, "Early Chishti Approach to Sama," 70-71.

other saints in and around Ajmer, became enthralled in the ecstatic spirit that prevailed in the gathering.[5]

Although *sama* came to uphold the internal reality of union with God, through the efforts of the lover-saint, its permissibility posed a problem in the hierarchy of religious rituals attached to the pursuit of spiritual aims. Whether Sufis of the subcontinent considered *sama* as superior to other religious practices, most importantly prayer (*salaat*), as a means of nearness to God, is something which is open to debates and discussions.[6] But it remains undeniable that *sama* was considered to be an inseparable part of the Chishtia spiritual practice, evolving into an exclusive domain of the Chishtia Sufis and their numerous disciples spread across the subcontinent, who many a times rendered a passionate defense for the ritual as an inseparable component of their spiritual discipline incumbent upon all the Sufis of the order.[7]

Such an attempt at legitimizing a ritual–which, since its inception, has been a favorite among legists and theorists alike, providing a continued supply of fodder for their tomes, in defense or censure of the practice– required a serious engagement with the subject, at multiple levels of intellectual thought, and literary output. The result being a forceful resistance towards any attempt at vulgarizing the ritual, while at the same time upholding its significance as an eminent symbol of Chishtia spiritual practice - both to other mystical orders, together with Sufis of the Chishtia family.

It is interesting that at a time when Moinuddin indulged in the practice of *sama* he faced little opposition from the *ulama* and legists. Rather it is known from sources, whatever meager we have on him, that the leading *ulama* and Sufis of his age like, Shaykh Shihabuddin Suhrawardi, Shaykh Muhammad Kirmani, Shaykh Muhammad Isfahani,

---

[5] P. M. Currie, *The Shrine and Cult of Muin al-din Chishti of Ajmer,* New Delhi: Oxford University Press, 2006, 69.

[6] While the Chishtia Sufis considered *sama* as a mystical exercise whose benefits surpassed any religious exercise of the Book, Suhrawardi masters like Shaykh Bahauddin Zakariyya considered prayer to be the most important spiritual exercise, emanating from the folds of religious tenets. See, Qamar ul Huda, *Striving for Divine Union: Spiritual Exercises for Suhrawardi Sufis,* London: Routledge Curzon, 2003, 56-58.

[7] Bruce Lawrence, "Early Chishti Approach to Sama", 73-74.

Shaykh Burhan al-din Chishti, Maulana Baha al-din Bukhari, Maulana Muhammad Baghdadi, the great Khwaja of Sijz, Shaykh Saifuddin Majuzi, Shaykh Jalaluddin Tabrezi, Shaykh Ahmed Wahid, Shaykh Burhan al-din Ghaznavi, Khwaja Sulaiman, and Abdur Rahman among others used to attend the *sama* of Khwaja Moinuddin. They came and kissed the feet of the Shaykh, to derive spiritual benefits.[8]

Sama is essentially an exercise for individuals who cherish a taste for it and are ready to sacrifice himself in the way of God. It is incumbent on such an individual to forget his 'self', so that he can lose his individual entity in the essence of God, and attain the station of annihilation (*fana*). In such a spiritual state the mystic completely immerses himself in the fire of the love of God, so that whatever he does is out of love for Him. Such a state of the mystic affects him directly, so that he hesitates little before surrendering himself in the path of his Lord.

Speaking of such a spiritual state, Shaykh Nizamuddin Awliya categorized *sama* into two types: Invasive (*hajim*) and non-invasive (*ghair hajim*). Invasive *sama* is that which invades the body quite easily stirring it towards agitation. This is likened to the reaction a heart may have on hearing accidentally a verse of poetry. While non-invasive *sama* is the one in which the intellect of the listener comes to play. In such an audition whenever one hears something that agitates him, he is drawn into a particular fold of contemplation where he equates the verses of poetry to a different non-material realm.[9] These can be the attributes of God, or the thoughts of his spiritual master. But the Shaykh also made it clear that the first form of *sama* is more impulsive and the resultant feeling that ruled the heart of the mystic cannot be explained by logical faculties.

In the light of the above it goes without saying that the spiritual practice of *sama* remained the *sine qua non* of the Chishtia mystical path, and being the primary ritual of the Chishtia mystics, *sama* essentially remained restricted to the initiates of the order – strictly distancing itself from the common masses. Thus we find a limited scope of expression on the part of the masses on the ritual of *sama,* which, perceived as a

---

[8] P. M. Currie, *The Shrine and Cult of Muin al-din Chishti of Ajmer,* 69.

[9] Amir Hasan Ala-Sijzi, *Fawaid ul-Fuad,* ed. Latif Malik, Lahore: Malik Siraj al-Din and Sons Publishers, 1966, 121-22.

highly organized mystical practice, if left opened to all can lead to an inevitable vulgarization of the spiritual fervor.[10]

4. *Sama* in the Cultural Milieu of the Subcontinent

An exclusivist approach does not necessarily imply that the mystics of the Chishtia order could keep themselves aloof from the influences of local culture and civilization, in their day to day spiritual exercises. Such a tradition of adaptation with indigenous cultural traits was attested by Bandanawaz Gesuderaz, the Chishtia torchbearer in the Deccan, who recalled that Nizamuddin Awliya used to listen to a variety of verses in Arabic, Persian, Hindavi and Urdu in an assembly of *sama.* Invariably he used to get overcome by the feelings of agitation that emanated from the interpretation of such verses. Being equipped with that degree of spiritual understanding, he could interpret those verses along the binaries of the lover-Beloved (*ashiq-mashuq*). He was bestowed with a natural ability to enjoy the flavor (*zauq*) of *sama,* which became rare after his time.[11]

However it was the genius of Amir Khusrau,[12] the poet laureate of medieval India, which made it possible, for the first time, to convey the feeling of an intense mystical love through the rich imagery of Hindavi and Urdu love poetry.

Tori surat ke balhari (Nijam)
Sab sakhian chundar mori maili
Dekh hansin narnari
Ab ke bahar chundar mori rang do
Rakh le laj hamari (Nijam Piya)
Sadqa Baba Ganj-e-Shakar ka

[10] Bruce Lawrence, "Early Chishti Approach to Sama," 74.

[11] Gesudaraz, *Khatima Adab ul-Muridin,* Delhi: Adabi Dunya, 2007, 130.

[12] A prolific classical poet associated with more than seven rulers of the Delhi Sultanate, Amir Khusrau Dehlvi (1253-1325 A. D.) is a household name in much of India and Pakistan through his rich lineage of songs and *qawwalis*. It is to him that we owe the invention of *qawwali* as a musical genre. His close relationship with one of the greatest Chishti saints of south Asia, Hazrat Nizamuddin Awliya, reflects his multi-cultural and pluralistic personality. For details, see Muhammad Habib, *Hazrat Amir Khusrau of Delhi*, New Delhi: Cosmo Publications, 2006.

Rakh le laj hamari (Nijam Piya)[13]
[Beholding your countenance I offer myself in sacrifice (Nijam)
All the other girls saw my soiled *chundar*
And together they laughed at me.
This springtime, dye my *chundar* for me
O protect my honour (Nijam Beloved)
In the name of Ganj-e-Shakar
Protect our honour (Nijam, Beloved)]

The most popular of the many verses composed by Amir Khusrau in Hindavi, for his spiritual master Hazrat Nizamuddin Awliya, this may seem to the untrained eye as nothing more than a flirtatious love poetry concerning individuals of flesh and blood - where a lover seeks his beloved through a secular love poem. But a deeper analysis reveals the metaphor of a mystic seeking union with his Beloved God. In this verse, the mystical experience is conveyed through a Hindu devotional idiom where the devotee speaks as a bride offering herself to the beloved- Hazrat Nizamuddin. The lover, while beholding the face of his Beloved, cries out to him, in a sense of surrender. This is an experience of vision, witnessed with the inner eye. The heart of the lover, sacrificed in the path of the Beloved, is held hostage – in complete trust to his Beloved. The lover appeals to save her grace, and her wish to get united with the patron saint is expressed through the metaphor of being painted in the same colour as that of her Beloved.

Although the opening line is distinctive by itself and epitomizes the entire song, the use of certain idioms heightens the spirit of mystical love and experience. Firstly, the usage of the spring season, the season of colour and festivities, more particularly the Spring Festival or the 'Basant Utsav', a traditional Hindu festival, which is celebrated, even today, with much liveliness at the dargah of Hazrat Nizamuddin. Secondly, together with the inclusion of a gender dimension – in this instance the female lover – the notion of etiquette (*adab*) is also emphasized through the usage of *chundar,* a traditional headgear among Muslim

[13] Regula Qureshi, *Sufi Music of India and Pakistan*, Karachi: Oxford University Press, 2006, 26.

women covering her head and chest, symbolizing culture and a subtle demeanor. It is a custom in south Asian dargahs that women are not allowed to enter the premises without a proper *chundar* covering her head and upper portion of the body. Thus, its usage in the poetical verse attests the purity of intentions, rather than trying to interpret as common love poetry. Thirdly, and most importantly the spiritual lineage of the Chishtia order is given due accordance – in this occasion through Baba Fariduddin Shakar Ganj, who is the spiritual guide (*pir*) of Nizamuddin Awliya. The lover in the verse above touches on the invocation of the spiritual seniors of Shaykh Nizamuddin Awliya, while imploring him to protect her honour.

Thus, as a master of the ritual of *sama,* Shaykh Nizamuddin Awliya not only incorporated elements from his immediate socio-linguistic and religious environment, enriching his mystical experience; but also upheld the sanctity of the ritual. Thus, while enumerating the finer qualities of the practice, Nizamuddin Awliya emphasized that for an assembly of *sama* to be proper (*jayez*), certain rules must be adhered to. Primary among them are that the *qawwal* or the reciter of poetry should be a matured individual, and should never be a young boy nor should he be a woman.[14] It is incumbent on the part of the audience to fill their hearts with the thought of God, and keep away from any sort of distraction that might hinder the effects derived from such a practice. The content of the ritual, precisely the verses read out in such an assembly should not be of frivolous or puerile character, nor incur banter and lightheartedness in the mind of the listener. The ambience of *sama* should be strictly maintained as in the case of any other spiritual exercise, thereby musical instruments (*mazamir*) should be kept away from such an assembly.[15] Nizamuddin Awliya censured the use of instruments like *chang* and *rabab,* in particular, and any musical instruments in general. Such were the parameters laid down by the great shaykh within which the exercise was to be performed, for it to be permissible (*halal*). Else it should be termed as questionable.

[14] Mir Khwurd, *Siyar ul-Awliya,* ed. Chiranjilal, Delhi: Matba-i Muhibb-i Hind, 1885, 511.

[15] Mir Khwurd, *Siyar ul-Awliya,* 511.

After such elaborate regulations the shaykh questioned the permissibility of *sama,* and stated that since it was a sacred rendition of the voice, why should it be termed as unlawful in the eyes of religion.[16] Like any other religious duty, *sama* too, for Nizamuddin Awliya, was essentially an exercise meant for the realization of divine blessings by the individual worshipper. It necessitated an engagement with the feelings of compassion, which came to play only when there was a bestowal of divine mercy and beneficence on the assembly. No amount of poetical verses and musical instruments are capable of making the 'heart stir in the love for God.' Only when it is divinely ordained that an assembly of *sama* reaches the heights of success. The arousal of the heart therefore depended entirely on the will of the Lord. The blessings of the divine, together with maintaining the sanctity and hierarchy in such devotional assemblies, are absolutely crucial if one desired to undertake a successful exercise of *sama.*[17]

5. Opposition of the *Ulama*

Such liberal arguments germinating within the folds of Islamic mystical thought sounded alien to the puritanical guardians of the faith, who chose to remain wedded to the literal interpretations of texts and beliefs. Islam to them represented an exclusive, politicized and closed arena, where external influences and meaningful 'diversions' are to be strictly abhorred. Eventually such an inward looking mentality developed into a confrontational attitude where Sufis were portrayed as individuals' contra to theologians and religious leaders. The twain shall never meet.

Chishtia Sufi manuals containing the words and accounts of their north Indian seers recognized, very well, the skeptical attitude shown by the *ulama* towards such a practice. While they kept themselves aloof from such an exercise, on the pretext that it is a forbidden/blasphemous practice, and advocated that none should engage in it.[18] However Sufi manuals also argued that an exercise which is conducted at the residence, or *khanqah,* of a dervish cannot possibly cross the limits of religious

---

[16] Mir Khwurd, *Siyar ul-Awliya,* 511.
[17] Mir Khwurd, *Siyar ul-Awliya,* 514.
[18] Amir Hasan, *Fawaid ul-Fuad,* 190.

and ethical sanctity.[19] Therefore even if the *ulama* condemned such a practice as beyond the parameters of religious ethics, they, under no circumstances could impose a ban upon its performance; or stop people from participating in *sama*. Sufis and dervishes are blessed from the Unseen, and it is not judicious to engage in a forced confrontation with them. Nizamuddin Awliya argued that it is not always that the *ulama* were opposed to the practice of audition. While some were accommodating towards such an exercise, many tended to act brashly without taking into consideration the logic operating behind such a ritual.[20] He further argued that even if *sama* was accepted as a permitted exercise in the eyes of law and religion, skeptics would never have engaged in it; for participation in *sama* required a certain conditioning of the heart, which only mystics can attain through prolonged austerity in the path of God.[21] Men of the material world would find little success in it, and thus remain deprived from the taste of *sama*.

6. The Practice of *Sama* in the Deccan

This discussion would remain incomplete if we do not look into the spread of the practice from the hallowed Chishtia *jamaat khanas* of north India, to a new socio-political environment in the south. The ritual made immortal through the support of its greatest benefactor – Shaykh Nizamuddin Awliya, received a new lease of life across the Vindhyas, courtesy the untiring genius of Shaykh Burhanuddin Gharib, the virtuous disciple of the legendary north Indian *wali*. Burhanuddin was instrumental in making the ritual central to the spiritual pursuits of the Chishtia order in the south, much in accordance to what his master had successfully done in the neighborhood of the Delhi Sultans.

His efforts bore fruit and reached their apogee under the masterful guidance of his successor, the leading and the most enigmatic of the Chishtia masters in the south – Khwaja Bandanawaz Gesudaraz. Following up on the hard work of Burhanuddin, Gesudaraz, laid down the ideals and principles of the Chishtia order, which in subsequent years came to constitute the most authoritative manual of the *silsila,*

[19] Amir Hasan, *Fawaid ul-Fuad,* 190
[20] Amir Hasan, *Fawaid ul-Fuad,* 190
[21] Amir Hasan, *Fawaid ul-Fuad,* 190

guiding masters and disciples alike towards the tough path of spiritual maturity.[22] Although Gesudaraz witnessed the popularity of the ritual of *sama,* while making preparations for his new life in the south, his lasting contribution lies in the institutionalization of the ritual, as a highly cherished spiritual practice of the Chishtia order. With this he also took initiatives to formulate the doctrines and articulate the traditions behind this ritual, together with according it at a hallowed place in the myriad lanes of Chishtia ritualistic practices.[23] This succeeded in providing a shape and backbone to the numerous writings he undertook on the subject of mysticism, more particularly *sama.*

Like his north Indian spiritual progenitor, Gesudaraz too could not free himself from the two essential registers of *sama* – the use of indigenous dialect and the confrontation with the *ulama.* Being a prolific author in both Indian and non Indian languages, Gesudaraz's assembly of *sama* reverberated with odes, poems and hymns in Persian and Hindavi (Deccani Urdu). Although the Shaykh preferred Persian as a medium of *sama* for 'Only in the sweet and tender melody of Persian poetry is it possible to do justice to the feelings and emotions surging in the heart of the singer'[24]; he nonetheless was aware of the age and could not free himself from the socio-cultural milieu he had situated himself into. Thus, in spite of characterizing *sama* as a ritual unfit for the uninitiated, Khwaja Gesudaraz took measures to widen its popular base through an effort of making the verses intelligible to the common masses. Towards this end he encouraged the inclusion of Hindavi verses in assemblies of *sama* arguing that 'Hindavi verses are usually soft, sweet and touching. The tunes are also soft and tender like the couplets, which induce humility and submission.'[25] Khwaja Bandanawaz Gesudaraz therefore became the first among the Chishtia mystics of south India to actively communicate and express his thoughts and ideas through the use Hindavi and Deccani Urdu poetry.

Thus, in the assembly of *sama,* even to this day, couplets written in Deccani Urdu by Khwaja Sahib himself together with his disciples are

[22] See, Gesudaraz, *Khatimah i-Adab al-Muridin*, 135.

[23] Gesudaraz, *Khatimah i-Adab al-Muridin*, 135.

[24] Ali Samani, *Siyar i-Muhammadi,* Hyderabad, 1928, 71.

[25] Ali Samani, *Siyar i-Muhammadi,* 71.

recited with the accompaniment of the tambourine, invoking the spiritual blessings of the great Chishtia masters.[26] An analysis of one such verse, recited in the assembly of *sama* would provide us with some idea as to the mystical ideals and attributes the shaykh adhered to throughout his lifetime.

> Aj birahe ki aag mujtane laage re
> Mu ka dikhlaye kar radi kursi lagaye
> Aj birahe ki aag mujtane laage re
> Ud batti ka shor mor ujala re
> Nisdin jalti mor mashakh mor sala re
>
> [The fire of separation has kindled
> Today in my body and soul
> My Beloved is on the throne
> Himself and His splendor on display
> I am burning in the fire of love today
> Incense burns night and day
> Likewise I am being burnt always.]

This verse above, ably express Gesudaraz's spiritual maturity together with the emotions that surge in his heart, in an assembly of audition. Gesudaraz says that *sama* is a blessing from the Unseen, which burns in the heart of the listener feelings of separation and longing for the Beloved.[27] It is under the influence of such emotions, as Baba Fariduddin Shakrganj had rightly remarked, that a mystic continues to burn in the fire that separates him from his Beloved.[28] It is this condition of separation that, in the words of Khwaja Bandanawaz, motivates an individual in the assembly of *sama* on his spiritual journey. So that, when he actually beholds his Lord, he is overrun by emotions of ecstasy. So that nothing remains of the mystic, for he completely annihilates himself in the essence of the Lord. The lover, who places himself in the pyre of contemplation, day and night, waits for his Beloved to unveil

---

[26] Syed Shah Khusro Hussaini, "Bund Sama", *Islamic Culture,* July 1970, 181.
[27] Syed Shah Khusro Hussaini, "Bund Sama," 178-79.
[28] Mir Khwurd, *Siyar ul-Awliya*, 535.

His glory. In this mystical path towards experiencing the divine, *sama* provides the most effective way of expressing love for the Almighty Lord, who blesses his creations through enlightenment of knowledge and divine beneficence. *Sama* is essentially a means of offering love to God who, in turn, makes his devoted worshipper burn and suffer in the pyre of separation, where only the spiritual adept are allowed to enter and participate.

7. Criticisms from the *Ulama* and the Defense of Gesudaraz

Such ideas fetched for Gesudaraz nothing better than an extreme hatred and ire of the *ulama,* who, similar to their north Indian counterparts, left no stone unturned to denigrate the spiritual valor of the Chishtia mystic. Such an intolerant attitude of the *ulama* seems to have rested on the pretext that *sama* was an innovation by Sufis within the religious profile of Islam, and their indulgence in such a practice with the accompaniment of music was completely illegal in the tenets of the *shariah* and hence blasphemous for any devout Muslim. Time and again the *ulama* approached the Sultans to issue verdicts opposing the practice of *sama* among the Sufis, particularly of the Chishtia order.[29] The *ulama* continued to make unsuccessful attempts to officially regulate the practice of *sama* on the ground that it was in conformity to the musical tradition of the resident Hindu population, and sought to pollute the faith of Islam by attempting 'a synthesis between the Muslim and Hindu artistic traditions.'[30] Chishtia Sufis, on the other hand, strived relentlessly to push themselves beyond the confines of dry religious practices and at the same time elevate themselves to a higher spiritual plane – stressing on the profound individuality of spiritual exercises like *sama* while at the same time successfully retaining its sacred character.

A more direct allegation was leveled against Gesudaraz by the *ulama* during the reign of Sultan Firuz Shah Tughlaq (1351-1388 A.D.), in the sense that the Chishtia mystic entertained listeners who prostrated before him in the assembly of *sama.* Although they tried their best to impose a ban on the spiritual assembly of the Chishtia master, the Sultan

[29] Khusro Hussaini, *Sayyid Muhammad al-Husayni i-Gisudaraz: On Sufism,* Delhi: Idarah-i-Adabiyat-i-Delli, 1983, 124.

[30] Khusro Hussaini, *Sayyid Muhammad al-Husayni i-Gisudaraz*, 124.

refrained from taking such an extreme step, and requested the saint to participate in *sama* in seclusion, so that the ambience of the assembly does not get polluted through un-Islamic practices. Gesudaraz acceded to the request and henceforth enjoyed *sama* from within a room with a curtain separating him from the rest of the participants.[31]

In the light of such interminable debates on, and profound qualities attached to, a particular mystical ritual, the question which naturally shores up, concern the reasons behind its importance. What sort of advantage, spiritual and otherwise, does *sama* have over the mandatory religious disciplines? Why is it considered to be more effective in realizing spiritual truths? And lastly, Why do mystics seem to prefer it over the mandatory religious tenets of Islam? The answer provided by Gesudaraz, in his writings, attempts to dissolve all doubts raised by the questions above. While conforming to the views, expressed by earlier Chishti masters, that together with prayer (*salaat*), fasting (*sawm*), and reciting of the Quran (*telawat*), *sama* too leads an individual closer to God[32], Gesudaraz argued that the primary necessity for a mystic traveling on the road of spirituality towards God was to interiorize the qualities of contemplation and thought – centering on the attributes and essence of the Lord. *Sama* being an assembly of audition, is possibly the best way to achieve this 'unity' of thought and contemplation (*tawajjuh*), which in turn are the supreme of all the fortunes (*jami i- sa'adatha*) which a mystic can hope to achieve in this path of God. Gesudaraz further asserted that 'triumph in my affair' (*fath-i kar-i man*) was achieved through extensive recitation of the Quran and participation in *sama.*[33]

Being a stickler for rules, Gesudaraz followed the tenets of religion very closely. But at the same time he was not ready to accept any criticism against *sama.* Replying to the criticisms leveled by the *ulama* that *sama* essentially bred blasphemy within the ranks of Islam, Gesudaraz argued that the most appropriate exercise for a Sufi in his search for the divine was a combination of the recitation of the Quran together with participation in *sama.* Such an exercise bore more fruit than engaging simply in daily prayers and recitation of the Quran. These dry religious

---

[31] Samani, *Siyar-i-Muhammadi*, 87-88.
[32] Mir Khwurd, *Siyar ul-Awliya,* 492.
[33] Samani, *Siyar i-Muhammadi,* 90.

exercises are meant only for those who spend their thoughts between the opposing forces of 'fear' (*khwaf*) and 'hope' (*raji*).[34] Mystics, who engage themselves in nothing but the love of God, prefer the earlier path. Thus, Gesudaraz was emphatic when advocating his support in favor of *sama* and always begun and ended the exercise with a recitation of the Quran.

When enquired on the efficacy of *sama* over prayers, Gesudaraz replied in the words of the great Chishti master Shaykh Maudud Chishti who had remarked that when a person observes prayers with all the formalities of the practice, he swings between extreme emotions of fear and hope. He remains unsure whether his prayers will be accepted or not. *Sama* on the other hand is a ritual that is considered to be one of the 'attractions' (*jadhbah*) emanating from the all Merciful (*al- rahman*)[35], where material creations and worldly emotions hold little importance in such divine engagements. While prayers are doubtful of being heard and accepted (*qabul*), engagement with *sama* is an acceptance within itself (*ayn i- qabul*). Thus, for Gesudaraz, 'remembrance' (*dhikr*), 'meditation' (*muraqabah*) and 'prayer' (*salaat*) being the essentialities of religious discipline, cannot under any circumstances supersede *sama* which is an exercise in the presence of the Divine, in the glory of His essences.[36]

Severely criticizing the *ulama* and theologians, who are foremost in labeling *sama* as nothing more than a means of indulging in pleasure and frivolity, Gesudaraz questions their right to declare such a practice as unlawful, since they are not aware of the means and aims that *sama* caters to. They are men of the world, and hence their point of view is limited to worldly parameters, incapable to discerning beyond it, into the sphere of the Unseen. They are alien to the path of spiritual enlightenment, and hence oblivious to the significance of terms like, pain (*dard*), seeking (*talabi*) and burning (*suzi*), as they bear for the Sufi. The satire of Gesudaraz is revealing in his statement where he says 'What a strange (*ajab*) person he is! He refers to agitation (*idtirab*), crying (*giryah*), grief (*andih*) and sorrow (*huzn*) as a sport.'[37] These emotions,

---

[34] Gesudaraz, *Khatimah i-Adab al-Muridin,* 70.

[35] Gesudaraz, *Asmar ul-Asrar,* Hyderabad, 1931, 103-04.

[36] Gesudaraz, *Asmar ul-Asrar,* 103-04.

[37] Gesudaraz, *Asmar ul-Asrar,* 103-04.

raging in the heart of the mystic, hold the key towards understanding the essence of the ritual from the eyes of a Sufi. Since the theologians are unworthy to fathom out the spiritual significance of this ritual, vis-à-vis the listener, it is prudent that they observe silence on such divine matters.

8. Conclusion

Such forceful diatribes by religious bigots, who 're'presented an extreme face of Islam, in the long run, worked as a qualifier for the mystical dimension of the religion. Sufism began to be characterized more and more as an ideal that was opposed to the essential tenets of Islam, being led by individuals who *preach* Islam in the wrong sense, and *practice* a faith that has little or no resemblance with the creed of Muhammad (SAW). In turn Sufis contribute little but inflict enormous harm upon the beliefs of common individuals who follow them in search of a pure faith. This unequivocal hatred quite unfortunately undermined the possibility of any independent voice that may be heard from the side of the mystics themselves. With conservative Islamic trends being largely overestimated, there continues to be an underestimation of the size and vigor of the mystical voice.

This paper while engaging with the sacred realm of Islamic mystical practices, has tried to carry the idea beyond the dialectics of strait-jacketed profanity. Islam presented itself to the inhabitants of the subcontinent in the garb of a mystical belief. It goes without saying that such individuals who were castigated as perpetrators of blasphemy succeeded in popularizing, not only their spiritual order, but also the monotheistic faith of the Arabian prophet among millions of idol worshippers of the subcontinent. In our discussion above, we have tried to harp upon the genius of the Chishtia saints of south Asia towards an institutionalization, not only of their order, but also of its most defining spiritual exercise, *sama.* It was to the untiring efforts of the Chishtia masters, that at a time when this ritual was mired in legal bitterness and royal controversies, they successfully upheld the sanctity of the practice, through strict conformation to both the classical mystical tradition and the Chishtia lineage, stretching beyond territorial borders.

Saints like Muinuddin Chishti, Nizamuddin Awliya, Burhanuddin Gharib, and Bandanawaz Gesudaraz were instrumental in placing much importance on the ethical standards of the individual participants of *sama,* so that an insistence on proper spiritual interpretation of poetical verses became the thumb rule in the intellectual realm of Chishtia *sama* practices. While determining the psychological basis of *sama* as one of the most profound spiritual exercises in the realm of Islamic mysticism, they laid utmost emphasis on contextualizing *sama* as an exercise on Sufi ethics, which must never be compromised if one was to derive divine benefits from such an assembly. The details of etiquette (*adab*), concerning this exercise, iaid a strong anti-pollutant platform for a regularization of the discipline, while eliminating from its path any traces of egotism and self importance which might infiltrate tiie heart of the lay individual. Thus, one finds the purity with which *sama* was practiced in the Chishtia cradle of north India, being emulated in the south, while maintaining similar standards of discipline and unadulterated intentions, which continued to inspire young mystics in the path towards a higher spiritual experience.

References

01. Currie, P.M., *The Shrine and Cult of Muin al-din Chishti of Ajmer,* New Delhi: Oxford University Press, 2006.
02. Ernst, Carl, *Eternal Garden: Mysticism, History and Politics at a South Asian Sufi Center,* New Delhi: Oxford University Press, 2004.
03. Gesudaraz, *Khatima Adab ul-Muridin,* Delhi: Adabi Dunya, 2007.
04. Habib, Muhammad, *Hazrat Amir Khusrau of Delhi*, New Delhi: Cosmo Publications, 2006.
05. Hasan Ala-Sijzi, Amir, Fawaid *ul-Fuad,* ed. Latif Malik, Lahore: Malik Siraj al-Din and Sons Publishers, 1966.
06. Hussaini, Syed Shah Khusro, Sayyid *Muhammad al-Husayni i-Gisudaraz: On Sufism,* Delhi: Idarah-i-Adabiyat-i-Delli, 1983.
07. Hussaini, Syed Shah Khusro, "Bund Sama", *Islamic Culture,* July 1970.
08. Khwurd, Mir, Siyar *ul-Awliya,* ed. Chiranjilal, Delhi: Matba-i Muhibb-i Hind, 1885.
09. Lawrence, Bruce, "Early Chishti Approach to Sama", in Milton Israel and N. K. Wagle, eds. *Islamic Society and Culture: Essays in Honour of Professor Aziz Ahmad,* Delhi: Manohar, 1983.

10. Qamar ul Huda, *Striving for Divine Union: Spiritual Exercises for Suhrawardi Sufis,* London: Routledge Curzon, 2003.
11. Qureshi, Regula, *Sufi Music of India and Pakistan*, Karachi: Oxford University Press, 2006.
12. Qushayri, Al, *Al Risala al Qushayriyya fi ilm al-Tasawwuf*, trans. Alexander Knysh, Lebanon: Garnet Publishing Limited, 2007.
13. Samani, Ali, *Siyar i-Muhammadi,* Hyderabad, 1928.

11

Significance of "You Have No Part with Me" in John 13:8

A Potential Mystical Interpretation

Sr. Bincy Mathew

Katholieke Universiteit Leuven, Leuven, Belgium

Since early centuries of the Christian era John's Gospel has been regarded as a 'mystical' Gospel. Nevertheless, scholars in the modern period have set aside the subject of mysticism in the Fourth Gospel.[1] One possible reason for this reservation can be attributed to the ambiguity of the term 'mysticism' itself.[2] For Christianity this term neither appears in OT nor in NT.[3] No one can, however, deny that the Scripture points to eternal truths and the mystery of God. Research has been undertaken, though to a limited extent, through the centuries to examine the mystical expressions in the Fourth Gospel. However, in this study we attempt to

[1] Jey J. Kanagaraj, *'Mysticism' in the Gospel of John: An Inquiry into Its Background*, Sheffield: Sheffield Academic Press, 1998, 20.

[2] Gershom G. Scholem, *Major Trends in Jewish Mysticism*, 3ed. London: Thames and Hudson, 1955, 6, observes that there is no mysticism as such and mysticism always related to a particular religious system.

[3] J. T. Pring, "Mystikismos," in *The Oxford Dictionary of Modern Greek: Greek-English and English-Greek*, Oxford: Clarendon, 1982, 207. The dictionary provides *mustikismos* as the Greek counterpart to the term mysticism. In the OT its cognate terms occur in Wis 8:4 (*mustis*); 12:5 (*mustēs*); and in 3 Macc 3:10 *mustikōs*. The Symmachus version of Isa 3:3 has different understanding of the term. In all these instances we don't have clear meaning of the term mysticism rather different contexts give different meanings.

explore an unnoticed phrase *echeis meros met' emou*[4] (have a part with me) in the footwashing episode in John 13:1-38. This is a potentially mystical expression which lies in v.8 and strengthens some of the past research.

1. A Historical Note on the 'Mysticism' in the Fourth Gospel

The idea that the Gospel of John holds 'mystical' elements was present in patristic circle.[5] Clement of Alexandria, in the second century, referred to John as 'the spiritual Gospel.'[6] Heracleon, the first commentator of the Fourth Gospel, gives a spiritual interpretation of the Gospel.[7] Origen regarded John as a mystical document and for him 'knowing' in the biblical usage is more than intellectual recognition. According to Origen, knowing God is being known by God that is union of God to those who know him and this knowledge gives them a share in his divinity. So, 'knowing God' means divinization that is having the image of God, a transforming vision.[8] Augustine, under the influence of Neo-Platonism, gave a spiritual interpretation to John.[9] Gnostic commentators found support for their idea of mysticism in John.[10]

The concept of mysticism in the Fourth Gospel has fallen into oblivion in the long debates on the historical value of the Gospel in the nineteenth century. However, some scholars never gave up the idea of mysticism in the Fourth Gospel. W. R. Inge tried to read the

---

[4] *Meros* in secular Greek means "to get as a share" or "to have a share in." In the NT it is also used as 'part' or 'share.' Jn 13:8 is translated as 'to have a part with.' C. K. Barret explains *meros* as a share in the community and connects it with baptism. R. Brown translates *meros* as 'heritage' and connects it with eternal life. George R. Beasley-Murray explains it as 'part with me' and the development of this can be seen in 14:3; 17:24.

[5] Andrew Louth, *The Origins of the Christian Mystical Tradition: From Plato to Denys*, Oxford: Oxford University Press, 1981, 2007, x.

[6] As quoted in Eusebius, *Historia Ecclesiatica*, 6.14.7.

[7] Einar Thomassen, *Heracleon*, ed. Tuomas Rasimus, NovtSup, vol. 132, Leiden-Bosten: Brill, 2010, 198.

[8] C. W. Macleod, "Allegory and Mysticism in Origen and Gregory of Nyssa," *JTS* 22, no. 2 (1971), 368-369.

[9] St. Augustine, *Tractates on the Gospel of John 1-10*, ed. Thomas P. Halton, trans. John W. Retting, The Fathers of the Church, Washington: C. U. Press, 1988, 3-38.

[10] Louth, *The Origins of the Christian Mystical Tradition*, 60-74.

Gospel as the 'charter of Christian mysticism,' and for him mysticism is the 'centralizing factor' of the Gospel around which the whole aspect of unity and diversity is fixed. Mysticism is not one of the exclusive relationships between believer and God, but a collective and ecclesiological one, that is, the union that exists between Christ and the church collectively, and between one another as members of Christ.[11] B. von Hügel is of the opinion that the Fourth Gospel is filled with mystic symbolism.[12] E. Underhill recognizes the Fourth Gospel as having a poetic and devotional nature rather than a historical and dialectical one. Underhill reads the Gospel from the perspective of mysticism. She finds a steady approximation of the human consciousness to perfect the union with spiritual reality. This genuine and deepest experience of a Christian mystic is reflected in a supreme literary experience in the Fourth Gospel. Therefore, John is the pioneer of Christian mysticism. Through an emphasis on the 'sense of the presence' as the ruling principle of the Fourth Gospel, Underhill heightens the mystical nature of the Fourth Gospel.[13] Although R. Bultman perceived an influence of mystic language in John, he discouraged any form of mystical interpretation.[14] He supposes that the *en hēmin* of Jn 1:14 refers to the indwelling of the *Logos* in the soul of the gnostic or of the mystic. According to C. K. Barrett 'proper mysticism' is absent in the Fourth Gospel and 'implied mysticism' can be found throughout the Gospel. The Gospel never takes flight from this world to a heavenly abode, but it indeed offers communion with God mediated through the salvation history. He presents a Christ-mysticism rather than eschatological mysticism. Johannine mystical expressions can be envisaged in the vocabularies such as: to know, to see, and to remain, which reflect the idea of an intimacy and communion

---

[11] William Ralph Inge, *Christian Mysticism*, London: Methues, 1899, 39-51. For a detailed analysis of some scholarship, see, Wilbert Francis Howard, *The Fourth Gospel in Recent Criticism and Interpretation*, London: The Epworth Press, 1955, 195-212.

[12] B. F. von Hügel, "The Gospel of St. John," in *Encyclopedia Britannica*, Cambridge: C. U. Press, 1911, 455.

[13] Evelyn Underhill, *The Mystic Way: A Psychological Study in Christian Origins*, Whitefish: Kessinger, 1913, 213-234.

[14] Rudolf Bultmann, *Theology of the New Testament*, vol. 2. London: SCM Press, 1955, 84. Rudolf Bultmann, *The Gospel of John: A Commentary*, trans. G. R. Beasley-Murray, Oxford: Blackwell, 1971, 16 n. 6, 69, 382, 536, 541, 605-606, 613-614.

with God. He also emphasizes the centrality of the historical Jesus.[15] M. Charan Singh in his commentary on John maintains the view that God is in everyone, and what we need is to realize this presence through Jesus. Every word spoken by Christ had deep mystical meaning and it is specific to the Gospel of John.[16] McPolin made a thorough study of Johannine mysticism. According to McPolin the traditional definition of mysticism is not feasible in the Fourth Gospel. The components of traditional mysticism describe an incommunicable and inexpressible knowledge and love of God or of religious truth, received in the spirit without precedent effort or reasoning. But the Fourth Evangelist does not portray this kind of mysticism between God and the human person. Moreover, he is not concerned with those extraordinary mystical graces as recorded by John of the Cross or Theresa of Avila. But, the Fourth Evangelist gives special attention to the theme of communion of the believer with the Father. He presents communion with God as an essential constitutive principle of the Christian life.[17]

In Rudolf Schnackenburg's understanding the Fourth Evangelist gives a Christian answer to the mystical desires and language of his time. According to Schnackenburg, Johannine mysticism is concerned with the believers 'being in' and 'abiding in' Christ and through him in God. The living and fruitful union in grace is not timeless and detached from history, but rather it is realized fully in the fellowship of Jesus with his disciples. 'The immanence formula' (14:19) explains it well. Johannine mysticism which speaks about union with Christ and God is intrinsically concurrent to the Christology of the Fourth Gospel. Fellowship with Christ is inseparable from the ethical qualities like love and obedience (13:14-15, 34; 15:4-10).[18] L. W. Countryman renders the Fourth Gospel as a progression toward the mystical union in the person of Jesus. He perceived the gospel as a mystic's experience of theology

---

[15] C. K. Barrett, *The Gospel According to St. John*, London: SPCK, 1958, 71-72.

[16] Maharaj Charan Singh, *St. John the Great Mystic*, Punjab: Radha Soami Satsang Beas, 1974, 2. Though his small 'Commentary on the Gospel of John' admits it as a mystic document, does he realize Christ as the realization of God is disputable.

[17] James McPolin, "Johannine Mysticism," *The Way* 1, 1978, 25-35.

[18] Rudolf Schnackenburg, *The Gospel According to St. John: Commentary on Chapters 13-21*, HTCNT, vol. 3. New York NY: Crossroad Publishing Company, 1982, 161-162.

and not as an intellectual theology in the abstract sense.[19] J. Kanakaraj's study on 'Mysticism in the Gospel of John' avowed the past researches on Jewish heritage of the Fourth Gospel and an analysis of the vocabularies of mystical expressions.[20] S. Schneiders presents the Fourth Gospel as 'mysterious and beautiful' and exploration of 'the spiritual world of mysterious mutual indwelling of Jesus and his disciples.'[21]

As the objectives of this Seminar indicates "Mysticism [...] is the pursuit of communion with, identity with, or conscious awareness of an ultimate reality, divinity, spiritual truth, or God through direct experience, intuition or insight."[22] We would like to take this definition as a starting point for the present paper. The analysis of scholarship on the Fourth Gospel indicates two kinds of scholarship: those who explicitly opt for 'Mysticism' in the Fourth Gospel and those who see a mysterious nature but call it as spiritual gospel. Scholars have two view points: one is traditional mysticism and the other is normal or implied mysticism. We take the latter as the matrix of the present paper. If Mysticism is the pursuit of communion with, identity with, or conscious awareness of an ultimate reality, divinity, spiritual truth, or God through direct experience, intuition or insight, is it legitimate to interpret Jn13:8 with a potentially 'mystical' connotation? Before an exploration of 13:8 we should make a brief survey of possible influences on the Fourth Evangelist.

2. Legacy of John's Mystical Expressions

Scholars point to two possible influences of John's mystical language: Hellenistic mysticism[23] and Jewish mysticism.[24] In the Hellenistic

---

[19] L. William Countryman, *The Mystical Way in the Fourth Gospel*, Philadelphia: Fortress Press, 1987, 11.

[20] Kanagaraj, 'Mysticism' in the Gospel of John.

[21] Sandra M. Schneiders, *Written That You May Believe: Encountering Jesus in the Fourth Gospel*, New York NY: The Crossroad, 1999, 1-3.

[22] http://www.mwb2011bangalore.in/Objectives.php, accessed on 01-10-2010.

[23] To name a few, Albert Schweitzer, *The Mysticism of Paul the Apostle*, London: Black, 1931. C. H. Dodd, *The Interpretation of the Fourth Gospel*, Cambridge: Cambridge University press, 1960; David L. Mealand, "The Language of Mystical Union in the Johannine Writings," *The Downside Review* 95. 1977.

[24] To name a few, Schnackenburg, *The Gospel According to St. John*; Edwyn Clement Hoskyns, *The Fourth Gospel*, ed. Francis Noel Davey, 2 ed. London: Faber and Faber,

mysticism, knowledge of God is related to mystical vision. Knowledge of God is an experience of entering into God by an ascent. Finally, the mystic experiences close unity with God which results in the deification, that is, the mystic becomes God. The final destination of the mystic is entry into *to phōs and hē zōē*. C. H. Dodd considers Hellenistic mysticism as an entry into *to phōs and hē zōē*. According to Dodd, this concept is adapted in the letter to the Ephesians and by the Fourth Evangelist.[25] For him, 'in God' in Hellenistic mysticism can be connected to the Johannine mutual indwelling. Union with God is a general thought of Hellenistic mysticism and one who is not in God has no secure existence. When we compare this view with the Fourth Gospel, it is plausible to argue that John gives a Christian sense to personal union with God that consists in *agapē*.[26]

Philo's mystical teachings highlight two important themes: the desire of the human mind to see God and to have union with Him. As in the Hellenistic mysticism, in Philo in the idea of union with God is explained through the principle of light, more exactly through the *Logos*.[27] *Logos*, as Philo regards, holds the fullness of light. For, the human mind can only see *Logos* that presents God as he is and the human mind can never perceive God as He is. In order to see God, the human mind has to transcend from this sensible world to the intelligible world. This transcendence is possible when the soul is freed from the bondage of matter. Therefore, he advocates ascetic practice as a prerequisite for mystical ascent. The idea that God's disclosure happens through 'light' and *Logos*, occurs both in John and Philo.[28] The concept of divine indwelling is also evident in both. Philo's concept of mystical union is analogous to John's concept of 'abiding in' and 'knowing.'[29] L. Mealand explains that Philo, through his concept 'God dwelling within the human souls,' has a strong inclination towards Hellenistic mysticism.[30]

1956. For a detailed study of this see Kanagaraj, *'Mysticism' in the Gospel of John*.

[25] Dodd, *The Interpretation of the Fourth Gospel*, 210.

[26] Kanagaraj, *'Mysticism' in the Gospel of John*, 200.

[27] Erwin R. Goodenough, *By Light, Light: The Mystical Gospel of Hellenistic Judaism*, New Haven: Yale University, 1935, 6-8. See also Kanagaraj, 71.

[28] Kanagaraj, *'Mysticism' in the Gospel of John*, 69-77.

[29] Mealand, "The Language of Mystical Union," 19-34.

[30] Mealand, "The Language of Mystical Union," 22.

Moreover, it is to be noted that Philo speaks of divine indwelling rather than mutual indwelling.

There was a strong influence of Hellenistic thought in the Judaism of the NT period. Johannine vocabulary might have been influenced by Greek thought. Platonism, which holds a dualistic understanding of reality, shows an affinity for the vertical dualistic nature of Judaism as heavenly and earthly. But, the *Logos* concept that was prevalent in stoicism did not influence John as it was used in the Stoic circle. Moreover, Philo's understanding of mysticism can have phraseological and conceptual links with John, but essentially differs from it. Even the *Hermetica* cannot be compared with John since its composition in the 2nd and 3rd CE becomes problematic. Furthermore, some of the important terms of *Hermetica* are absent in John. A statistical comparison also proved the same fact that John is inclined more to the thought pattern of the OT. Therefore, these two backgrounds do not play much role in the Fourth Gospel.[31]

Jewish Mysticism: A large number of scholars agree that Hellenistic-Jewish mysticism does not give an adequate answer to the question of Johannine mysticism.[32] The research of the last hundred years to explore the Jewish background of Christianity in the light of ancient Jewish sources gives considerable reliability to the Jewish background of John. This is evident in John's presentation of the OT ideas of Jesus as the Messiah, the servant of Yahweh, the King of Israel, and the Prophet. Influence of the prophetic literature, Psalms, Proverbs, Sirach and Wisdom of Solomon on the Gospel is undisputable. Though the rabbinic literature was written in the Christian era or later, it contains elements

---

31 Raymond Brown, *The Gospel According to John I-XII*, AB, vol. 29, London: Yale, 1966, 52-64.

32 J. Abelson, *Jewish Mysticism*, London: G. Bell and Sons, 1913, 48-49; H. Odeberg, *The Fourth Gospel Interpreted in Its Relation to Contemporaneous Religious Currents in Palestine and the Hellenistic Oriental World*, Uppsala-Och-Stockholm: 1929, 48ff.; T. Preiss, *Life in Christ*, London: SCM Press, 1954, 11-31; Gershom G. Scholem, *Jewish Gnosticism, Merkabah Mysticism, and Talmudic Tradition*, New York: JTSA, 1960, N. A. Dahl, "The Johannine Church and History," in Current Issues in New Testament Interpretation: Essays in Honour of O. A. Piper, ed. W. Klassen and G. F. Snyder, New York: Harper Row, 1962, 14-30; P. Borgen, *Bread from Heaven: An Exegetical Study of the Concept of Manna in the Gospel of John and the Writing of Philo*, NovtSup, vol. 10, Leiden: E. J. Brill, 1965, 2, 147, 177.

that go back to Jesus' time. The discoveries of the Dead Sea scrolls from caves 4 and 11 describe heavenly temple, heavenly liturgy, angels having intimate knowledge of divine secrets etc. Worship of different grades of angels gives considerable support to the extensive interest in the heavenly world. Moreover, a Dead Sea *Merkabah* fragment speaks about the movement of the divine throne chariot and the glorious chariot. In that sense, it exceeds the apocalyptic literature and comes closer to *Hekhalot* literature.[33]

Late first century Palestinian mysticism, as described in the *Hekhalot* literature,[34] points to the *Merkabah* (chariot) mysticism. *Merkabah* mysticism was characterized by an ascent to heaven and a vision of God. But the disputable date of *Hekhalot* literature (200-700CE) raises serious questions. Nonetheless, affinity with earlier apocalyptic that goes back to the second century BCE, seen in the Pseudepigrapha are antecedents to the later Jewish 'theosophic' and cosmological speculations.[35] Gnostic literature and esoteric description of certain particular spiritual experience as in Ezekiel 1 and Isaiah 6, and Daniel brought up the tradition which existed much before the written *Hekhalot* literature. The early form of *Merkhabah* mysticism which was in practice in the first century Palestine is evident from 4 QShirShabb, 2 Cor 12, The Exagoge, Pseudo-Philo, The Similitude of Enoch, Enoch, 4 Ezra, The Apocalypse of Abraham, The Testament of Abraham, The Book of Revelation 4-5, the Ascension of Isaiah 6-11, and the mystical tradition of the school of Yohanan ben Zakkai (1-80 CE).[36] For this reason, *Merkabah* mysticism in Palestinian Judaism that came much before the time of the Fourth Gospel shows reliable dependence of John.[37]

---

[33] Christopher Rowland and R. A. Christopher Morray-Jones, *The Mystery of God: Early Jewish Mysticism and the New Testament*, Leiden, Boston: Brill, 2009, 30-31.

[34] A collection of Jewish mystical writings composed plausibly around 200-700 CE.

[35] Rowland and Morray-Jones, *The Mystery of God*, 28-29. Authors argue for an extensive mystical tradition antecedent of the *Tannaitic* period.

[36] Jey J. Kanagaraj, "Jesus the King, *Merkabah* Mysticism and the Gospel of John," *TB* 47, no. 2 (1996), 351.

[37] Raymond E. Brown, *The Gospel According to John XIII-XXI*, AB, vol. 29 A. London: Yale, 1970, 56-64. April D. DeConick, *Voices of the Mystics: Early Christian Discourse in the Gospels of John and Thomas and Other Ancient Christian Literature*, ed. Stanley E. Porter, JSNTsup, Sheffield: Sheffield, 2001. Though many studies give

Having refuted the mystical influence of the world behind and in the Fourth Gospel, in the following session, we try to concentrate on a central and much debated episode in the Fourth Gospel, the footwashing. Though there are some detailed studies on the theme of mysticism in the Fourth Gospel, there has been little attention paid to the footwashing episode.[38]

3. Footwashing and Having Part with Jesus

Among the canonical gospels, only the Fourth Gospel contains the account of Jesus washing the feet of the disciples (13:1-38).[39] The act of footwashing, ripe with meaning, exhibits a unique incident without parallel. The importance of this section of the Fourth Gospel is that the whole section can be seen against the background of the farewell tradition in the OT that gives resonance to the immediacy of departure.[40] The whole section of farewell discourses (ch. 13-17) describes a situation where Jesus is with 'his own.' Moreover, the whole farewell material is framed in a temporal unit 'before the Passover,' a meal context gives a spatial unit, and the culmination of his action and discourse reaches toward the love commandment.

3.1. Footwashing: A Macro Context

Footwashing falls in the second part of the Fourth Gospel, namely, the Book of Glory (ch. 13-20). Scholars have considered the washing of the feet in the first part of the farewell discourse (ch. 13-17).[41] There

---

enough reasons to read the Fourth Gospel against the Palestinian Judaism, we must also take into consideration Hellenistic thoughts and Hellenistic Judaism. See, Forg Frey, "The Bible and the Dead Sea Scrolls: The Second Princeton Symposium on Judaism and Christian Origins." in The Scrolls and Christian Origins, ed. James H. Charlesworth, Waco: Baylor University, 2006, 442.

[38] E. Underhill, J. Kanakaraj, etc. do not give particular reference to the footwashing in their discussion on Mysticism and the Fourth Gospel.

[39] We will see later the reasons to take 13:1-38 as a whole unit.

[40] For instance, the Farewell Speeches of Isaac (Gen 27, Jacob (Gen 49) Moses (Deut 31-33), Joshua (Josh 24) and Samuel (I Sam 12).

[41] The structural division of the Fourth Gospel by Raymond E. Brown limits the footwashing in 13:1-20. While some other scholars argue for the inclusive character (*agapē* in v1 and in 34-35 and the question of Peter 36-38 is closely connected to the 13:33, 'his going away') of this chapter in 13:1, 34:36, 36-38 and read 13:1-38 as a

are opposing views about whether the footwashing episode constitutes a literary unit or not.[42] According to Bultmann, it is the task of exegetes to demonstrate the inner unity of the two interpretations.[43] Brown takes vv.2-11 as a unit and regards vv.12-20 as a second interpretation of the footwashing.[44] But B. Lindars opt for the unity of the whole section and appreciates John's method of building on traditional material.[45] In 1982, based on the 'Leuven Hypothesis,'[46] M. Sabbe defended the dependence of John on the Synoptics by analyzing Jn 13:1-20. Sabbe argues for a direct dependence of John on the Synoptic Gospels as a literary model to better explain the whole chapter of 13. Sabbe, however, assigns an important specific influence upon John to the redactional elaboration of Luke based on his Marken source.[47] An analysis of the 'Johannine stylistic characteristics' gives approval to his findings.[48]

As much as the debate exists in the unity of the text, the meaning and interpretation of the footwashing also differs without final consensus. In

---

literary unit. See, George Mlakuzhiyil, *The Christocentric Literary Structure of the Fourth Gospel*, Rome: Editrice Pontificio Instituto Biblico, 1987, 221-222.

42 For instance, Ernst Lohmeyer, "Die Fusswaschung," *ZNW* 38 (1939), 74-94; A. Weiser, "Joh 13, 12-20 -Zufügung Eines Späteren Herausgebers?," *BZ* 12 (1968), 252-57; J. D. G. Dunn, „The Washing of the Disciples' Feet in John 13,1-20," *ZNW* 61 (1970),247-252, support the unity of the text. M.-É. Boismard, "Le Lavement Des Pieds," *Revue Biblique* 71 (1964), 5-24, in his commentary of 1977, distinguishes three authors and a fourfold redaction.

43 Bultmann, *The Gospel of John*, 559-560.

44 Brown, *The Gospel According to John*, 561-562.

45 Lindars Barnabas, *The Gospel of John*, Grand Rapids: Eerdmans, 1987, 441-442.

46 Proponents of this theory argue that the Fourth Gospel is indeed based on written sources and that the primary sources that can be identified are the synoptic gospels. See, Robert T. Fortna and Tom Thatcher, *Jesus in Johannine Tradition*, Louisville: West Minister John Knox, 2001, 1-14. The re-emergence of this theory can be found in the 26th Colloquium Biblicum Louvaniense in 1975. At this international conference Frans Neirynck presented a paper proposing the synoptic gospels as the main sources behind John 20:1-18. See, Frans Neirynck, "John and the Synoptics," in *BETL*, ed. F. Van Segbroeck, Leuven University Press, 1982, 364-400. The dependence of John on the Synoptics is also well presented by G. Van Belle in the presidential address in the 54th Colloquium Biblicum Louvaniense in 2005. See, Gilbert Van Belle, "The Death of Jesus in the Fourth Gospel," in *BETL*, Leuven: University Press, 2007, 3-64.

47 Sabbe, "The Footwashing in Jn 13 and Its Relation to the Synoptic Gospels," 279-308.

48 Van Belle, "The Signs Source in the Fourth Gospel," 405-417.

fact a variety of interpretations have been given to this pericope. Of the many interpretations, one of the most prominent views is that in the footwashing episode Jesus offers a lesson in humility to his disciples.[49] The commandment of love and service is another important aspect that the interpreters point out.[50] There are also several scholars who have seen in the footwashing a reference to the Eucharist.[51] The Footwashing is also closely associated with baptism.[52] The idea that footwashing serves as a symbol of cleansing from sin, is another interpretation of Jn 13:1-20 which received a great deal of attention.[53] The connection between the footwashing and Jesus' death on the cross is an important dimension of the pericope that emphasises the footwashing as a soteriological sign as many scholars emphasise.[54] However, modern scholarship undeniably connects it with the passion, death and resurrection of Jesus.

3.2. Footwashing in the Micro Context

Considering the inclusive character of the narrative, we take 13:1-38 as a self contained unit,[55] without engaging the textual problems that had been discussed much in the earlier scholarship. Scholars have the opinion that 13:1-38 can be seen as unit that consists of the symbolic act of the hour vv.1-17; the prediction of the betrayal vv.18-30; the parting love commandment vv. 31-35 and the denial vv.36-38.[56] Four important characters in the Fourth Gospel (Jesus, Peter, Judas and the beloved disciple), the misunderstanding of the disciple, knowledge comes

---

[49] Brown, *The Gospel According to John*, 561-562.

[50] For instance, M. J. Lagrange, H. Windish, and C. K. Barrett.

[51] For instance, W. Bauer, O. Cullmann, A. Maynard, and J. N. Suggit.

[52] For instance, E. von Dobschütz, C.T. Craig, M. Werner, R. H. Lightfoot, W. F. Howard, and R. Brown.

[53] For instance, E. W. Hengstenberg, F. Godet, F. Spitta, J. Grill, T. Zahn, J. D. G. Dunn, H. Weiss, and G. Beasley-Murray.

[54] For instance, F. M. Braun, E.C. Hoskyns, A. Wikenhauser, R. Schnackenburg, and E. Haenchen.

[55] Interpretation of the footwashing is intelligible if we read it on the basis of discipleship. V.1-20 provides the picture of Jesus as the model of Discipleship and vv.20-30 complete failure of discipleship are again repeated in vv.31-35 and vv.36-38 respectively. Therefore, for a better understanding we take 13:1-38 as one unit. See, Mlakuzhiyil, *The Christocentric Literary Structure*, 222.

[56] Mlakuzhiyil, *The Christocentric Literary Structure*, 223.

later, strong negation (Peter) and strong affirmation (Jesus) regarding the act of the footwashing, the mandatory nature of the act, allusion to the betrayal, appearance of the betrayer, deep intimacy of the beloved disciple with Jesus and the love commandment posit a challenge to the reader to go deeper into the symbolism/intentionality of the text. Many scholars have suggested that Jn 13:6-11 can be said to be 'the key to the symbolism of the Footwashing.'[57] We do agree with this opinion at the same time we understand that this key opens a wide horizon to the reader. Crucial to vv.6-11 is v.8 where Jesus says to Peter: *ean mē vipsō se, ouk echeis meros met' emou*. If Brown is right, the conversation between Jesus and Peter gives us the clue to the interpretation of the footwashing. V.8 is the response to v.7 where Peter strongly refuses to be subjected to the washing. At first, we concentrate on v.8 and this verse can be subdivided into five parts.

8a. *legei autōi Petros·*
8b. *ou mē nipsēis mous podas eis tov aiōna.*
8c. *apekrithē Iēsous autōi·*
8d. ean mē nipsō se,
8e. *ouk echeis meros met' emou.*

4. Literary Analysis of V. 8:

The immediate context of v.8a is the act of footwashing. Peter is the dialogue partner for Jesus.[58] Peter in the Fourth Gospel is not the first disciple to follow Jesus or acknowledge his messianic statues except in 1:42 and 6:68 in the Book of Signs.[59] It is possible here that Peter acts as a spokesperson for the disciples and also behaves impulsively (6:68; 18:10; 21:7). Importance of the use of the terms in the question of Peter in v.6 *kyrie, su mou nipteis tous podas* is significant that he stresses the

[57] Brown, *The Gospel According to John*, 565.

[58] The occasions where Peter is present are 1:42- a new name; 6:68- affirms faith in Jesus;13:6- misunderstanding of Jesus' action; 13:36-38- Peters denial prediction; 18:10-misunderstaning; 18:15-18:25-27- denies Jesus; 20:1-10- goes to the empty tomb; 21:1-14- swimming from fishing boat to Jesus; 21:15-19- reinstatement and commissioning (believe-faith-life).

[59] John Christopher Thomas, *Foot-washing in John 13 and the Johannine Community*, Sheffield: Sheffield, 1991, 90-92.

Lordship of Jesus. The vocative *kyrie* combined with *su* points to an emphatic tone, emphasizing the paradoxical reversal of roles. Peter's objection to the act of footwashing starts in v.6. At first sight, Peter's objection to the act of footwashing will not surprise the reader because of the unusual sequence of the events. These extraordinary elements include the background of a festive meal (v.1), the action is not before the meal as one would have expected but the structure of two consecutive genitive absolutes cause one to infer that the action is in between the supper[60] and the change of role (lord and slave).[61] But it can be assumed from the context that Peter was not the first to be washed. Therefore, it is typical of John that he uses the misunderstanding character for the revelation of the messianic identity of Jesus.[62] *Arti*[63] and *meta tauta* points to the temporal tension that exists in the Fourth Gospel. V.7 is ambiguous and plausibly we can understand it on the basis of 12:16. Here we get the first clue that the footwashing is not a simple washing; and they will not understand it until *meta tauta*. This is an indication to the future dimension of *meta tauta*. As typical in many of Johannine episodes, the footwashing can only be understood entirely after the crucifixion and resurrection. Jesus' words in v.7 have no effect on Peter, but he reacts with strong resistance. This highest form of negation draws immediate attention to the answer given to this negation. 8d puts forward a condition to accept or to reject (*ean*). The distribution of pronouns *me*, *se* and *emou* make it emphatic and personal. If the condition is accepted, the act *nipsō* makes Peter to have a *meros* with Jesus. The central point of washing is have a share/part and the entire passage is linked to *meros*.[64]

---

[60] Brown, *The Gospel According to John*, 551. Washing before the meal was common in the first century Judaism but washing in between the supper in the footwashing evokes extraordinariness of the action.

[61] Brown, *The Gospel According to John*, 551.

[62] Hugo Zorrilla, "A Service of Sacrificial Love: Footwashing (John 13:1-11)," *Direction* 24, no. 1 (1995), 82.

[63] Missing in OS^{sin} some OL copies; P^{66} shows confusion.

[64] It is interesting to note that μέρος is used in the Septuagint to translate ql,xe (ḥēleq), the word that describes the God-given portion to each tribe of Israel. Num18:20 points to the special blessing of God to Aaron. The share which Levi could expect is replaced by a special relationship with God. God becomes their inheritance (Deut 12:12; 14:27). See, Johann Michl, "Der Sinn der Fusswaschung," *Biblica* (1959), 697-708; Ronald B.

4.1. Meros and hē hōra

Unlike the Synoptics, *hē hōra*[65] bears deep theological significance in the Fourth Gospel.[66] In Jn 13:1 the temporal idea expressed through *hōra* reveals that it is the appointed time for the completion of Jesus' mission and his return to where he had come from. It is an *anabasis*, being elevated because of the *katabasis*. The whole life of Jesus irrevocably was an orientation towards this particular time willed by the Father. Jesus accepts this hour during his prayer in 12:27. The motivation of this hour is to glorify the Father (12:28). Moreover what is going to happen in the hour is explained in v.13. Two things are clearly indicated by the narrator that Jesus will depart from this world and will go to the Father. The solemn introduction in 13:1 and opening words of the 17:1 give the idea that glorification of the Son is the glorification of the Father and the glorification is only through the death and resurrection of Jesus (the hour). 19:14 gives a numerical understanding that is, the sixth hour, the time when Pilate proclaimed that Jesus is the 'king of the Jews,' the hour when the paschal lamb was being killed in the temple. Before the finishing of the hour, the mother of Jesus becomes the mother of the disciple and the disciple of Jesus becomes the son of Jesus' mother (19:26, 27). Therefore, as G. Mlakuzhiyil observes, the hour of Jesus coincides with the hour of the spiritual maternity of Mary and the inauguration of the hour of the Church, the household of the Father.[67] Disciples are invited to enter into new realm of relationship. Therefore, the community is at the center of the hour where the clear revelation of the Father is expected (16:25) and the Father will be worshipped in Spirit and Truth (4:21-23). The disciples are, therefore, incorporated into the highest communion ever possible with freedom. *Meros met' emou* is an invitation to participate in the *hōra* of Jesus and its fruit, the highest communion. This sharing with Jesus points to their appointment in the Kingdom where they share at the table and will be seated on the throne to judge. Sabbe connects it with Lk 12:51 and Mt 24:51 which

---

Allen, *Numbers*, ed. Frank E. Gaebelenin, *The Expositor's Bible Commentary*, vol. 2. Michigan: Zondervan, 1990, 855.

[65] Jn 2:4; 7:30; 8:20; 11:9; 12:23; 13:1; 17:1.

[66] The word occurs 26 times in the Gospel.

[67] Mlakuzhiyil, *The Christocentric Literary Structure*, 162-164.

evidently tell about two 'parts' or 'shares': one is of eternal life and the other one is of eternal damnation.[68] Knowledge about and participation in Jesus' hour are the prerequisites for 'have a share or part with Jesus.'

4.2. Meros and hoi idioi

The entire farewell discourse spins around the theme of Jesus' *hōra* and his love for 'his own.' But who are 'his own' in the Johannine sense? His own can be explained through the good shepherd imagery (10:4,12,27).[69] Sheep and shepherd imagery is classical in the OT.[70] This striking expression of the shepherding imagery frequently occurs in the NT.[71] While the Synoptics ends with the prophecy of the death and resurrection of the good shepherd, the Fourth Gospel expresses the supreme truth of revelation in picturing the good shepherd as one who lays down his life for 'his own' (sheep) that he may take it again (10:15-28). Laying down his life is not an end in itself, but it points towards life. Subsequently, in the Fourth Gospel the parable of the Good Shepherd continues until sheep ('his own') witnessed the death and resurrection. It is important to note here that the courtyard adjoining a house serves as the fold for the sheep. Therefore access to the house both for the shepherd and to the sheep were provided by a single door. Identification of the shepherd's voice, knowledge of the names of each sheep, leading them out, and following of sheep are given absolute tone to the intimate relationship between the sheep and shepherd. Jesus calls *hoi idioi* by name. 'His own' hear his voice and hearing the voice and believing in Jesus is a sign of life.[72] The beloved disciple in 13:23 represents his own through an intimate relationship with Jesus as 1:18 where Jesus was in the bosom of the Father. The phrase 'his own' connotes mutual intimate knowledge and personal relationship between Jesus and the disciples.

---

[68] Sabbe, "The Footwashing in Jn 13 and Its Relation to the Synoptic Gospels," 297.

[69] Chennattu, *Johannine Discipleship as a Covenant Relationship*, 90.

[70] OT pictures Israel as God's flock (Ps 23, 74:1; Is 40:11; Jer 23: 1-4), and a good shepherd David or a branch from the stem of David will save the flock from the hands of a false shepherd (Jer 23:1-8; Ezek 34:22; I Enoch 35).

[71] Mk 6:34, 14:27; Lk 12:32, 15:3-7; Matt 9:35, 36, 15:24, 18:12, 26:31; Heb 13:20; 1Pet 2:25, 5:4; Rev 12:5.

[72] Hoskyns, *The Fourth Gospel*, 366-378.

Mutual intimate knowledge and personal relationship between Jesus and disciples closely related to the *agapaō* terminology in John. We find a tripartite union in *agapaō* expressions in the farewell materials; union between the Father and the Son, union between the Son and the disciples and through Jesus the disciples' union with the Father and union between the disciples based on love (13:1, 34; 14:21; 15:9, 12, 17; 14:31 cf. 11:5). Increased use of the 'love' terminology in the second part of the Gospel also gives some important clues to it.[73] Love is directed towards 'his own' and the characteristic of this love is *eis telos* (to the very end). Scholars agree that *eis telos* can be taken both temporally (to the end of his life) and modaly (as fully, wholly or completely) and consequently it denotes the intensity,[74] that is, his perfect love. If we interpret the act of footwashing against vv.1-3, it is definitely drawing one to the loving intimacy and communion with Jesus.

4.3. Meros and Washing/Water

The conditional clause, *ean mē nipsō se* (13:8d), expresses the importance of washing, consequently the importance of water. He pours water into a basin.[75] The fountain in the Hebrew Bible is used as a figure of speech to indicate God or ways of the wise. Ps 36:10 describes God as fountain or source of life. Isaiah calls forth people to come to the thirst quenching water.[76] In Johannine understanding the life giving water has saving powers and it is intrinsically related to Christ. Jesus' dialogue with a Samaritan woman signifies eternal life (4:10,14). Water in 7:37-39 is a symbol for that which quenches a human's search for life and drinking points to the personal acceptance of the believer to what it signifies.

---

[73] In the first twelve chapters of the Fourth Gospel 'life' appears 50 times and 'love' only 6 times where as in chapters 13-21 'life' appears 6 times and 'love' appears 31 times.

[74] E. Stauffer, "Eis," in *TDNT*, ed. Kittel Gerhard, Michigan: Eerdmans, 1964, 426-427.

[75] The word used here for basin is νιπτῆρ. νιπτῆρ is derived from the verb νίπτω meaning 'to wash.' Although the precise word for water □δωπ appears only once in chapter 13 (v.5), νίπτω appears eight times (vv.5, 6, 8x2, 10, 12, 14x2; λούω appears once in v.10).

[76] Kelley Coblentz Bautch, *A Study of the Geography of I Enoch 17-19: No One Has Seen What I Have Seen*, ed. John J. Collins, JSJSup, vol. 81, Leiden: Brill, 2003, 76.

Water is therefore, emblematic of a new life (4:14; 6:51,54). The life-giving water symbolizes the Spirit, because John explicitly explains this symbolism in 7:39. In Jn 9 the man born blind is healed when he is immersed into the water of *Siloha* (*apestalmenos*) which means 'one who is sent.' In Johannine understanding the one who is sent is Christ. Therefore healing points to Jesus and washing effected to see everything properly.[77] Thus, pouring water on the feet of the disciples emphasizes the pouring of the Spirit after his death and the resurrection. It insists that while the disciples were slow to understand during the ministry of Jesus (12:16), they were subsequently led by the Spirit into all truth (14:26; 16:13). For John Jesus is the well of water for eternal life and the rivers of living water mediate life.[78] John 4:10 presents water as a gift or reward for the thirsty. In the Book of Revelation water is presented as a gift (Rev 21:6; 22:17) to the martyrs (7:17), and the victors (Rev 21:6). Water depicts life as a love relationship with God.[79] Therefore, the meaning of washing can be understood only when washing is understood as a sign. It is clear that a refusal to the washing is a refusal to the relationship with Jesus.[80] *Meta tauta* in v.7 makes it clear that true symbolic character can be grasped oniy later. 'Understanding later' necessarily points to the meaning of 'the hour,' glorification and bestowal of the Spirit (2:22; 7:37-39). The referent of the washing is *meros met'emou*. Therefore, an acceptance of the washing gives them a continued union with Jesus and that is his death on the cross. F. Segovia understood the washing in the whole spectrum of believing and non-believing. The Fourth Gospel presents the disciples until this point as persons who have believed in Jesus (1:35-51; 2:1-11; 6:66-71).[81] But their 'believe' will come to its fullness when they receive the Spirit.

[77] Cf. Joseph T. Pamplaniyil, *Crossing the Abysses: An exegetical Study of John 20:19 in the Light of the Johannine Notion of Discipleship*, Leuven: Katholieke Universiteit, 2006, 65-67, 213,214.

[78] Bautch, A Study of the Geography of I Enoch 17-19: No One Has Seen What I Have Seen, 78.

[79] Bautch, *A Study of the Geography of I Enoch 17-19: No One Has Seen What I Have Seen*, 78-79. Herold Weiss, "Foot Washing in the Johannine Community," *NovT* 21 (1979), 304.

[80] Segovia, "John 13 1-20," 43.

[81] Fernando F. Segovia, "John 13 1-20, the Footwashing in the Johannine Tradition," *ZNW* 73 (1982), 38.

Spirit enables them to know and accept the meaning of the hour thus come to fellowship with Jesus. Knowing and believing interconnected and to know is to have deep personal relationship[82]

4.4. Meros and Eternal Life:

The above analysis connects *meros* with eternal life. When Jesus washes the feet of Peter, it is clear that only by accepting the action of the master, the disciple can have any part with him. The whole Gospel points directly and indirectly the theme of eternal life. The inclusive character of the Gospel based on the theme of 'life' makes it clear (1:4 and 20:30-31). Significance of the phrase *eis tov aiōna* (NRSV renders the meaning as 'never' but literally it means 'unto the age' / 'unto eternity') makes the point clear. *eis tov aiōna* appears twelve times in the Fourth Gospel (4:14, 6:51; 6:58; 8:35x2 51; 52 10:28, 11:26; 12:34;13:8; 14:16 and 1Jn 2:17). Among this eleven times the phrase appears when Jesus teaches about the eternal life. Notably, 13:8 is the only place where the phrase is not virtually related to the eternal life. The phrase *eis tov aiōna* both in the non-biblical usage and in the biblical sense points to a timeless eternal reality.[83] Why does the author use this particular phrase in this section even though the double negatives already give an emphatic negation? From the twelve instances we may rightly conclude that here the opposition is not a simple negation of the washing, but the negation of the referent of *niptō*, *he hōra*, and *agapaō* that is the eternal life.[84]

The purpose of the Son's mission and the purpose of the Gospel can be summarized in terms of giving life (1:4; 20:30-31).[85] Washing of the feet is not only a prophetic prefiguration of Jesus' death on the cross,

---

[82] Hartwig, Thyen, "Das Johannesevangelium," in *HNT* 6, Tübingen: Mohr Siebeck, 2005, 684.

[83] Hermann Sasse, "Aieon," in *TDNT*, ed. Kittel Gerhard, Michigan: Eerdmans, 1964, 198.

[84] The new relationship through the participation in 'Jesus' having' will make the believer participate in the first resurrection as it is explained in Rev 20:6. The believer who has a part in the first resurrection will then have a share in the tree of life (Rev 22:19). Entry into paradise and share in the fruits of the tree belongs to those who are cleansed by the blood of Christ Rev 22:14. In Jewish thought, paradise is a future abode of believers and blessed ones are called to eat the tree of life.

[85] David A. Ihenacho, *The Community of Eternal Life: The Study of the Meaning of Life for the Johannine Community*, Lanham: University Press of America, 2001, xx.

but also enables 'his own' to inherit the eternal life. Because, the power to give eternal life is part of the power that the Father has given him (13:1; 17:2). John 1:3-4 depicts *Logos* as source of 'life' and describes 'life' as a light of men. Whereas, 1:12-13 reveals the nature of this life as divine life of those who receive the revealed *Logos* of God in faith which makes them children of God. Though participation of a believer in God's life is God's own love, humans are not passive. Believing in Jesus is the condition and disobeying will remove one from the life. The qualifier 'eternal' not only points to (3:15; 16:36) an infinite duration after death but also qualitatively new life which even death cannot destroy. Even the absence of the qualifier reflects this same reality (3:36a and 3:36b). Jn 10:10 and 14-15 reflect that life consists of mutual intimate knowledge of Jesus and 'his own.' Eternal life is knowledge in the Johannine sense. Knowledge means communion of Christ and through him with the Father.[86] This knowledge is the knowledge of Jesus as the way, the truth and the life (14:6). It is the knowledge which 'his own' will have later through the gift of the Holy Spirit, make them inheritors of life. Therefore a life lived in communion with Jesus and the Father experiences the result of this life in this life itself. Peter's negation is a clear negation of the gift of communion which the Father gives through Jesus. The gift of communion is not only of a vertical relationship but a horizontal one which reflects on the *hypodeigma* of Jesus.

5. Meros and Morality in the Fourth Gospel

Intimate communion explained in the footwashing is inseparable from the morality of the Fourth Gospel. *Meros meta* presupposes love and faithfulness as it is explained in vv.12-17. Ethics of brotherly/sisterly love exemplified and perfected in the earthly Jesus is prefigured in the act of footwashing. Jesus gives supreme proof of his love as depicted in 13:1; 17:26 and ultimately it becomes eternal and fruitful. This supreme love obliges 'his own' to practice the same love.[87] Therefore, Johannine

[86] For a detailed analysis of Eternal Life see, Marianne Meye Thompson,"Eternal Life in the Gospel of John," *Ex auditu* 5 (1989), 35-55; Mlakuzhiyil, *The Christocentric Literary Structure*, 291-298.
[87] Schnackenburg, *The Gospel According to St. John*, 162.

ethics is Christological[88] and communitarian in character. The life to which believers are called is a life of obedience which is perfected in love.[89] Johannine expressions of intimate communion with God are not exclusively spiritual; rather it takes the other seriously. In addition to that, in footwashing we see an obligatory service that arises from the washing which is offered to the disciples by their master.[90] The relationship of the disciples with Jesus is one in which he calls them his friends. But this does not negate his call to service, rather, it heightens it. The disciples call him Teacher and Lord, and it is so (13:13). Therefore, the act of footwashing leads the disciples to the loving service in the model of Jesus.[91] The two unparallel terms (master, slave) became perfectly balanced when an ontological change of disciples as brothers of the Son in the household of the Father.

Does footwashing present an ontological change in relationship? We are tempted to say 'yes' as we are informed by the interpretation given by S. Schneiders who points out three models of services. The first model denotes what the server must do for the served because of some right or power that the latter has. This kind of service contains the elements of inequality and domination. It can become exploitative and oppressive because of the power of the served. In the second model of service, service is rendered freely for the served in times of need because the server has the power to do it. Here, inequality also pervades in the sphere of service. As Schneiders notes, the service that surpasses these pervasions is that of friendship based on equality; and domination is totally foreign to friendship. According to her, this is because Johannine Jesus commands not love of enemies, but love unto death. In friendship, the gift of one's life is experienced as enrichment rather than the

---

[88] Raymond F. Collins, *Christian Morality: Biblical Foundations*, Notre Dame: University of Notre Dame, 1986, 41.

[89] Barrett, *The Gospel According to St. John*, 72.

[90] Alan R. Culpepper, "The Johannine "Hypodeigma": A Reading of John 13," *Semeia* 53 (1991), 146. This service includes the footwashing/love/death for one another as he has done. It is by the imitation of the pattern of Jesus' life and death that all will know that they are his disciples (13:35).

[91] R. Melvyn Hillmer, "They Believed in Him: Discipleship in the Johannine Tradition," in *Patterns of Discipleship in the New Testament*, ed. Richard N. Longenecker, Cambridge: Eerdmans, 1989, 31.

impoverishment of oneself. 'To die that a friend might live is to live in a transcendent way.' Therefore Jesus established an intimacy with them that superseded his superiority and gave access to the disciples to all he has. He made the believer his friend without any form of inequality; this genuine love for humankind must be our point of discussion.[92]

Have a part with Jesus is an invitation to 'remain in'. It presents an everlasting communion between the Father, the Son and life sharing union of the disciples with Jesus and the Father.[93] This is a fruit bearing union (15:8) which is not merely an excellence of character but a will and capacity for sharing the life as well.[94] This moral nature is advised not because of its general goodness but it is a natural outflow of an experience of salvation. In many instances of the word *opheilō* indicates the link between human obligations and the experienced act of salvation.[95] Scholars agree that remain in' perfectly symbolizes the Johannine motif of indwelling and this indwelling is the essential constitutive principle of all Christian life. Johannine use of the eternal life or indwelling can be easily grasped into an individualistic relationship with God. But the very personal relationship signifies an inescapable social dimension of the concept of life. T. W. Manson puts it rightly that the divine life is a self giving love. As a result those who have committed to life or possess it are obliged to impart it in the world to have life in abundance (10:10). It is to be noted that John's is not merely a contemplative mysticism held in Neo-Platonism. For John, as other NT writers hold, Christianity has its application in the realm of morality, just as moral conduct finds its motivation in God.[96] The friendship with Christ and the living example

---

92 Schneiders, *Written That You May Believe* 170-174.

93 Kanagaraj, *'Mysticism' in the Gospel of John*, 265.

94 Christopher Thomas, *Footwashing in John 13*, 109, 150. I Jn 2:6 also gives the binding nature of moral conduct. Ignatius of Antioch mentions it in the epistle to Polycarp and the Martyrdom of Polycarp 14.2. He suggests that to share a person's *meros* is to share his /her identity or destiny and ultimately in sharing in his/her reward. See also, Bernard H. John, *Critical and Exegetical Commentary on the Gospel According to St. John*, Edinburg: T. and T. Clark, 1928, 461.

95 F. Hauck. '□φείλω,' in *TDNT*, 563. In Lk we have this word in 17:10 to indicate obligatory service of a slave to his master. See also R. H. Lightfoot, *St. John's Gospel: A Commentary*, Oxford: Clarendon, 1956, 270.

96 Culpepper, "The Johannine "Hypodeigma," 133-152.

of this friendship in love renders mysticism and morality inseparable for John.[97]

A strange silence on the word 'mysticism' in the third part of this paper is intentional because of the concern that the text must be spoken. But the exposition makes it evident that the footwashing is deeply mystical. The literary and exegetical analysis of the pericope shows that as a sign of 'complete love' the footwashing signifies the disciples' continued friendship with Jesus. Peter stands as a literary figure through whom the readers come to a greater revelation, that they are not 'low-level beings' but have the inherent potential to be children of God. Thus, they are invited to have a part in the Divine Life. A remote and distancing God becomes an intimate friend in the daily life of the believer. This relationship is one of mutual belonging, intimate and faithful commitment.

The new commandment places 'his own' in the very ordinariness of life of relationship. All these aspects are interwoven in the Christo-centric, soteriological and communitarian (ethical) aspects of the Fourth Gospel. 'To have a part' one needs a right understanding and acceptance of the hour of Jesus. This knowledge of the hour in Johannine thought and washing in the Holy Spirit is a transformative experience of communion with, identity with Jesus. This transformative experience is not inclusive rather other-centered. Therefore, the footwashing is a sign of continued fellowship with Jesus, but it also functions as a sign of their continued readiness for participation and sharing in his identity, mission and destiny. Thus we find a new way of experiencing God in one's life. Therefore the *echeis meros met'emou* echoes the objectives of this seminar. 'Mysticism [...] is the pursuit of communion with, identity with, or conscious awareness of an ultimate reality, divinity, spiritual truth, or God through direct experience, intuition or insight.'

---

[97] McPolin, "Johannine Mysticism," 30.

References

01. Abelson, J., *Jewish Mysticism*, London: G. Bell and Sons, 1913.
02. Allen, Ronald B., *Numbers*. Vol. 2, *The Expositor's Bible Commentary*, ed. Frank E. Gaebelenin, Michigan: Zondervan, 1990.
03. Augustine, St., *Tractates on the Gospel of John 1-10*, trans. John W. Retting, The Fathers of the Church, ed. Thomas P. Halton, Washington: C. U. Press, 1988.
04. Barnabas, Lindars, *The Gospel of John*, Grand Rapids: Eerdmans, 1987.
05. Barrett, C. K., *The Gospel According to St. John*, London: SPCK, 1958.
06. Bautch, Kelley Coblentz, *A Study of the Geography of I Enoch 17-19: No One Has Seen What I Have Seen*, Vol. 81 JsjSup, ed. John J. Collins, Leiden: Brill, 2003.
07. Bieringer, Reimund, and Mary Elsbernd, *Normativity of the Future: Reading Biblical and Other Authoritative Texts in an Eschatological Perspective*, Leuven: Peeters, 2010.
08. Boismard, M. É., "Le Lavement Des Pieds," *Revue Biblique* 71 (1964), 5-24.
09. Borgen, P., *Bread from Heaven: An Exegetical Study of the Concept of Manna in the Gospel of John and the Writing of Philo*, Vol. 10 NovtSup, Leiden: E.J. Brill, 1965.
10. Brown, Raymond E., *The Gospel According to John I-XII*, Vol. 29AB, London: Yale, 1966.
11. Brown, Raymond, *The Gospel According to John (XIII-XXI)*, Vol. 29A AB, London: Yale University Press, 2008.
12. Bultmann, Rudolf, *Theology of the New Testament*, Vol. 2, London: SCM Press, 1955.
13. Bultmann, Rudolf, *The Gospel of John: A Commentary*, trans. G. R. Beasley-Murray, Oxford: Blackwell, 1971.
14. Charan Singh, Maharaj, *St. John the Great Mystic*, Punjab: Radha Soami Satsang Beas, 1974.
15. Chennattu, Rekha M., *Johannine Discipleship as a Covenant Relationship*, Peabody MS: Hendrickson, 2006.
16. Collins, Raymond F., *Christian Morality: Biblical Foundations*. Notre Dame: University of Notre Dame, 1986.
17. Countryman, L. William, *The Mystical Way in the Fourth Gospel*, Philadelphia: Fortress Press, 1987.
18. Culpepper, Alan R., "The Johannine "Hypodeigma": A Reading of John 13," *Semeia* 53 (1991), 133-152.
19. Dahl, N.A., "The Johannine Church and History," in *Current Issues in New Testament Interpretation: Essays in Honour of O.A. Piper*, ed. W. Klassen and G. F. Snyder, 14-30, New York: Harper Row, 1962.

20. DeConick, April D., *Voices of the Mystics: Early Christian Discourse in the Gospels of John and Thomas and Other Ancient Christian Literature* JsntSup, ed. Stanley E. Porter, Sheffield: Sheffield, 2001.
21. Dodd, C.H., *The Interpretation of the Fourth Gospel*, Cambridge: Cambridge University Press, 1960.
22. Dunn, J.D.G., "The Washing of the Disciples' Feet in John 13, 1-20," *ZNW* 61 (1970).
23. Ford, Massyngberde J., "Revelation," in *AB*, New York: Doubleday, 1975.
24. Fortna, Robert T. and Tom Thatcher, *Jesus in Johannine Tradition*, Louisville: West Minister John Knox, 2001.
25. Frey, Forg, "The Bible and the Dead Sea Scrolls: The Second Princeton Symposium on Judaism and Christian Origins," in *The Scrolls and Christian Origins*, ed. James H. Charlesworth, 3, 407-461, Waco: Baylor University press, 2006.
26. Goodenough, Erwin R., *By Light, Light: The Mystical Gospel of Hellenistic Judaism*. New Haven: Yale University, 1935.
27. Hillmer, R. Melvyn, "They Believed in Him: Discipleship in the Johannine Tradition," in *Patterns of Discipleship in the New Testament*, ed. Richard N. Longenecker, 15-37, Cambridge: Eerdmans, 1989.
28. Hoskyns, Edwyn Clement, *The Fourth Gospel*, 2 ed., ed. Francis Noel Davey, London: Faber and Faber, 1956.
29. Howard, Wilbert Francis, *The Fourth Gospel in Recent Criticism and Interpretation*, London: The Epworth Press, 1955.
30. Inge, William Ralph, *Christian Mysticism*, London: Methues, 1899.
31. John, Bernard H., *Critical and Exegetical Commentary on the Gospel According to St. John*, Edinburg: T. and T. Clark, 1928.
32. Kanagaraj, Jey J., "Jesus the King, Merkabah Mysticism and the Gospel of John," *TB* 47/ 2 (1996), 349-366.
33. Kanagaraj, Jey J., *'Mysticism' in the Gospel of John: An Inquiry into Its Background*, Sheffield: Sheffield Academic Press, 1998.
34. Lienhard, Joseph T., *Exodus, Leviticus, Numbers, Deuteronomy*, ed. Thomas C. Oden, Ancient Christian Commentary on Scripture, Illinois: Intervarsity Press, 2001.
35. Lightfoot, R. H., *St. John's Gospel: A Commentary*, Oxford: Clarendon, 1956.
36. Lohmeyer, Ernst, "Die Fusswaschung," *ZNW* 38 (1939), 74-94.
37. Louth, Andrew, *The Origins of the Christian Mystical Tradition: From Plato to Denys*, Oxford: Oxford University Press, 1981, 2007.
38. Macleod, C. W., "Allegory and Mysticism in Origen and Gregory of Nyssa," *JTS* 22/2 (1971), 362-379.
39. McPolin, James, "Johannine Mysticism," *The Way* 1 (1978), 25-35.

40. Mealand, David L., "The Language of Mystical Union in the Johannine Writings," *The Downside Review* 95 (1977), 19-34.
41. Michl, Johann, "Der Sinn Der Fusswaschung," *Biblica* (1959), 697-708.
42. Mlakuzhyil, George, *The Christocentric Literary Structure of the Fourth Gospel*, Rome: Editrice Pontificio Instituto Biblico, 1987.
43. Neirynck, Frans, "John and the Synoptics," In *BETL*, ed. F. Van Segbroeck, 364-400, Leuven University Press, 1982.
44. Odeberg, H., *The Fourth Gospel Interpreted in Its Relation to Contemporaneous Religious Currents in Palestine and the Hellenistic Oriental World*, Uppsala-Och-Stockholm, 1929.
45. Preiss, T., *Life in Christ*, London: SCM Press, 1954.
46. Pring, J.T., "Mystikismos," in *The Oxford Dictionary of Modern Greek: Greek-English and English-Greek*, 207, Oxford: Clarendon, 1982.
47. Richter, G., "Die Fusswaschung: John 13, 1-20," *MThZ* 16 (1965), 13-26.
48. Rowland, Christopher and R. A. Christopher Morray-Jones, *The Mystery of God: Early Jewish Mysticism and the New Testament*, Leiden, Boston: Brill, 2009.
49. Sabbe, Maurits, "Johan and the Synoptists: Neirynck vs Boismard," *ETL* 56 (1980), 125-139.
50. Sabbe, Maurits, "The Footwashing in John 13 and Its Relation to the Synoptic Gospels," *ETL* 58 (1982), 279-308.
51. Sasse, Hermann, "Aieon," in *TDNT*, ed. Kittel Gerhard, 1, 197-209, Michigan: Eerdmans, 1964.
52. Schnackenburg, Rudolf, *The Gospel According to St. John: Commentary on Chapters 13-21*, Vol. 3, HTCNT, New York: Crossroad Publishing Company, 1982.
53. Schneider, J., "Xylon," in *TDNT*, ed. Kittel Gerhard, 4, 37-40, Michigan: Eerdmans, 1967.
54. Schneiders, Sandra M., *Written That You May Believe: Encountering Jesus in the Fourth Gospel,* New York: The Crossroad, 1999.
55. Scholem, Gershom G., *Major Trends in Jewish Mysticism,* London: Thames and Hudson, 1955.
56. Schweitzer, Albert, *The Mysticism of Paul the Apostle*, London: Black, 1931.
57. Segovia, Fernando F., "John 13 1-20, the Footwashing in the Johannine Tradition," *ZNW* 73 (1982), 31-51.
58. Stauffer, E., "Eis," in *TDNT*, ed. Kittel Gerhard, 2, 420-442, Michigan: Eerdmans, 1964.
59. Thomas, John Christopher, *Footwashing in John 13 and the Johannine Community*, Sheffield: Sheffield, 1991.

60. Thomassen, Einar, *Heracleon*, Vol. 132 NovtSup, ed. Tuomas Rasimus, Leiden-Boston: Brill, 2010.
61. Thompson, Marianne Meye, "Eternal Life in the Gospel of John," *Ex auditu* 5 (1989), 35-55.
62. Underhill, Evelyn, *Mystic Way: A Psychological Study in Christian Origins*, Whitefish: Kessinger, 1913.
63. Van Belle, Gilbert, "Johannine Bibliography 1966-1985: A Cumulative Bibliography on the Fourth Gospel," in *BETL*, 82, 1-500, Leuven: University Press, 1988.
64. Van Belle, Gilbert, "The Signs Source in the Fourth Gospel: Historical Survey and Critical Evaluation of the Semeia Hypothesis," in *BETL*, 116, 1-503, Leuven: University Press, 1994.
65. von Hügel, B. F., "The Gospel of St. John," in *Encyclopedia Britannica*, 15, Cambridge: Cambridge University Press, 1911.
66. Weiser, A., "Joh 13, 12-20 -Zufügung Eines Späteren Herausgebers?" *BZ* 12 (1968), 252-57.
67. Weiss, Herold, "Foot Washing in the Johannine Community," *NovT* 21 (1979), 298-325.
68. Zorrilla, Hugo, "A Service of Sacrificial Love: Footwashing (John 13:1-11)," *Direction* 24/1 (1995), 74-84.

12

Dialogue along Mystics' Spirituality

Models of Effective Interreligious Dialogue in Religious Pluralistic Societies

Dr. Marinus C. Iwuchukwu
Assistant Professor of Theology
Duquesne University, Pittsburgh, USA

1. Introduction

Reflecting on the importance of mysticism and its values in religion, with special reference to the Abrahamic religions and religions that originated from the Indian subcontinent, Wayne Teasdale said, "All these religious traditions emerge out of mystical experience [...] One can almost say that the real *religion* of humankind isn't religion at all; rather, it is mystical spirituality, the bosom out of which the religions themselves have been born" (91). This statement underscores the importance and premiere value, placed by most religious traditions on mystics and mysticism. The popularity of mystics in every religion and society at large, and the respect they command from both adherents and admirers are common knowledge. Mystics are known to identify union with the Ultimate Reality or God (as is known in the Abrahamic religions) as a need that transcends particular religious persuasion; an indispensable need for every creature. This paper will critically examine the dialogic values decipherable from mystics like Francis of Assisi, Rabia al-Adawiyya, Sri Ram Thakur, Kabir, and Azriel ben Menahem that will benefit people living in religious pluralistic societies. It will also focus extensively on how the exemplary lives of these mystics provide valuable lessons for effectively implementing the dialogue of life and dialogue of action[1] in religious pluralistic societies. Those two forms of dialogue, as this paper will illustrate, are invariably contingent on as well as promote the social, economic, and political realities of the society. Finally, this paper will propose ways, followers and admirers of these mystics can collaborate with people of other faith traditions in the society towards achieving the kind of humane, godly, non-violent, and peaceful society, which the mystics would advocate.

2. The Spirituality of Mystics in Response to the World Around Them

At this juncture, brief biography of the mystics earlier mentioned will be presented, with the intent of highlighting some of their spiritual and human attributes that lend them to us as models for effective interreligious dialogue. It is important to state upfront, at this point, that the choice of these mystics is both random and deliberate. They are random selections, because the mystics referenced in this paper did not unequivocally teach or advocate interreligious dialogue as we understand the term today. However, knowing what we know today about other religions and the indispensability of interreligious dialogue in our religious pluralistic societies and looking closing into the lives of many mystics of different religions, it is implied and logically deducible that they will not be adverse to dialogic activities between peoples of different faith traditions. They are also deliberate selections, because each of the mystic identified in this essay reflects in either her or his spirituality, philosophy of life or theological assumptions, concepts and ideas that will promote healthy interreligious dialogue in a milieu of religious pluralism.

---

[1] See the Pontifical Council for Inter-Religious Dialogue and the Congregation for the Evangelization of Peoples, *Dialogue and Proclamation*, 42 (19 May, 1991). The English translation is obtainable in William Burrows, ed. *Redemption and Dialogue: Reading Redemptoris Missio and Dialogue and Proclamation*. Maryknoll, N.Y: Orbis Books, 1993, 93-118. This document identifies four different forms of interreligious dialogue, namely: the dialogue of life; dialogue of action, dialogue of theological exchange; and dialogue of religious experience.

3. Rabia al-Adawiyya (c. 718-801 C.E)

Rabi'a al-Adawiyya of Basra was born about a century after the beginning of Islam (c. 718 C.E.) and died in 801 C.E. She has been described as a "model of piety and love of God" by both Islamic and non-Islamic scholars (Smith xxvi). Accounts of her spiritually heroic and exemplary life and thoughts emerged and circulated around Europe from the fourteenth century.[2] Although not much of historical record or texts are available of her, but as Annemarie Schimmel rightly observed, "her legendary biography has served as the ideal pattern for the way of someone who strives for unconditional love of God and surrender to the will of the Divine Beloved, and the absoluteness of her devotion has inspired thousands of men and women on the mystical path (Smith xxviii)."

Rabi'a was born into a Sufi home, her father is said to have reflected the Sufi spirituality of totally depending on God as the sole provider of all one has even in dire conditions.[3] It is speculated that Rabi'a lost both parents at an early age and was separated from her sister due to a severe feminine in Basra. It was during this separation that she was sold into slavery by a stranger. Her intense spirituality, which her master witnessed, led to her regaining her freedom. She chose to be celibate in a society where that was rare, notwithstanding the pressures she received from suitors (Smith 12). As an ascetic Sufi, Rabi'a chose to live a life of poverty and self-denial. She had disciples and admirers who consulted with her on many spiritual matters. She was reputed with very sharp wit and deep insight on religious and spiritual matters. She was known to spend hours in prayers and contemplation.[4]

Although Rabi'a was ascetic, she still had strong sense of solidarity with the needy and poor in the society. She did not measure the value of people by their material possession or worth. She was known to be

[2] Joinville, the chancellor of King Louis IX of France wrote stories about her. Depiction of her image carrying water and fire on the street is also engraved in a European painting. See Smith, xxvii ff.

[3] There is a story of the father refusing to ask from anyone the swaddling cloth the wife asked for after the delivery of Rabi'a hoping that God will provide, which eventually became the case through an unsolicited donation from the Emir (Cf. Sells, 155-156).

[4] For the Sufis such prayer is not simply the traditional *salat* but contemplative prayers (Cf. Smith, 26).

generous to those in need and provided as much as she could to the poor and needy when she came across them. There is a story of her giving out the only two loaves of bread she had, which were for two sheikhs who visited her home, to a beggar who came to her door. She later received some fresh supplies to meet the hungry needs of her guests (Smith). Appropriately, she considered kindness to the beggar as pleasing God. Therefore, for Rabi'a works of charity and other good works for the common good are considered as pleasing God.

Rabi'a is most popular for her views and practical demonstration of love for God. The Sufi concept of God as the Beloved evolved from Rabi'a's deep commitment to God in love and reference to God as her Beloved. Rabi'a's passion and devotion to loving God is described as the "disinterested love" of God; a spirituality that is original to her in the Sufi tradition. She advocates a love of God, which transcends the fear of punishment or hope of reward. Al-Hujwiri appropriately outlines the differences between an ordinary believer and that of a mystic in their relationship to God and according to him the relationship of the mystic is defined by love and intimacy (Smith 91). To demonstrate Rabi'a's commitment to intimacy with God she said, "The groaning and the yearning of the lover of God will not be satisfied until it is satisfied in the Beloved" (Smith 98). These words parallel St. Augustine of Hippo's popular saying, "for thou hast made us for thyself and restless is our heart until it comes to rest in thee" (Augustine 31).

To underscore her strong stand on loving God, she maintained that God is absolutely deserving of love not on the basis of the expectation of reward or avoidance of punishment. It is therefore, understandable that Rabi'a has been very popularly associated with saying: "O Lord, if I worship you out of fear of hell, burn me in hell. If I worship you in the hope of paradise, forbid it to me. And if I worship you for your own sake, do not deprive me of your eternal beauty."[5]

---

[5] See Sells (169). These words are re-echoed from a Christian theological worldview in the "Hymn of Love" of Francis Xavier as follows: O GOD, I love Thee for Thyself,/ And not that I may Heaven gain,/ Nor because those who love Thee not,/ Must suffer Hell's eternal pain./ Thou O my Jesus! Thou didst me Upon the Cross embrace;/For me didst bear the nails and spear/ And manifold disgrace;/ And griefs and torments numberless, And sweat of agony;/E'en death itself - and all for one Who was Thine enemy./Then why, O blessed Jesus Christ, Should I not love Thee well:/Not for the

As a mystic, love was at the heart of Rabi'a's search for union with God. She left for her followers and admirers lots to learn about complete commitment to loving God. More importantly, she is a vivid reminder that loving God is a duty and responsibility that all human beings must exercise, as a gesture of reciprocation to a God who is all loving. Loving God should not be for a reward or fear of punishment.

4. Azriel Ben Menahem (1160-1238)

He is the founder of the speculative Kabbalah and was popularly called "The Saint." He was born in Gerona. At an early age, he was attracted to the mystical studies that had started to spread in Spain. He however left Spain to southern France to become a student of the renowned Kabbalist, Isaac the Blind. When he left France he traveled extensively in Spain promoting the spirituality of the Kabbalah movement. That mission did not yield much. He returned to his place of birth, Gerona, to establish a Kabbalah school. Following the speculative pattern of theology, he wrote a commentary on the Ten *Sefirot*, in the form of questions and answers. He also wrote another commentary in which the 613 Jewish mitzvoth are explained as originating from the Torah.

Theologically, he argued that God can best be understood through negative reference. That is a theological assumption, which echoes the Apophatic theology of Eastern Orthodox Christianity. According to him what God is not can easily be ascertained not what God is, hence for him the greatest qualification for God is "Endlessness" (Jewish 373).

Using the philosophy of "*En-Sof*," he attempted to explain the being of God, which is neither dependent on anything nor diminished by God's act of creation. He denies the eternal existence of the universe, while strongly affirming the infinite nature of God. He also rejected the Platonic idea of God as a primary matter. Rather, he embraced the Neo-platonic view of emanation as the principle of God's creative work of the universe. According to the emanation theory of Azriel:

---

sake of winning Heaven, Or of escaping Hell;/Not with the hope of gaining aught, not seeking a reward;/But, as Thyself hast loved me, O ever-loving Lord?/E'en so I love Thee, and will love, and in Thy praise will sing. See http://www.2heartsnetwork.org/Xavier.htm.

> [...] the act of creation did not consist in producing an absolutely new thing; it was merely a transformation of potential existence into realized existence [...] This material world, being limited and not perfect, could not proceed directly from the *En-Sof*; neither could it be independent of Him; for in that case He would be imperfect. There must have been, therefore, intermediaries between the *En-Sof* and the material world; and those intermediaries were the Ten *Sefirot* (Jewish 374).

The Ten *Sefirot* are divided according to their nature to three main groups. The first consist of the first three, which are considered superior and come from the world of thought, the next three from the world of soul, and the last four represent the corporal world. They all depend upon one another and linked in a chain like formation. They all have positive and passive qualities, namely emanating and receiving abilities. Azriel qualifies the first Sefirah as the "Will." According to Azriel, these ten *Sefirot* correspond to the ten parts of the human organism and different ten refractions of light (ibid.).

Azriel's speculative Kabbalistic philosophy emphasizes divine relationship with creation through emanation and the human search for union with the immutable and infinite God (the *En-Sof*). This is a philosophical assumption he shares with the Neo-Platonists. Azriel therefore, finds spiritual companionship with the Neo-Platonists, as well as with followers of Pseudo-Dynosius and Western theologians who are attracted to the theology and spirituality of *via negativa*. With these groups, Azriel is able to demonstrate the positive impact of their spiritual disposition on the quality of life followers of his brand of spirituality impact the society with. The Kabbalah movement ceased from being a path for select few and spiritual elites to become a spiritual path many ordinary Jews espoused because of its pragmatic impact on the quality of life of its adherents. People were able to recognize and appreciate the dove-tailed nature of the theoretical Kabbalah and the practical Kabbalah (Birnbaum 533). This merge or development is not accidental but consistent with the origin of Kabbalah and its dependence on the Hebrew scripture for illumination (*zohar*).

5. Francis of Assisi (1182-1226)

Francis of Assisi is one of the few Christian saints who command universal appeal and respect from people of different religious traditions. From the moment he received his call to serve the need of rebuilding the Church, he was determined to live strictly by the standards of the Good News proclaimed by Christ. He was born to a wealthy merchant Pietro Bernardone and his wife Pica in Umbria, Assisi in 1182. As a young man Francis had all the trappings of one born with a silver spoon; flamboyantly showing off his family's wealth in the little town of Assisi. At age 20 as one of the local soldiers he had a firsthand experience of the horror of war as he was captured as a prisoner of war by the Perugians. He remained in Perugia for about a year and fell ill during the period. His period of recovery from the attack of fever afforded him the time for deeper reflection on life and what he wanted from life. Francis cut back on his extravagant lifestyle and began to spend his money in support of charitable causes and providing for needy people he came across. He had a life changing experience at the little country chapel of San Damiano. While praying in that chapel one day he heard a voice asking him to rebuild God's church that was in ruin. He took the message literarily and embarked on selling some of his father's business items to raise money towards reconstructing the country chapel. This action infuriated his father and created a rift between him and his father for a while. However, Francis was now convinced that he had a divine calling to help the poor and support good causes that will evoke positive image for the Church. Francis was reputed to have vowed spousal relationship with "Lady Poverty" (Robinson). Therefore, he was satisfied living without any attachment to material things. Nonetheless, he went out of his way to care for the sick, especially lepers and provided for the poor. He will later have a group of followers who admired his spirituality and works of charity and eventually form a community of friars, who considered each other as equals and vowed to a life of poverty.

On April 16, 1209, Pope Innocent III officially approved the Order of Friars Minor. Although this was the era of the Crusades, Francis, while in favor of seeking the conversion of Muslims (popularly known as the Saracens), was neither in favor of the violence of the Crusade nor of forced conversion.

Francis made two failed attempts to bring the Gospel to the Saracens between 1212 and 1214. The first was to Syria and the second was to Morocco. Francis finally made a successful trip to Damietta, Egypt in the heat of the Fifth Crusade, August 1219. He intended to stop the crusaders from fighting the Saracens, but was unsuccessful. After the defeat of the Crusaders by the Saracens Francis succeeded in gaining access into the Saracens' camp. He and his companions were taken prisoners and brought before Sultan Malek Al-Kamil. However, the sultan received him and his companions as free people having satisfactorily concluded on the innocuous personality of Francis. Francis spent a few days with the Sultan and his court and made a deep impression on them. This dialogic encounter must have deeply influenced Francis and changed his perception of Muslims favorably and positively. Francis went back to Italy a completely changed person, changes that will be reflected in the modifications made in the rules guiding the Friar Minors as well as Francis' decision to step down as the General of the order.

Among the changes made in the rules of the Friar Minors after Francis' return from meeting with the Sultan include the following: (i) The encounter with the Saracens is primarily to be one of pure presence: serving, peacefully, non-violent, indeed obedient, and subservient presence, which attests and confesses the Christian faith simply as solidarity lived out between brothers and sisters. (ii) However, the explicit preaching of the gospel is secondary. It may take place only if an additional inner impulse, the recognized will of God, is behind it (Rotzetter 108).

It is fair to surmise that Francis' meeting with Sultan Malek offered him a genuine opportunity for dialogue of life, dialogue of theological exchange, and dialogue of religious experience. He emerged out of that dialogic encounter thoroughly embracing Muslims as brothers and sisters. It is observed that Francis tried to implement some of the ideas he got from his dialogic encounter with the Saracens in their Islamic liturgy to some of his spiritual exercises.[6]

[6] In her book, Kathleen A. Warren strongly speculates that Francis tried to emulate some of the Islamic acts of piety and theology of God in his teachings and religious practices. Warren argues that Francis was particularly intrigued with the Islamic concept of total submission to the will of Allah.

Francis of Assisi leaves behind a wealth of lessons for the world of his time. And many of those lessons are relevant to the focus of this paper, especially in the area of seeking better relationship and understanding with people of different religious faith traditions. It is certainly in honor of the personality of St. Francis as the bridge between Christianity and brothers and sisters of other faith traditions and his stand for global and ecological peace that in the fall of 1986 Pope John Paul II invited religious leaders of different faith traditions to Assisi for a day of prayer for peace.

6. Sri Ram Thakur (1860-1949)

Sri Ram Thakur was born in 1860 at Dingamanik in the district of Faridpur, Bangladesh into a Brahmin family and was little known outside Bengal. His followers came from all walks of life and religious persuasions. He was widely regarded as a saintly figure and among Hindus considered as an avatar of one of the deities. He must have imbibed deep spiritual and ascetic life from his father. His father was an ascetic, who was devoted to penance in the tradition of the tantras (Kaibalyadham). Ram Thakur was known to have predicted some major events of global proportion, like the beginning of World War II, dropping of the bomb in Hiroshima in 1945, and the assignation of Mahatma Gandhi in 1948 (Kaibalyadham). He was revered by his followers many of whom were dalits and people of non-Hindu religions. He understood his mission to be one of helping people find relief from the hardship and difficulties of life. Therefore, he focused on feeding the poor and needy, providing education and medical care for the less privileged. These charities are still carried on by his followers today. On his followers' homepage, some of the activities the group listed following the instruction of their founder include: (i) To lay emphasis on rendering welfare services to the society with a spiritual outlook. (ii) To propagate the ideas of Sri Thakur to develop and extend the philanthropic and charitable activities of Dhams/Ashrams. (iii) To arrange for the free education of the poor and needy people of the society. (iv) To arrange for the free treatment and medicines for the poor people of the society through a Charitable dispensary of Dham (Kaibalyadham).

Sri Thakur considered his spiritual message as universally applicable to people of every religion. Therefore, the set up of the worship space was such that people of other faith traditions could use it to pray according to their traditions and find spiritual fulfillment. Sri Thakur died in 1949. His followers reflecting on his life and mission said this about him:

> To save and salvage human beings from the unending and unbearable pains and misery, injustice and corruption of the materialistic world, the Almighty God comes in human form to this world from time to time. The Saviour shows the right path to set them free from their predicament. By His divine love and by demonstrating the ideal way of life. He uplifts the ordinary human folk to extra-ordinary level of spiritual enlightenment and God-consciousness. Sri Sri Ramthakur is such a great soul (Kaibalyadham).

7. Kabir (1440-1518)

Kabir is an Indian mystical poet, who used songs to reflect the depth of his understanding about the divine and relationship with the divine. He is referenced in this discussion, not merely because he stands out as a bridge mender between Islamic, Sikh, and Hindu spiritualities, but more importantly, because of what I consider his thoroughness in reflecting the essence of human spirituality. One not necessarily based on religious affiliation but rather one that transcends mere loyalty to a religious tradition. According to him, God is directly accessible to everyone regardless of people's religious affiliations and even in the absence of religious rituals. According to Nabhadas, one of his ardent followers and biographer, "Never did Kabir accept the distinctions of caste or the four stages of life, nor did he revere the six philosophers. 'Religion devoid of love is heresy,' he declared. 'Yoga and penance, fasting and alms-giving are, without meditation, empty,' he affirmed" (Cf. Sethi, 4). Kabir, was born a low caste of Muslim parents. He rejected the caste system not only because of the disadvantage he personally suffered being a low caste but also because he was completely against the social philosophy of dehumanizing people, which the caste system does. He was a strong believer in equality of everyone, stemming from his understanding of the dignity each individual possesses as creatures of one God. His belief in the dignity of every human person based on the divine touch in each person eventually made his Guru, Ramanand, who was known to resent low caste people, to change his attitude towards and perception of people of low caste. Guru Ramanand finally came to appreciate and embrace Kabir, despite his low caste status and even admitted other low caste disciples subsequently (Sethi, 11ff).

Although Kabir was strongly influenced by both Hindu and Islamic mysticism, he did not consider either of them as absolutely necessary for effective communication and relationship with God. Like many mystics, his universe consisted of three orders: becoming, being, and God. He was convinced about the immanence of God, hence his saying: "The Lord is in me, the Lord is in you, seek for Him within you" (Ferguson 99). In his songs and poetry, he profoundly enunciated the indispensability of love and loving relationship in the search for union with God. He stated that God is revealed in life, but more eminently in love. Therefore, he said, "One Love it is that pervades the whole world, few there are who know it fully" (ibid.). This statement is the underpinning of all mystics referenced in this work. More importantly, it goes to explain how union with God is best attained through loving relationship with God. And in the case of Kabir, as with other mystics like Francis of Assisi, Ram Thakur, Azriel Ben Menahem, and Rabi'a Al-Awadiyya, the love for God is synchronous with the love for fellow human beings. And as Kabir, will state, this love is universal, embracing all creatures of God as Francis of Assisi empirically demonstrated.

8. Solidarity of Mystics as Exemplary for Dialogue of Action and Life

According to Swidler, Duran, and Firestone:

> [...] the mystics appear to all meet together on a high level of unity with the Ultimate Reality no matter how it is described, including even in the more philosophical systems like Neoplatonism. The greatest of the Muslim Sufis, Jewish Kabbalists, Hindu Bhaktas, Christian Mystics, Buddhist Bodhisattvas, and Platonist Philosophers all seem to be at

> one in their striving for and experience of unity with the One, which in the West is called God, *Theos*" (19).

The words of these authors summarize the solidarity mystics share with each other notwithstanding differences in faith traditions. Normatively, mystics practice more thorough religious rituals and implement arduous efforts towards their search for union with the divine or ultimate reality. Hindu religion credits mystics among the few who are able to attain *Moksha* and the same holds true of the search to reach either *Nirvana* or transformation for Buddhists or union with God for people of the Abrahamic religions. Characteristically, mystics are known to overcome many limitations, including those imposed by their particular religious traditions. Teasdale succinctly states,

> The mystical life, in its maturity, is characteristically, naturally, even organically interspiritual because of the inner freedom and liberation the mystical journey ignites in the depths of the person. It frees us from the obstacles within us that would hold us back from the generosity and willingness to partake in the mystical springs of other religions (92).

This unique characteristic of mystics unquestionably presents them as credible models of effective dialogue with people of other faith traditions. This is because dialogue at its best explores the good of the other and invites the interlocutors to willfully appreciate the good of the order. The Vatican document *Dialogue and Proclamation* alludes to this development in the dialogic process and encounter (Pontifical #32).

Ordinarily, mystics will seamlessly collaborate with each other towards dialogue of theological exchange as well as dialogue of religious experience. The choice to focus on how they will promote dialogues of action and life in solidarity is borne out of the need to expand the usefulness of these saintly people to the broader society. Dialogues of action and life are those forms of dialogue every person in the society should engage in to promote the needs of the individual, community, and common goods.

Each of the mystics reviewed above was transparently friendly and accepting of the people they lived with and demonstrated genuine and honest characteristics of good neighbors. However, with the exception of the Indian mystics, all others reviewed in this study lived in very culturally and religiously homogenous societies. In the case of the Azriel Ben Menahem of Gerona, he lived in a Middle Age society where people were confined to particular ethnic/religious communities, so that as a Jew, he was limited, for the most part, in his interactions with non-Jews. Notwithstanding his physical, social, and religious limitations, he actually made overtures to the philosophers of his milieu, whom he thought will appreciate the philosophy of his theological assumption, but was turned down. The Indian and Bangladeshi mystics, Kabir and Sri Thakur, had extensive relationship with people from different religious traditions found in their worlds at the time.

Although Sri Thakur was born into a Brahmin family, he engaged in positive relationship and friendship with dalits and non-Hindu religious people. Kabir, on his part, conveniently related with Muslims and Hindus alike. Although, Francis of Assisi considered himself a person with a mission to convert sinners to the Church and God, he did not relate with people he met on the streets from the perspective of sinners and saints. Hence his support and charitable disposition was not focused on people's faith or religious identity. His embrace of the life of poverty was to share with the poor the experience of non-dependence on material possession as well as to identify with the life of severe depravity of the poor. The poor and needy do not need any religious label to merit his support, affection, and affinity. Francis' trip to Egypt to meet with Sultan Malik al-Kamil, although motivated by the desire to seek the conversion of the Muslim, offered him a unique opportunity of a dialogue of life. In his interactions with his guest, he became better informed about Islam and the religious practices of Muslims and that experience changed his perception of Muslims. This change in perception resulted in the modification of the rule of his order about the people they ordinarily identified as the Saracens. Francis apparently became opposed not only to a forced conversion of the Saracens but also of encountering them with the primary intention to convert them to Christianity.

It is therefore imperative that dialogue of life and dialogue of action call for solidarity with people of other faith traditions. It is also imperative from the philosophical and theological assumptions of the mystics considered in this study, that engaging in dialogue of action with people of other faith traditions will receive the mystics' approval. Azriel's concept of human relationship with God underscores the common origin and destiny of all people as well as the universality of the invitation to demonstrate human response of love towards God through loving relationship with people. In the light of this understanding, joint activities by people of different faith traditions for the common good and service to human community will certainly be approved by Azriel.

According to *Dialogue and Proclamation*, dialogue of action calls for Christians and people of other faith traditions collaborating "for the integral development and liberation of people" (Pontifical, 42). Therefore, based on the spirituality and theological worldviews of Azriel, Rabi'a Al-Awadiyya, Sri Thakur, Francis, and Kabir, collaboration of religions and people of different faith traditions towards projects intended to provide education, health services, shelter, food, and clothing to the poor and needy are not only acceptable but recommended. Sri Thakur and Francis spent their lives caring for the needs of the poor and less privileged. In the case of Francis, Kabir, and Rabi'a, they chose to experience the social and living conditions of the poor by willfully living in poverty. Rabi'a, Kabir, and Francis shared and gave out their own personal belongings to the poor they came across. Kabir would require from people who love God, manifest acts of charity and emphatically stated that those are actions and services recommended to all moral beings regardless of their faith tradition.

Smith reflects on the thoughts of a renowned Muslim mystic, Al-Qushayri, who defines love as "the enduring inclination of the love-intoxicated heart, the preference of the Beloved over all companions, harmony with the Beloved, whether present or absent, the effacement of the lover's qualities and the establishment of the Beloved's essence, and finally the agreement of the heart with the Will of the Lord" (93). It is understood, especially from the impression given by Smith and the references to the thoughts of many Sufi Muslims, that love is synonymous with God (Smith 88-136). This is certainly synchronous with a Judeo-Christian understanding of the relationship between God and love. Therefore, the epistle of John summarizes the ontology of love thus "He who loves lives in God and God lives in him" (1Jn. 4:16).

The philosophy of "disinterested love" of God, which Rabi'a strongly advocated can be applied to support the needs of the common good. Therefore, if dialogue of action will promote this good, then it is both expedient and recommended for people of every religion in the society to be involved in it and encourage it. To do so, there is need for total and unbiased commitment to the processes of dialogue of action and dialogue of life, regardless of the length of time it takes or the rigors they entail to become realized. The principle of "disinterested love" is necessary for a complete focus on ones goals and objectives in life.

The ultimate transformation and union with the divine will, which results from "disinterested love" leaves everyone involved with only one choice in life, namely acting in accord with the will of God. Although the desired ultimate union requires that mystics divest in human and material needs, they are not removed from empathizing or finding solidarity with the poor, oppressed, and victims of social injustice in the society. In reality, many mystics have more passionately identified with the lowest of the low at the height of bonding with the divine.

9. Invaluable Need for Dialogues of Action and Life

At the heart of the search for ongoing and healthy interreligious dialogue in pluralistic societies is also the search for solidarity among the different religions.[7] To achieve such solidarity, which addresses the common good and goals of human society, the dialogues of action and dialogue of live are indispensable. Human societies have continued to drift away from the old mono-cultural and mono-religious settings. Religious pluralism has become a norm of post-modern society by default. It is not conceivable to see societies become less pluralistic given the way the world is developing (except ethnic/religious cleansing or genocide

[7] See John Paul II, *Redemptoris Missio*. John Paul II strongly advocated interreligious dialogue between Christians and people of all faith traditions because he strongly believed in not only the presence of the Spirit in the lives of people of other faith traditions but also in their religion. Therefore, it is only logical, that Christians work together with these people in search for more peaceful world and a world where social justice and concern for human dignity and respect are of premier importance.

become an acceptable social order). The economic and social factors that are driving migration and settlement of people are no longer dependent on religious or cultural identities of people. While we may not be able to stop the spread of pluralism, we can significantly determine how to best live with each other in the interest of the common good and for the benefit of the community. Therefore, promotion of effective dialogues of action and life, is necessary to maintain peace, non-violence, social justice, preservation of human dignity and equality of all people of diverse faith traditions living in the same geo-political space.

The Federation of the Asian Bishop' Conference (FABC) recommends the exercise of dialogue in three different areas of life in Asia, which are: dialogue with the Asian poor, intercultural dialogue, and interreligious dialogue. This body of religious leaders appears to comprehend the need for collaboration with other religious groups in Asia towards effective dialogue of action and dialogue of life. According to its 1992 plenary session, the FABC was strongly convinced about its role in the Asian continent as "a Church that faithfully and lovingly witnesses to the Risen Lord Jesus and reaches out to the people of other faiths and persuasions in a dialogue of life towards the integral liberation of all" (Eilers 287-288). Such collaboration will be helpful to promote education for the youth, establishment of health clinics and hospitals, and running cooperatives that provide affordable food, clothing, and household needs. These collaborative efforts will not only serve the needs of the community and common good, they will also strengthen and foster healthier and better relationship among the religions and their followers.

There are a number of such joint projects serving the needs of the community and the common good in different cities in the United States of America and parts of Asia. Among the ones that come to mind are: (i) Global Peace Works, with main office in New York, but actively functioning in Asia;[8] (ii) The Dorothy Day Center Food Ministry in Oklahoma City, Oklahoma, USA;[9] (iii) Interfaith Families Project of

---

[8] To learn more about this organization go to their webpage: http://globalpeaceworks.org.

[9] The website of this organization is: http://www.peaceforlife.org/projects/palestine/about.html.

the Greater Washington, DC Areas in USA;[10] (iv) Project Interfaith is a multi-faith organization geared towards better understanding of different faith tradition and providing training and education in the community. It is located in Omaha, Nebraska, USA;[11] (v) Palestine in Solidarity – Peace for Life, a group of people of faith interested in the Palestinian struggle based in Quezon City, Philippines.[12]

10. Conclusion

At the heart of the mystics' relationship with the other was a strong moral sense to love. In addition, their support for the needy and poor originates from devout compassion. Francis of Assisi strongly underlined his marriage to "Lady Poverty." Rabi'a, Kabir, and Sri Thakur all had deep sense of affinity with the poor and happily lived lives that were devoid of dependence on material possessions. Azriel's insight into loving God can be interpreted to have empirically translated into strong sense of obligation to love people through service and support for the needy.

Therefore, to successfully engage in dialogue of life with people of other faith traditions, one has to genuinely love them and desire good neighborly relationship with them. In the same vein choosing to collaborate with people of other faith traditions to promote just cause and bring liberation to the less privileged in the society, a compassionate disposition is indispensable. It follows then that imbibing a strong sense of obligation to love and be compassionate, which the mystics had, people living in religious pluralistic societies will be able to engage in meaningful dialogues of life to promote better human relationships and respect for each other, as well as collaborate with each other to achieve noble goals for the common good. Mystics therefore, can be seen as great role models for the promotion of the desired progressive interreligious dialogue in religious pluralistic societies today. Since mystics generally enjoy loyalty and credibility from followers and admirers, they can use their influence and respect to urge their followers and admirers to

[10] For more detailed information about this organization, which is one of its kind in the USA visit their website, http://iffp.net/.

[11] For more information about this organization visit their website on: http://projectinterfaith.blogspot.com/.

[12] For more information visit this organization's website: http://www.peaceforlife.org/projects/palestine/about.html.

comprehend what they appreciate in others who are different, towards more healthy dialogues among the followers of different faith traditions in the pluralist societies today.

References

01. Augustine, *Confessions and Enchiridion*, trans. Albert Cook Outler, Louisville, Kentucky: Westminster John Knox Press, 2006.
02. Birnbaum, Philip, *Encyclopedia of Jewish Concepts*, New York: Hebrew Publishing Company, 1995.
03. Eilers, Franz-Josef, ed. *For All the People of Asia*, vol. 2, Documents from 1992 to 1996, Quezon City: Claretian Publication, 1997.
04. Ferguson, John, *An Illustrated Encyclopedia of Mysticism and the Mystery Religions*, New York: A Continuum Book, The Seabury Press, 1977.
05. John Paul II. *Redemptoris Missio*, On the permanent Validity of the Church's Missionary Mandate, December 07, 1990, http://www.vatican.va/ holy_father/ john_paul_ii/encyclicals/documents/hf_jp-ii_enc_07121990_redemptoris-missio_en.html. Accessed 10/10/2010.
06. Kaibalyadham, Sri Sri. "Sri Sri Ramthakur – Life Sketch," Sri Sri Ramthakur The Great Saviour, 2006-2010. http://www.srisriramthakur.org/ page.asp? GoToPage=10002&SP=1. Accessed 10/09/ 2010.
07. Pontifical Council for Inter-Religious Dialogue and the Congregation for the Evangelization of Peoples. *Dialogue and Proclamation* (19 may, 1991), ed. William Burrows. *Redemption and Dialogue: Reading Redemptoris Missio and Dialogue and Proclamation*. Maryknoll, N.Y: Orbis Books, 1993, 93-118.
08. Robinson, Paschal, "St. Francis of Assisi." *The Catholic Encyclopedia*. Vol. 6, New York: Robert Appleton Company, 1909. 5 Nov. 2010 <http://www. newadvent.org/ cathen/06221a.htm>. Accessed 10/08/2010.
09. Rotzetter, Anton, "Francis of Assisi: A Bridge To Islam." *Frontier Violations*, eds. Felix Wilfred and Oscar Beozzo, London: SCM Press and Maryknoll, New York: Orbis Books, 1999.
10. Sells, Michael A., ed. *Early Islamic Mysticism – Sufi, Qur'an, Mi'Raj, Poetic and Theological Writings*, New York and Mahwah, NJ: Paulist Press, 1996.
11. Sethi, V.K: *Kabir - The Weaver of God's Name*, Punjab, India: Radha Soami Satsang Beas, 1984.
12. Smith, Margaret, *Rabi'a the Mystic and her Fellow-saints in Islam*, London and New York: Cambridge University Press, 1984.
13. Swidler, Leonard, Khalid Duran, and Reuven Firestone, *Trialogue: Jews, Christians, and Muslims in Dialogue*, New London, Connecticut: Twenty-Third Publications, 2007.

14. Teasdale, Wayne, "Mysticism as the Crossing of Ultimate Boundaries: A Theological Reflection," *Frontier Violations*, eds. Felix Wilfred and Oscar Beozzo, London: SCM Press and Maryknoll, New York: Orbis Books, 1999.
15. *The Jewish Encyclopedia*, Vol. 11, New York and London: Funk and Wagnalls Company, 1916.
16. Warren, Kathleen A., *Daring to Cross the Threshold: Francis of Assisi Encounters Sultan Malek al-Kamil*, Rochester, Minnesota: Sisters of St. Francis, 2003.

Contributors

Swami Paramananda is the founder of Satyam Gyanam Anandam Society (SGAS), which is a Charitable Organization. Swamiji is an accomplished meditation master who currently imparts teachings to more than 1200 persons at the Prashant Ashram and Lao Tzu Meditation Centres at Dubreuil and Beau-Climat, La Flora (Mauritius). He is well known for his great spiritual attainments and his ability to interpret complex spiritual truths in a simple and logical manner. Recently Swamiji participated in a conference on *"Proposing Self-Education as the Missing Dimension in Education"* in Paris, organized by ICIE, France. Swami Paramananda is a prolific Mauritian writer who has published 21 books during the past 10 years. He also publishes the bi-annual magazine 'Know Thyself'.

Dr. Jakub Urbaniak is Professor of the Department of Church History and Church Polity, University of Pretoria, South Africa. He has served as Lecturer at St Augustine College of South Africa (Johannesburg - RSA), Literary Agent at Sw. Wojciech Publishing House (Poznan - PL) and Translator (French – Polish / English – Polish). He successfully completed his D. Phil from the Université Européene de Bretagne, Brest with the dissertation on "Buddhist and Christian intuition of the wretchedness of the human condition in the life and writings of Emile Cioran." Some of his research interests include 'Sacral/Secular – Present Imagery', 'Bioethical questions with reference to the visions of old age and death in Buddhism and Christianity', and Buddhist-Christian Dialogue'.

Dr. Barbara A. Amodio is a visiting Professor at Fairfiled University, fairfield, CT, USA, where she teaches introductory and advanced courses in 'Comparative Philosophy'. She also teaches 'World Religions' at Housatonic Community College. She has also taught at Fordham Unversity, new York, Loyola University, Chicago, University of Chicago, and the University of Connecticut, USA. She is an initiate of Kriya Yoga under Swami Paramahamsa Hariharananda Giri, and has served for 20 years as Human Rights Commissioner in the city o Norwalk, USA. Her areas of research and publication include Indian, Middle Eastern and Chinese traditions, and western Aesthetics.

Dr. Emilio Giuseppe Platti is Professor Emeritus of Islamic Studies at the Katholieke Universiteit Leuven, Belgium. He is a member of the Dominican Institute in Cairo, Research Center for Dialogue with Muslims and Study of the Islamic Literary Heritage. He serves as the Editor of the Journal *Mélanges de l'Institut Dominicain d'études orientales*. He is a profilic writer with many books and research articles to his credit. Some of his books include *Christen und Muslime: Freunde oder Feinde? Herausforderung an die Moderne* (2010), *Islam, Friend or Foe?* (2008), and *Christian-Muslim Relations: A Bibliographical History* (2010).

Dr. Luke Emehielechukwu Ijezie is currently Professor of Biblical Theology and Biblical Languages at the Catholic Institute of West Africa, Port Harcourt, Nigeria. He holds a Licentiate in Sacred Scripture from the Pontifical Biblical Institute - Biblicum, Rome and a doctorate in Scared Scripture from the Gregorian University Rome. He also taught Sacred Scripture for two years at the Pontifical Urban University, Rome (2000-02) and at St Mary's Seminary, Umuowa - Orlu (1988), and at Bonus Pastor Seminary, Osina (1989-91).

Dr. Hoang Thi Tho is the Head of the Department of Oriental Philosophy, Institute of Philosophy, Vietnam Academy of Social Sciences (VASS), Hanoi, Vietnam. He holds a Ph.D. from the Institute of Philosophy, Vietnamese Academy of Social Sciences, Vietnam, with the dissertation "History of Buddhist Zen Thought: from Vedas in India to Buddhist

Zen Sect in China" (2004). He has organized international conferences, workshops, symposia, and seminars, and delivered lectures at various national and international conferences. Among the several publications – both books and articles - include *History of Buddhist Zen Thought: from Vedas in India to Buddhist Zen Sect in China* (2005) and *K. Marx, F. Engels and Lenin on Dialectical Logics* (1985).

Dr. Gnanapragasam Lazar a Reader in the Faculty of Philosophy, JDV, Pune, India and a Visiting Faculty in the Regional Philosophate, Visakapatinam, AP, and in the Yara College, Melbourne, Australia. He took his Ph.D in World Religions from the University of Lancaster, UK, with the thesis, "Phenomenology of Priesthood in Shaivism and Christianity." His academic contributions include the book, *Phenomenology of Priesthood in Shaivism*, and several articles on world religions published in both national and international magazines, and presentation of scholarly papers on world religions in Japan, Papua New Guinea, and Jakarta.

Dr. Romualdas Dulskis is Doctor of Theology and Professor at the Catholic Theology Faculty in Vytautas Magnus University, in Kaunas, Lithuania, and a Visiting Faculty at the St. Joseph Diocesan Seminary, Vilnius. He is a member of the Curatorium of European Society for Catholic Theology and a Member of Polish Society for Spiritual Theology. He is the author of five scholarly books and over fifty academic articles. Professional interests include Ecumenism, Spirituality, Interreligious Dialogue and Theology of Vocation. He also serves as an expert in Lituanistika International Data Base.

Dr. Kashshaf Ghani is a doctoral fellow at the Centre for Advanced Studies, Department of History, University of Calcutta, India. He has served as Research Assistant to Prof. Suranjan Das, Prof. Basudeb Chattopadhyay, (2005-06), and to Prof. Bhaskar Chakravorty (2006-07), and as Editorial Assistant, Global South SEPHIS (South-South Exchange Programme for Research on the History of Development). He holds a Diploma in Software Technology and in Web Designing from Curelife Infotech Pvt. Ltd. He has published several articles in academic journals and magazines, and presented several scholarly papers at international conferences.

Sr. Bincy Mathew is a doctoral fellow at the Faculty of Theology, Katholieke Universiteit Leuven, Belgium. She has served as the sub-editor of *Ratio* and has been assisting in writing the history of the Sacred Heart Congregation. Her research interests include 'family life and evangelization' and she has presented some research papers, like "Toward a Culture of Life" and "The Family as the Basic Ecclesial Community."

Dr. Marinus C. Iwuchukwu is Assistant Professor of Systematic Theology in the Theology Department of Duquesne University, Pittsburgh, USA. Dr. Iwuchukwu holds a Masters in Journalism and Ph.D. in Systematic Theology from Marquette University, Milwaukee, Wisconsin, USA. His areas of specialization and research include 'theology of religions with special interest in interreligious and intercultural dialogue' as well as 'religious pluralism' and 'media, religion, culture and dialogue in Africa'. Among his recent publications is the book, *Media Ecology and Religious Pluralism* (2010).

Index of Subjects

Abrahamic 197, 208
Absolute 11, 14, 17, 20, 40, 49, 53, 62, 80, 86, 107, 121-122, 126-128, 131-132, 134, 141, 183, 185, 199
Absolute Love 49, 53
Action and Inaction 14
Aesthetics 4, 53, 55-58, 65-67, 218
Alms-giving 206
Ambiguity 171
Analogous 176
Anatta 29
Ancestry 75
Angel 57, 63, 98, 178
Annihilation 41, 47, 66-67, 122-123, 157
Aphoristic 28
Appearing World 54, 60
Approximation 173
Art form/s 1
Ascetic 34, 36, 40, 44, 75, 154, 176, 199, 205
Atma 11
Audition 6, 62, 91, 155, 157, 162, 164, 166
Authentic 4, 54, 56, 58, 60, 64-65, 134, 142, 152
Authenticity 60
Awakening 30
Awareness 1, 3, 7, 19, 29, 35, 46, 59, 61, 63, 90-91, 137, 175, 192

Beatitude 28, 136
Behaviour/s 2, 15-16, 133
Belief and Disbelief 14
Blessed 33, 41, 55, 121, 162, 188, 200
Blessed Fault 23
Bliss 11, 13, 19, 37, 66, 121
Body 11, 14-15, 17-18, 32-33, 37, 41, 64, 79, 95, 103-105, 136, 157, 160, 164
Bonding 211
Boundaries 6, 61, 215
Bounds xi, 1-2, 5, 7, 9, 19, 46, 117-139
Brahman 5, 14, 54, 61, 124, 132, 136
Brahmin 205, 209
Brotherhood 70-72, 74-79
Buddha 13, 22, 27-31, 50-51, 102, 106, 109-110
Buddhahood 9, 114
Buddhism 1, 4-5, 21-22, 24-31, 35-37, 46-49, 52, 101-103, 105-116, 217

Calligraphy 56, 59, 62, 64-65
Catharsis 41, 43, 47

Celibate 14, 199
Character 25, 37, 49, 72, 97, 109, 113, 115, 147, 160, 165, 179, 181, 183, 187-188, 190-191
Charitable 203, 205, 209, 217
Charter of Christian Mysticism 173
Christian Faith 23-24, 40, 50, 204
Christian Theology 23-24, 36, 50
Christianity 1, 4, 21-23, 25-27, 31, 34, 46-47, 49, 57, 87, 134, 145-146, 151, 171, 177, 191, 201, 205, 209, 217, 219
Christocentrism 32, 34
Cognitions 2
Collaboration 210, 212
Commandment 15, 179, 181-182, 192
Commitment 29, 81, 192, 200-201, 211
Commitment to God 200
Common Good 200, 208, 210-213
Communion 1, 59, 61, 83, 87, 91-92, 97-99, 136, 173-175, 184, 186, 189-192
Community 6, 37, 58, 85, 137, 144-145, 172, 182, 184, 187-188, 195-196, 203, 208, 210, 212-213, 218, 220
Companions 63, 122, 204, 210
Compassion 7, 16, 25, 33, 38, 41, 65, 109, 125-126, 130, 145, 161, 213
Conflict/s 5, 58
Conscious 1, 12, 17, 41, 55, 60, 91, 97, 105, 175, 192
Consciousness 1, 3-4, 10-11, 13-15, 16-19, 22, 35-37, 46-47, 54, 58, 61, 67, 90, 103-107, 112, 115-116, 120, 122, 132-133, 136, 173, 206
Contemplation 3-4, 27-28, 32-33, 35, 37, 42-43, 45, 51, 105, 120, 124, 157, 164, 166, 199
Contemplative 3, 26, 42, 45, 47, 49, 63-64, 124, 135, 137-138, 141, 191, 199
Contemplative Seeing 3
Contradictory 10
Conversion 203, 209
Convulsion 28
Corporal World 202
Cosmic Consciousness 10, 61
Cosmic Disaster 22
Cosmic Divine 55
Cosmology 40, 50-51, 54, 58-60, 96-98, 134, 139
Creation 11-12, 24-25, 41, 50, 54-55, 59-60, 65, 80, 87-90, 93, 95, 98, 125, 128, 130, 133, 138, 165, 167, 201-202
Cross 23, 26-27, 31-32, 34, 43-45, 148, 161, 174, 181, 187-188, 200, 215
Cross-cultural 3
Crucifixion 30-31, 33-34, 46, 67, 183
Crusaders 204
Cultural Identities 212

Dance 1, 16, 56
Daoism xi, 6, 141-152
Darkness 17, 36, 39, 44-45, 54-55, 57, 121
Death 5, 18, 21, 24, 29-30, 34, 36-43, 49-50, 66, 97-98, 103-104, 110, 113, 117, 122, 148, 180-181, 184-185, 187-190, 200, 217
Destination 4, 10, 19, 60, 176
Destiny 96-97, 191-192, 210
Destructibility 37
Detached 28, 147, 174
Devotee 17, 72, 74, 159
Devotion 5, 70-72, 75, 78, 81, 138-139, 148, 199-200

Devotional xi, 5, 69-81, 159, 161, 173
Devotional Islam xi, 5, 69-81
Dharma 15, 22, 25, 29, 61, 64-65, 110, 114
Dialectical 173, 219
Dialogic Encounter 204
Dialogue of Action 198, 207-212
Dialogue of Life 198, 204, 209-213
Didactic Meaning 25
Dignity 207, 211-212
Dimension/s 5-6, 16, 23, 29, 46, 57, 61-62, 64-65, 81, 88, 92, 96, 117-118, 120, 130-131, 133-135, 137, 139, 145-146, 159, 168, 181, 183, 191, 217
Discourse 27, 50, 57, 88, 92, 150, 178-179, 185, 194
Disinterested 6, 200, 211
Dissolution 12
Divine Indwelling 176-177
Divine Life 136, 189, 191-192
Divinity 1, 42, 45, 123, 132, 172, 175, 192
Divinization 172
Doctrines 2, 60, 70, 109, 154, 163
Domination 109, 190
Dread 39
Duality 14-15, 17, 19, 59-60, 66, 129
Dukkha xi, 4, 21-51, 103
Dwij 10

Ecological 205
Ecstasy 42, 91, 120-121, 123, 164
Effort 19, 29-30, 104, 120, 135, 138, 149, 156, 162-163, 168, 174, 208, 212
Ego 11, 14, 19, 27-31, 47, 66, 97, 103-104, 122
Elevation 31-35, 60, 153
Emanation 89, 201-202
Emotions 2, 18, 163-164, 167
Empathy 38
Empirical Existence 21, 25
Endlessness 201
Energy 12-14, 16, 18, 94, 107, 142, 144
Enjoyment 14, 17
Enlightenment 4-5, 9-10, 13-17, 19-20, 26, 29, 31, 39, 46, 59, 66, 103, 106, 110, 112, 165, 167, 206
Environment 4, 10, 24, 160, 162
Epistemology xi, 5, 101-116, 123
Equality 148, 190, 207, 212
Equanimity 26-27, 48
Esoteric 3, 16, 20, 55, 62-63, 66, 102, 120, 122, 135, 137, 178
Eternal 11, 22, 64, 80, 105, 112, 146, 155, 169, 171, 185, 188-189, 200-201
Eternal Life 10, 25, 42, 172, 185-189, 191, 196
Ethical 22, 35, 37, 109, 162, 169, 174, 192
Evolution 4, 10, 12, 59-61
Exemplary Life 199
Existence 11-12, 17-19, 21-23, 25, 30-31, 35-36, 49, 87, 94, 110, 120, 126, 131, 133, 135-136, 138, 141, 144, 149-151, 154, 176, 201-202
Existentialist 28
Exoteric 3, 63, 122, 133, 135
Experience xi, 1, 3-7, 9-13, 18-52, 54-56, 59, 61-62, 65-67, 80, 83-99, 105, 107, 115, 117-119, 122-123, 126, 129, 135, 137, 146, 150, 152-153, 155, 159-160, 169, 173-176, 178, 189-190, 191-192, 197-198, 203-204, 208-210
Explicate Order 13
Extraversion 26

Eye of Reason 3
Eye of the Flesh 3
Eye of Understanding 3

Faith 7, 23-24, 26, 36, 40, 50, 94, 117-119, 135, 161, 165, 168, 182, 189, 198, 204-206, 208-214
Faith Traditions 7, 198, 205-206, 208, 210-214
Family 5, 72-76, 81, 112, 156, 203, 205, 209, 220
Feeling 4, 18, 27, 30, 33, 35, 47, 102-104, 110, 112, 115-116, 157-158, 161, 163-164
Fellowship 174, 188, 192
Feminine 62-63, 199
Festivities 69, 78, 159
Figure of Speech 186
First-order 3
Foot Washing 6, 182, 187, 196
Footwashing Episode 172, 179-181
Forced Conversion 203, 209
Formless 11, 53-54, 63
Formlessness 53-54, 59, 61-62
Four Elements 30, 110
Freedom 13-17, 19, 25, 42, 56, 94, 104, 184, 199, 208

Genealogy 74-76, 80
Generosity 208
Genuine Mysticisms 63
Glorification 184, 187
God xi, 1, 3, 5-6, 9-19, 23-26, 31, 33-34, 41-45, 47-48, 51, 53, 55-57, 60-61, 64, 67, 73, 77-79, 81, 83-99, 117-139, 142, 146, 148, 153-157, 159-162, 165-167, 171-176, 178, 183, 185-187, 189-192, 195, 197, 199-204, 206-211, 213-214
God Friends 58-59, 81
God's Mercy 23, 131
God-consciousness 206
God-experience 7
Godhead 34, 53, 56-57, 59-61, 66
God-intoxication 56
God-realisation 15
Goodness 24, 41, 50, 55, 88, 191
Gospel 6-7, 31, 92-94, 97, 141, 171-196, 204
Great Death 21, 39-40
Great Light 39

Harmonizing 6
Harmony 19, 26, 116, 130, 144-145, 149, 151-152, 210
Hellenistic 175-177, 179, 194-195
Heresy 206
Hinduism 1
Homogeneous 13
Human Condition 22, 24, 50, 217
Human Dignity 211-212
Human Life 17, 59, 123, 134-135, 138, 152
Human Nature 10, 102, 121
Human Sin 23-24
Humility 14, 19, 145-148, 163, 181
Humility and Arrogance 14
Hyletic Substance 55, 60

Iconography 57
Icons 5, 56, 58, 62
Identity 1, 66-67, 92, 132, 175, 183, 191-192, 209

Idol Worship 53, 56, 58, 62-63, 66, 168
Idolatry 6, 90, 118
Ignorance 10, 17, 22-23, 102-104, 112
Illiterate 10-11

Illusion 15, 17, 19, 30, 39, 61, 108, 127, 150
Image of God 172
Imagery 158, 185, 217
Immanence 6, 118, 124-135, 138, 174, 207
Immediacy of Departure 179
Immutable 202
Impermanence 36-37, 50, 103, 107, 109
Implicate Order 13
Implication/s 5, 59
Incarnate 4-5, 10, 87, 92, 94, 96
Indian Thinking 5, 101
Individual 2, 4, 6, 9, 14-16, 19, 30, 40, 47, 96-99, 114, 137-138, 144, 153, 157, 159-161, 164, 166, 168-169, 191, 207-208
Individuality 6, 19, 47, 123, 154, 165
Individuation 7
Indwelling 173, 175-177, 191
Ineffable Peace 13
Inequality 145, 190-191
Infinite 11-14, 18, 38, 66, 124, 129-130, 132, 189, 201-202
Inner Experience 3
Inner Impulse 204
Inner Self 6, 48, 117, 154
Insight 1, 29, 49, 105, 107, 117, 119, 122, 127, 143, 148-150, 175, 192, 199, 213
Institution 2-3, 69-70, 81, 97, 149
Instrument 23, 62, 95, 160-161
Integral Development 210
Intellectual 10, 32, 43, 49, 62, 111, 125, 136, 156, 169, 172, 175
Intense Experience 4, 27
Intercultural 5, 53
Intercultural Dialogue 212, 220
Intermediaries 32, 202
Internal Being 6
Internal Experience 62
Internal Life 6, 114
Interreligious Dialogue xii, 7, 197-215, 219
Intimacy 57, 173, 182, 186, 191, 200
Introspection 5, 87, 102, 104, 106, 111, 113
Intuition 1, 36-37, 46, 105-108, 111, 114-115, 119, 127, 136, 175, 192, 217
Inward-looking 104
Islam xi, 1, 5-6, 53, 56, 58, 60-61, 64, 67, 69-81, 117-120, 125, 130-131, 133-135, 137-139, 153-154, 161, 165-166, 168, 199, 209, 214, 218
Islamic xi, 4-6, 53-68, 71-72, 74, 77-81, 117-139, 154-155, 161, 164, 166, 168-169, 204, 206-207, 214, 218
Islamic and Non-Islamic 199

Judaism 1, 57, 176-179, 183, 194
Justice 2, 23, 127, 129, 149, 163, 211-212

Karmic 22, 36
Knowing 10, 19-20, 152, 172, 176, 188, 198

Lady Poverty 203, 213
Lawlessness 63
Legendary 101, 162, 199
Liberation 4, 27, 29-30, 39, 42, 51, 208, 210, 212-213
Life 3, 6-7, 10, 17-19, 23-28, 30-31, 33, 37, 39-40, 42-46, 50, 56, 59, 61, 67, 75, 78, 84, 89, 93-95, 98, 102, 107, 109-110, 114-116, 121-124, 129-130, 132-139, 142, 144-154, 162, 172, 174, 177, 184-192,

195-196, 198-199, 202-214, 217, 220
Lifestyle 141-142, 147-148, 151, 203
Light xi, 2, 4, 12, 17, 24, 39, 44, 53-68, 77, 88, 90, 94, 121, 126, 128, 132, 144, 157, 166, 176-177, 187, 189, 194, 202, 210
Light and Sound xi, 4, 53-68
Logic 1, 13, 17, 22, 49, 66, 88, 92, 108, 129, 157, 162, 198, 211, 217, 219
Logos 80, 92, 94, 98, 173, 176-177, 189
Love 7, 10, 16, 19, 26, 33-34, 41-46, 48-49, 53, 55-57, 65-66, 77, 87, 92, 96, 114, 119-123, 125-126, 131, 133, 136, 138, 151, 161, 164-165, 167, 174, 179, 181-183, 185-187, 189-192, 196, 199-201, 206-207, 211, 213
Love-intoxicate 210
Low Caste 206-207
Luminous 4, 54-55, 59, 61, 65-66
Luminous Black Light xi, 53-68

Manifestation/s 25, 60, 80, 85, 120, 122, 126, 128, 133
Mantra 61-62, 64-65, 121
Martyrdom 42, 191
Masochist 40
Masochistic 40
Material Possession 154, 199, 209, 213
Matter 11-13, 16, 19, 30, 36, 46, 55, 84, 87-88, 98, 114, 168, 176, 199, 201, 207
Maya 19, 30, 61
Meditation 3, 9-10, 12-13, 29, 35-38, 49-51, 62, 66, 102, 108, 110-112, 115, 167, 206, 217
Mental 13, 18, 22, 30, 35, 38, 87, 91, 104, 119
Mental Affair 9
Mercy and Consolation 56
Merkhabah Mysticism 178
Meros 6-7, 172, 182-192
Message 10, 23, 56, 88-89, 91-92, 203, 206
Messianic Identity 183
Metaphysical 22, 26-27, 32, 37, 49, 54, 56, 62, 121, 127
Metaphysics 59, 134, 139
Method 4-5, 10, 18, 87, 106, 108, 120, 122, 180
Middle Way 29
Migration 212
Mind 9-15, 17-20, 23, 29, 31, 36-38, 42, 47-49, 51, 53, 57, 62, 70, 85, 87, 90, 102, 104-106, 111-116, 120, 136, 143, 148, 152, 160, 176, 212
Miniature 17, 66
Mirage 11, 55, 61
Miseries 28
Modern Society 5, 211
Monism 61
Mono-cultural 211
Mono-religious 211
Monotheism 61-62
Morality 16-17, 119, 189-193
Morality-immorality 14
Motivation 25, 184, 191
Movements 71
Music 1, 62, 65-66, 137, 154-155, 159, 165, 170
Mutual Indwelling 175-177
Mysterious 9, 11, 25, 27, 74, 109, 125, 136, 145, 175
Mystery 4, 9-12, 19, 22-27, 85-86, 90, 94, 142, 171, 178, 195, 214
Mystery of Suffering 24
Mystical Connotation 175
Mystical Consciousness 1, 3

Mystical Explanation 7
Mystical Failure 28
Mystical Movement 5, 117
Mystical Paradox 4, 54-55, 57-58, 63, 65-66
Mystical Path 27, 31, 33, 36, 46, 48, 157, 165, 199
Mystical Traditions 4, 26-28, 46-50, 64, 66
Mysticism xi, 1-2, 4-7, 9-10, 19-20, 26-31, 33, 35-37, 39-41, 46-52, 63-64, 66, 68-69, 74, 81, 83-88, 90-94, 96-98, 117-139, 141-152, 154-155, 163, 169, 171-179, 191-195, 197, 207, 214-215
Mysticism of Love 48-49

Nafs 53
Negative Reference 201
Neo-platonism 62-63, 172, 191
Neuroscience 1
New Testament 57, 83, 91-96, 98, 148, 151, 173, 177-178, 190, 193-195
Nirvana 9, 13, 25, 30, 110, 112, 208
Noble Truths 29, 102-103
No-mind Statem 10
Non-dependence 209
Non-Dual One 60
Non-Duality 49, 62, 65-66
Non-phenomenal 7
Non-violent 15, 198, 204
Nothing 10-12, 14, 19-20, 23, 27, 30, 51, 98, 118, 123-124, 129-130, 132, 141-142, 144-146, 159-165, 167,
Nothingness 11, 90, 102-103, 105-107, 110-111, 113-114

Obedience 174, 190
Oblivion 172
Old Testament 5, 23-24, 83, 88-93, 98,
Oneness 10, 17-18, 60-62, 66, 119, 128-130, 138, 143-144
Ontology of Love 211
Opportunities 17
Orthodox 5, 34, 117, 201

Painfulness 22, 24
Panorama 25
Paradox 4, 29, 44, 48, 54-55, 57-58, 63, 65-66, 124-126, 128, 142, 150
Participation 25, 33-34, 162, 166, 185, 188-189, 192
Passio xi, 4, 21-52
Passion of Christ 33
Passion/s 32-33, 40, 43, 155, 181, 200
Paths 3-4, 10
Patristic Circle 172
Peace 13, 18, 22, 31, 37, 142, 205, 212-213
Pedagogy 23
Perception 12, 17-19, 37, 102-103, 105-108, 118-119, 150, 204, 207, 209
Perfect Contemplation 32, 43
Personality 5, 23, 97, 115, 158, 204-205
Pessimistic 28
Phenomenal 7, 105
Phenomenon 1, 64-65, 84, 86, 90-91, 104-105, 107
Philanthropic 205
Philosophy 1-2, 7, 9, 17, 80, 85, 101, 106-107, 109, 113-114, 117-118, 127, 136, 149, 152, 198, 201-202, 206, 209, 211, 218-219
Philosophy of Life 7, 198
Physics 1, 11, 54, 59
Pilgrim 71, 73, 79
Pilgrimage 70

Platonic 128, 201
Platonism 177
Pluralism 198, 211-212, 220
Pluralist/s 3, 7
Pluralistic Societies xii, 7, 197-215
Poetry 1, 65, 67, 154-155, 157-158, 160, 163, 207
Politics 6, 59, 155, 169
Possibilities 17
Post-modern 211
Potential xii, 17-18, 40, 106, 112, 171-196, 202
Pragmatic 35, 202
Prakriti-Purusha 12
Preaching 6, 31, 204
Predicament 206
Presence 12, 32, 77, 88-90, 95, 98, 103, 117, 120, 128, 131, 155, 173-174, 204, 211
Presence of the Divine 6, 117, 167
Preservation 12, 212
Primary Matter 201
Primordial 4, 62, 97
Privation 44
Problem 6, 22-26, 84-87, 96, 118, 156
Process 17, 19, 23, 40, 47-49, 58-59, 86, 95, 103, 105, 107-109, 112-113, 116, 133, 152, 154, 208
Procession 71, 74, 78-79
Prophetic Religion 27
Prophets 10, 58, 60, 80, 91, 154
Psychology 1, 108, 116
Punishment 23, 40, 131, 150, 200-201
Purgation 35, 44, 57

Qualities 7, 13, 80, 126, 130, 146, 160, 166, 174, 202, 210,
Quality of Life 202
Quest xii, 6, 36, 86, 153-170

Rationality 26, 29
Realisation 16-17, 20, 37
Reciprocation 201
Recitations 72
Regeneration 18
Relationship/s 6-7, 83-84, 86-87, 91, 98, 124, 130, 132-134, 142, 144, 149-150, 158, 173, 183-193, 200, 202-203, 205-207, 209-213
Religion of Dogma 26
Religion of Faith 26
Religion, Definition of 3
Religion/s xi, 1-4, 6, 9-20, 22, 24-27, 36-37, 48, 50-51, 85, 87, 96-99, 101-102, 109, 114-115, 118, 133-134, 136-137, 161-162, 166, 168, 197-198, 205-206, 208, 210-212, 214, 218-220
Religious Consciousness 3
Religious Life 3, 84-85, 122, 154
Religious Persuasion 197, 205
Religious Pluralism 211
Religious Scriptures 11
Responsibility 146-148
Resurrection 39
Revelation 24, 31-32, 41, 65, 67, 85, 178, 187, 194
Ritual/s xii, 6, 153-170
Ruh 53-54

Sabbath 16
Sacred xii, 6, 67, 85, 153-170, 218, 220
Sacred Arts 4, 55, 58, 61
Sacred Mantrum 64
Sage 4, 26-28, 141-145, 147, 151
Saint 5, 26-28, 33-34, 43, 47, 51, 54 58, 64, 69-81, 121, 123, 125, 155-156, 158-159, 166, 168-169, 201, 203, 209, 214
Salafism 71

Salvation 27, 33, 45, 86, 94-95, 104-106, 112, 114, 122, 151, 173, 191
Sama 6, 56, 62, 66, 154-169
Samsara 22, 30, 35
Satan 57, 60
Sat-Cit-Ananda 11
Satti-Shiva 13
Saviour 28, 32-34, 43, 206, 214
Scholar/s 5, 19, 60, 65, 71-72, 75-76, 79, 91, 111, 113-115, 119, 150, 153, 171-172, 175, 177, 179, 181-182, 186, 191, 199
Science/s 1, 6, 10-13, 18, 59, 84, 108, 110, 117, 119, 139, 218
Scriptures 10-11, 17, 19-20, 83, 93, 102, 110, 125-126, 137, 149, 152, 171, 194, 202, 218
Second-order 3
Secular xii, 4, 6, 20, 58, 79, 151-170, 172, 217
Seeker 4, 10, 19, 141
Self-annihilation 47
Self-denial 40, 199
Self-luminous Light 55
Senses 11, 17-18, 28, 33, 40, 45, 47, 54-55, 58-59, 153
Sermons 42, 72
Servant of Yahweh 177
Service 43, 57, 67, 95-96, 121, 133, 181, 183, 190-191, 196, 205, 210, 213
Settlement 212
Shastras 61, 64
Sheer Bliss 13
Shepherd 185
Silence 4, 18-19, 27, 64-65, 90, 141, 168, 192
Sins 23, 147
Sirr 54
Sleepwalker 17
Social Injustice 211
Solidarity 199, 204, 207-211, 213
Solitude 41, 63
Soteriological 25, 181, 192
Sound xi, 4, 53-68, 88, 96, 147-148
Space 12-13, 15, 61-62, 78, 85, 206, 212
Spiritual 1, 3, 6, 11, 15, 18-20, 22, 26, 28-29, 33-34, 37-39, 41, 43-44, 48-49, 54, 57-61, 63-66, 70, 77-80, 87, 95, 106, 115, 117-120, 122-123, 125, 131-133, 138, 142, 145-146, 153-160, 162-170, 172-173, 175, 178, 184, 190, 192, 198-199, 202, 204-206, 217, 219
Spiritual Cultures 63-64
Spiritual Disposition 37, 202
Spiritual Fulfillment 206
Spirituality xii, 1, 3, 7, 9-10, 17, 20, 30, 33-34, 37, 51, 63, 67, 83, 153, 166, 197-215, 219
Spousal Relationship 203
Stages of Life 206
State of Consciousness 4, 14
Substance 12-13, 55, 60, 97
Subtle Stuff 12
Suffering xi, 4, 21-52, 102-104, 109, 114, 147
Sufi xi, 4-6, 53-81, 118-119, 121-127, 130, 136-139, 153-170, 199-200, 210, 214
Sufi in Union 66
Sufism 5-6, 64, 70-71, 74-75, 78, 80-81, 117-123, 126, 128-129, 132-135, 137-139, 153-154, 165, 168-169
Sunni Institution 69
Supra-rational 36
Supreme Enjoyer 17
Supreme Mind 12

Symbol/s 6, 15, 23, 40, 50, 53-54, 65, 67, 85, 109, 125, 128, 136, 143, 145, 156, 181, 186
Synoptics 180, 184-185, 195

Tantra 30, 51, 61, 64, 205
Tension/s 22, 56-57, 183
Theological Assumption 7, 198, 201, 209-210
Theology 1-2, 23-24, 26, 36, 48, 50, 69, 87, 93-96, 124-125, 129, 136, 173-175, 193-197, 201-202, 204, 218-220
Third-eye Seeing 3
Tong-len 38
Tradition/s 3-7, 22-24, 26-28, 35-37, 39, 44, 46-54, 56, 58-62, 64-67, 70, 72-74, 78, 83-84, 86-91, 96, 98, 114, 125-126, 130, 143-144, 146, 148, 154, 158, 163, 165, 168, 172, 177-180, 187, 190, 194-195, 197-198, 200, 203, 205-206, 208-214, 218
Transcendence 6, 36, 118, 124-132, 134-135, 138, 176
Trans-cultural 1
Transformation 13, 17-19, 36, 41-42, 45, 49, 51, 56, 58, 202, 208, 211
Transforming 17, 35-47, 143, 152
Transforming Vision 172
Truth 1, 4, 9-13, 17, 20, 22-24, 29, 36, 45, 55-56, 68, 102-103, 105-107, 112, 114, 117, 119-120, 123, 134, 139, 147, 153, 166, 171, 174-175, 184-185, 187, 189, 192, 217
Truth, Nature of 10
Twice-born 10

Ultimate Good 24
Ultimate Possibility 17
Ultimate Reality 1-2, 19, 117, 119, 175, 192, 197, 207-208
Unbound xii, 6, 153-170
Unconditional Love 45, 199
Unio Mystica 32, 41, 48
Unitive 3
Unity 7, 10, 25, 42, 45, 48, 56, 61-63, 80, 86, 137-138, 142, 144-145, 149-150, 166, 173, 176, 180, 207-208
Universe 9, 11-13, 17-18, 57-58, 60, 77, 80, 88-89, 102-103, 105, 110, 115, 123, 129-130, 133, 136, 152, 201, 207
Unmanifest 54, 59-60, 66
Unseen 55, 162, 164, 167
Upanishads 11, 20

Values 7, 47, 58, 96, 107, 135, 144, 197
Vedas 11, 20, 218-219
Vipassana xi, 5, 101-116
Virtue/s 10, 13, 18, 48, 84, 137, 142-146, 148-150
Visual Arts 1, 141
Voice 56, 89-90, 138, 161, 168, 178, 185, 194, 203
Void xi, 4, 12-13, 49, 53-68

Water 33, 55, 109, 121, 138, 141-146, 148, 186-188, 199
Welfare 16, 205
Willingness 43, 134, 208
Wisdom 6, 11, 26, 36, 48-51, 67, 77, 88-90, 94, 98, 104, 107, 112, 114-115, 122, 134, 143, 146, 149, 151, 177
Withdrawal 40
Word of God xi, 5, 83-99
Works of Charity 200, 203
Worship 2-3, 53, 56, 58, 62-63, 85, 121, 128, 178, 184, 200, 206

Index of Authors

Abd al-Ra'ûf Sa'd, Taha 72-73, 81
Abduh, Muhammad 79
Abelson, J. 177, 193
Achebe, Chinua 96-98
Adibe, Gabriel E. 97
Agnew, Una 2
Ahmad, Safwat Jawdat 81
al-Fârid, Ibn 79-80
Al-Ghazali 119, 121, 126, 132, 134, 137
al-Huwiri 123
al-Qasabî, Abd al-Hâdî 80
Aligwekwe, P. E. 96
Ali, Yusuf 73
Allen, Ronald B. 183-184, 193
Amodio, Barbara A. xi, 4, 53-68, 218
Aquinas, Thomas 57, 146, 152
Arabi, Ibn 60, 65, 67, 119, 126-128, 132, 137, 139
Arbery, A. J. 138-139
Arinze, Francis A. 98
Asanga 106
Augustine, Saint 132, 136, 172, 193, 200
Awliya, Shaykh Nizamuddin 157-162, 169
Azriel ben Menahem 7, 197, 201-202, 207, 209-210, 213
Bailey, Raymond 34, 36, 41, 44-45, 48, 50
Bancroft, Anne 45, 48, 50
Bannerth, Ernst 71-72, 75, 78-79
Barnabas, Lindars 180, 193
Barrett, C. K. 173-174, 181, 190, 193
Barry, Michael 67
Bautch, Kelley Coblentz 186-187, 193
Berger, Peter 40, 50
Bernard of Clairvaux, Saint 33, 42, 48
Biegman, Nicolaas 78
Bieringer, Reimund 2, 193
Birnbaum, Philip 214
Blake, William 13
Blakney, Raymond B. 41, 50
Bodhi, Bhikkhu 27, 50
Bohm, David 12-13
Boismard, M. É. 180, 193, 195
Bonaventure, Saint 33, 42
Bonnamy, Alain 69
Borgen, P. 177, 193
Bragt, Jan Van 26, 40, 51
Brown, Raymond E. 93, 172, 177-183, 193
Buber, Martin 7
Buddha, Gautama 22

Bultmann, Rudolf 173, 180, 193
Cam Thanh, Ven 112
Chah, Ajahn 36, 50
Charan Singh, Maharaj 174, 193
Chennattu, Rekha M. 185, 193
Chich, Rachida 81
Chishti, Khwaja Moinuddin 155-158, 169
Chishti, Shaykh Maudud 167
Chittick, W. C. 120, 139
Cioran, Emile 28, 50, 217
Cleary, T. 142, 152
Colledge, Edmund 32-33, 41, 50
Collins, Raymond F. 190, 193
Coomaraswamy, Anand K. 58
Countryman, L. William 174-175, 193
Culpepper, Alan R. 92, 190-191, 193
Currie, P. M. 156-157, 169
Cutler, Howard C. 21, 50

Da Todi, Jacopone 33
Dahl, Nils Alstrup 93, 177, 193
Dalai Lama 21, 24, 29-30, 35, 38-39, 49-50
Dao Hanh, Ven 112
Davies, Olivier 32
DeConick, April D. 178, 194
De Jong, Frederick 81
Deblaere, Albert 35
Derrida, Jacques 127-128
Dodd, C. H. 175-176, 194
Douglas, Mary 40, 50
Dulskis, Romualdas xi, 6, 141-152, 219
Dumoulin, Heinrich 29, 50
Dunn, J. D. G. 180-181, 194
Dupré, Louis 48
Duran 207, 214
Durkheim, Emile 84-85

Eboh, Simeon O. 97
Eckhart, Meister 26-27, 31-32, 34, 41-42, 50-51, 86
Egan, Harvey D. 86, 93
Eilers, Franz-Josef 212, 214
Einstein, Albert 9, 130
el-Aswad, Al-Sayed 80
El Kadi, Galila 69
Eliade, Mircea 48, 50, 85
Elsbernd, Mary 193
Ernst, Carl 118, 139, 155, 169
Fathî Abû Bakr, Muhammad 75, 81
Ferguson, John 207, 214
Firestone 207, 214
Ford, Massyngberde J. 194
Fortna, Robert T. 180, 194
Francis of Assisi 7, 33, 197, 203-205, 207, 209, 213-215
Francis of Assisi, Saint 26, 214
Frankl, Victor 21
Fredericks, James L. 36, 50
Frey, Forg 179, 194
Geoffroy, Eric 70, 76-77, 81
Gesudaraz, Khwaja Bandanawaz 158, 162-169
Ghani, Kashshaf xii, 6, 153-170, 219
Gharib, Shaykh Burhanuddin 162, 169
Ghazzali 67
Gobillot, Geneviève 77
Goldingay, John 89
Goodenough, Erwin R. 176, 194
Grand Sheikh Idries Shan 122
Gril, Denis 70, 74-75, 77, 81

Habib, Muhammad 158, 169
Hanh, Thich Nhat 51
Happold, F. C. 4
Harmless, William 31, 33-34, 51

Harvey, Andrew 33-34, 38, 40, 42-44, 51
Hasan Ala-Sijzi, Amir 157, 169
Hillmer, R. Melvyn 190, 194
Hoffman-Ladd, Valerie J. 81
Hoskyns, Edwyn Clement 175, 181, 185, 194
Howard, Wilbert Francis 173, 181, 194
Husayn, Taha 79
Hussaini, Syed Shah Khusro 164-165, 169

Ibn al-Arabi 119, 132
Ignatius of Loyola, Saint 27
Ijezie, Luke Emehiele xi, 5, 83-99, 218
Inge, William Ralph 172-173, 194
Isidore of Seville 145
Iwuchukwu, Marinus xii, 7, 197-215, 220

Jesus Christ 23, 92, 94, 200
John of the Cross, Saint 26-27, 43-44, 174
John Paul II 205, 211, 214
John, Bernard H. 191, 194
John, Saint 173-175, 189-191, 193-196
Julian of Norwich 32, 41, 50

Kabir 10-11, 136-137, 197, 206-207, 209-210, 213-214
Kachappilly, Kurian xi, 1-7
Kaibalyadham, Sri Sri 205-206, 214
Kanagaraj, Jey J. 171, 175-176, 178, 191, 194
Kersten, Holger 67
Khalili, Nasser D. 67
Khusrau, Amir 158-159, 169
Khwurd, Mir 160-161, 164, 166, 169
Knysh, Alexander 120, 139, 154, 170
Kohn, L. 149, 152
Kourie, Celia 93-94
Kraus, H. J. 88
Krishna 15-17
Krishnamurti, J. 18

Lau, D. C. 145-147, 152
Lawrence, Bruce 155-156, 158, 169
Lazar, Gnanapragasam xi, 5, 117-139, 219
Lienhard, Joseph T. 194
Lightfoot, R. H. 181, 191, 194
Lohmeyer, Ernst 180, 194
Lonergan, Bernard 87
Louth, Andrew 172, 194
Luizard, Pierre-Jean 81
Ly Anh Tong 112
Ly Thai Tong 112
Ly Thanh Tong 112

Macleod, C. W. 172, 194
Mansoor, Al-Hillaj 16
Marcel, Gabriel 25
Mathew, Bincy xii, 6-7, 171-196, 220
Mayeur-Jaouen, Catherine 69, 78, 80-81
McGinn, Bernard 2, 33, 42-44, 51
McGregor, Richard 70, 81
McPolin, James 174, 192, 194
Mealand, David L. 175-176, 195
Merton, Thomas 21, 25-26, 34, 36, 39, 41, 44-45, 48-51, 128-129, 139
Michl, Johann 183, 195
Mlakuzhyil, George 180, 195
Mommaers, Paul 26-27, 29, 32-35, 39-43, 45-49, 51
Moses 15, 88, 90, 92, 179
Mott, M. 139
Mouzi's *Li Huo Lun* 110

Moyaert, Paul 2
Muhammad, Prophet 5, 63, 72, 79, 117, 119-120
Muhammad, Sa'd Hasan 81
Muqaddasi, Sheikh Izzidin 67
Murata, Sachko 139
Murphy, Roland E. 89

Nagao, Gadjin M. 48, 51
Nagarjuna 106
Nasr, Sayeed Hossein 58, 67, 117-118, 139
Neirynck, Frans 180, 195
Nguyen Tai Thu 110-113
Nicholson, Reynold A. 71, 119

Odeberg, H. 177, 195
Ohtoshi, Tetsuya 70
Onwubiko, Oliver O. 98
Origen 48, 64, 172, 194
Otto, Rudolf 85-86

Pabongka, Rinpoche 30, 51
Padwick 139
Paramananda, Swami xi, 4, 9-20, 217
Patanjali 54, 59, 66, 102
Peers, Edgar Allison 43, 51
Petitot, Henry 28, 51
Petyt, Maria 34-35
Philo 86, 176-178, 193
Platti, Emilio Giuseppe xi, 5, 69-81, 218
Plotinus 58, 62, 64, 128, 136
Porphyry 62
Preiss, T. 177, 195
Pring, J. T. 171, 195

Qamar ul Huda 156, 170
Qureshi, Regula 159, 170
Qushayri, Al 154, 170, 210

Rabia al-Adawiyya 7, 197, 199-201
Rahman, Fazlur 133-135
Rama, Lord 15
Ramakrishna, Swami 10-11
Reese, W. L. 2
Renard, John 81
Richard of St. Victor 3
Richter, G. 195
Ringgren, Helmer 91
Rinpoche, Pabongka 30, 51
Robinson, Paschal 214
Rohr, Richard 3
Rolle, Richard 137
Rood, Rick 3
Rose, Seraphim 34
Rotzetter, Anton 204, 214
Rowland, Christopher 178, 195
Ruysbroeck 136

Sabbe, Maurits 180, 184-185, 195
Sabra, Adam 70, 81
Sahib, Khwaja 163
Samani, Ali 163, 170
San'ai, Hakim 68
Sankara, Acharya 86
Sasse, Hermann 188, 195
Scattolin, Giuseppe 79-80
Schallenbergh, Gino 72
Schimmel, Annemarie 120, 139, 199
Schnackenburg, Rudolf 174, 181, 195
Schneider, J. 195
Schneiders, Sandra M. 175, 190, 195
Scholem, Gershom G. 171, 177, 195
Schuon, F. 134, 139
Schweitzer, Albert 175, 195
Segovia, Fernando F. 187, 195

Sells, Michael A. 68, 214
Sethi, V. K. 214
Shah, Idries 68
Shakrganj, Baba Fariduddin 160, 164
Shih, Rashida 78
Smith, Margaret 121, 214
Socrates 11
Stauffer, E. 186, 195
Stevens, Edward 26-27, 29-30, 36-37, 40, 45, 47
Suzuki, Daisetsu Teitaro 26-27, 31, 39, 41, 46, 51, 105
Swidler, Leonard 214
Sze, Mai-mai 68

Teasdale, Wayne 37, 51, 197, 215
Teresa of Avila, Saint 26, 28, 41, 43, 51
Thakur, Sri Ram 7, 197, 205-207, 209-210, 213-214
Thao Duong 111-112
Thera, Nyanaponika 52
Thien Hoi, Ven 112
Tho, Hoang Thi xi, 5, 101-116, 218
Thomas, John Christopher 182, 195
Thomassen, Einar 172, 196
Thompson, Marianne Meye 189, 196
Tran Nhan Tong 109, 112
Tran Thai Tong 113
Truc Lam Yen Tu 111-112
Tyler, Peter 2

Underhill, Evelyn 124, 173, 179, 196
Urbaniak, Jakub xi, 4, 21-52, 217

Van Belle, Gilbert 180, 196
Van Bragt, Jan 26, 40, 51
Vashubandhu 106
Veervasantha, Swami 12-13
Vineeth, Francis 2
Vinitaruci 111-112
von Hügel, B. F. 173, 196
von Rad 90

Wagner, J. Ross 88
Walsh, James 32, 50
Warren, Kathleen A. 204, 215
Weiser, A. 180, 196
Weiss, Herold 181, 187, 196
Whitson, Robley Edward 52
Williams, Paul 46, 52
Wong, Eva 143, 152
Wu, Yantong 111-112

Yogacara 106-107
Yüan-wu 39

Ziedan, Youssef 76
Zorrilla, Hugo 183, 196